CLEP-13   COLLEGE-LEVEL EXAMINATION
          PROGRAM SERIES

This is your
PASSBOOK for...

Chemistry

Test Preparation Study Guide
Questions & Answers

NATIONAL LEARNING CORPORATION®

COPYRIGHT NOTICE

This book is SOLELY intended for, is sold ONLY to, and its use is RESTRICTED to individual, bona fide applicants or candidates who qualify by virtue of having seriously filed applications for appropriate license, certificate, professional and/or promotional advancement, higher school matriculation, scholarship, or other legitimate requirements of education and/or governmental authorities.

This book is NOT intended for use, class instruction, tutoring, training, duplication, copying, reprinting, excerption, or adaptation, etc., by:

1) Other publishers
2) Proprietors and/or Instructors of "Coaching" and/or Preparatory Courses
3) Personnel and/or Training Divisions of commercial, industrial, and governmental organizations
4) Schools, colleges, or universities and/or their departments and staffs, including teachers and other personnel
5) Testing Agencies or Bureaus
6) Study groups which seek by the purchase of a single volume to copy and/or duplicate and/or adapt this material for use by the group as a whole without having purchased individual volumes for each of the members of the group
7) Et al.

Such persons would be in violation of appropriate Federal and State statutes.

PROVISION OF LICENSING AGREEMENTS – Recognized educational, commercial, industrial, and governmental institutions and organizations, and others legitimately engaged in educational pursuits, including training, testing, and measurement activities, may address request for a licensing agreement to the copyright owners, who will determine whether, and under what conditions, including fees and charges, the materials in this book may be used them. In other words, a licensing facility exists for the legitimate use of the material in this book on other than an individual basis. However, it is asseverated and affirmed here that the material in this book CANNOT be used without the receipt of the express permission of such a licensing agreement from the Publishers. Inquiries re licensing should be addressed to the company, attention rights and permissions department.

All rights reserved, including the right of reproduction in whole or in part, in any form or by any means, electronic or mechanical, including photocopying, recording, or by any information storage and retrieval system, without permission in writing from the Publisher.

Copyright © 2025 by
National Learning Corporation

212 Michael Drive, Syosset, NY 11791
(516) 921-8888 • www.passbooks.com
E-mail: info@passbooks.com

PASSBOOK® SERIES

THE *PASSBOOK® SERIES* has been created to prepare applicants and candidates for the ultimate academic battlefield – the examination room.

At some time in our lives, each and every one of us may be required to take an examination – for validation, matriculation, admission, qualification, registration, certification, or licensure.

Based on the assumption that every applicant or candidate has met the basic formal educational standards, has taken the required number of courses, and read the necessary texts, the *PASSBOOK® SERIES* furnishes the one special preparation which may assure passing with confidence, instead of failing with insecurity. Examination questions – together with answers – are furnished as the basic vehicle for study so that the mysteries of the examination and its compounding difficulties may be eliminated or diminished by a sure method.

This book is meant to help you pass your examination provided that you qualify and are serious in your objective.

The entire field is reviewed through the huge store of content information which is succinctly presented through a provocative and challenging approach – the question-and-answer method.

A climate of success is established by furnishing the correct answers at the end of each test.

You soon learn to recognize types of questions, forms of questions, and patterns of questioning. You may even begin to anticipate expected outcomes.

You perceive that many questions are repeated or adapted so that you can gain acute insights, which may enable you to score many sure points.

You learn how to confront new questions, or types of questions, and to attack them confidently and work out the correct answers.

You note objectives and emphases, and recognize pitfalls and dangers, so that you may make positive educational adjustments.

Moreover, you are kept fully informed in relation to new concepts, methods, practices, and directions in the field.

You discover that you are actually taking the examination all the time: you are preparing for the examination by "taking" an examination, not by reading extraneous and/or supererogatory textbooks.

In short, this PASSBOOK®, used directedly, should be an important factor in helping you to pass your test.

NONTRADITIONAL EDUCATION

Students returning to school as adults bring more varied experience to their studies than do the teenagers who begin college shortly after graduating from high school. As a result, there are numerous programs for students with nontraditional learning curves. Hundreds of colleges and universities grant degrees to people who cannot attend classes at a regular campus or have already learned what the college is supposed to teach.

You can earn nontraditional education credits in many ways:
- Passing standardized exams
- Demonstrating knowledge gained through experience
- Completing campus-based coursework, and
- Taking courses off campus

Some methods of assessing learning for credit are objective, such as standardized tests. Others are more subjective, such as a review of life experiences.

With some help from four hypothetical characters – Alice, Vin, Lynette, and Jorge – this article describes nontraditional ways of earning educational credit. It begins by describing programs in which you can earn a high school diploma without spending 4 years in a classroom. The college picture is more complicated, so it is presented in two parts: one on gaining credit for what you know through course work or experience, and a second on college degree programs. The final section lists resources for locating more information.

Earning High School Credit

People who were prevented from finishing high school as teenagers have several options if they want to do so as adults. Some major cities have back-to-school programs that allow adults to attend high school classes with current students. But the more practical alternatives for most adults are to take the General Educational Development (GED) tests or to earn a high school diploma by demonstrating their skills or taking correspondence classes.

Of course, these options do not match the experience of staying in high school and graduating with one's friends. But they are viable alternatives for adult learners committed to meeting and, often, continuing their educational goals.

GED Program

Alice quit high school her sophomore year and took a job to help support herself, her younger brother, and their newly widowed mother. Now an adult, she wants to earn her high school diploma – and then go on to college. Because her job as head cook and her family responsibilities keep her busy during the day, she plans to get a high school equivalency diploma. She will study for, and take, the GED tests. Every year, about half a million adults earn their high school credentials this way. A GED diploma is accepted in lieu of a high school one by more than 90 percent of employers, colleges, and universities, so it is a good choice for someone like Alice.

The GED testing program is sponsored by the American Council on Education and State and local education departments. It consists of examinations in five subject areas: Writing, science, mathematics, social studies, and literature and the arts. The tests also measure skills such as analytical ability, problem solving, reading comprehension, and ability to understand and apply information. Most of the questions are multiple choice; the writing test includes an essay section on a topic of general interest.

Eligibility rules for taking the exams vary, but some states require that you must be at least 18. Tests are given in English, Spanish, and French. In addition to standard print, versions in large print, Braille, and audiocassette are also available. Total time allotted for the tests is 7 1/2 hours.

The GED tests are not easy. About one-fourth of those who complete the exams every year do not pass. Passing scores are established by administering the tests to a sample of graduating high school seniors. The minimum standard score is set so that about one-third of graduating seniors would not pass the tests if they took them.

Because of the difficulty of the tests, people need to prepare themselves to take them. Often, they start by taking the Official GED Practice Tests, usually available through a local adult education center. Centers are listed in your phone book's blue pages under "Adult Education," "Continuing Education," or "GED." Adult education centers also have information about GED preparation classes and self-study materials. Classes are generally arranged to accommodate adults' work schedules. National Learning Corporation publishes several study guides that aim to thoroughly prepare test-takers for the GED.

School districts, colleges, adult education centers, and community organizations have information about GED testing schedules and practice tests. For more information, contact them, your nearest GED testing center, or:

GED Testing Service
One Dupont Circle, NW, Suite 250
Washington, DC 20036-1163
1(800) 62-MY GED (626-9433)
(202) 939-9490

Skills Demonstration

Adults who have acquired high school level skills through experience might be eligible for the National External Diploma Program. This alternative to the GED does not involve any direct instruction. Instead, adults seeking a high school diploma must demonstrate mastery of 65 competencies in 8 general areas: Communication; computation; occupational preparedness; and self, social, consumer, scientific, and technological awareness.

Mastery is shown through the completion of the tasks. For example, a participant could prove competency in computation by measuring a room for carpeting, figuring out the amount of carpet needed, and computing the cost.

Before being accepted for the program, adults undergo an evaluation. Tests taken at one of the program's offices measure reading, writing, and mathematics abilities. A take-home segment includes a self-assessment of current skills, an individual skill evaluation, and an occupational interest and aptitude test.

Adults accepted for the program have weekly meetings with an assessor. At the meeting, the assessor reviews the participant's work from the previous week. If the task has not been completed properly, the assessor explains the mistake. Participants continue to correct their errors until they master each competency. A high school diploma is awarded upon proven mastery of all 65 competencies.

Fourteen States and the District of Columbia now offer the External Diploma Program. For more information, contact:

External Diploma Program
One Dupont Circle, NW, Suite 250
Washington, DC 20036-1193
(202) 939-9475

Correspondence and Distance Study

Vin dropped out of high school during his junior year because his family's frequent moves made it difficult for him to continue his studies. He promised himself at the time he dropped out that he would someday finish the courses needed for his diploma. For people like Vin, who prefer to earn a traditional diploma in a nontraditional way, there are about a dozen accredited courses of study for earning a high school diploma by correspondence, or distance study. The programs are either privately run, affiliated with a university, or administered by a State education department.

Distance study diploma programs have no residency requirements, allowing students to continue their studies from almost any location. Depending on the course of study, students need not be enrolled full time and usually have more flexible schedules for finishing their work. Selection of courses ranges from vo-tech to college prep, and some programs place different emphasis on the types of diplomas offered. University affiliated schools, for example, allow qualified students to take college courses along with their high school ones. Students can then apply the college credits toward a degree at that university or transfer them to another institution.

Taking courses by distance study is often more challenging and time consuming than attending classes, especially for adults who have other obligations. Success depends on each student's motivation. Students usually do reading assignments on their own. Written exercises, which they complete and send to an instructor for grading, supplement their reading material.

A list of some accredited high schools that offer diplomas by distance study is available free from the Distance Education and Training Council, formerly known as the National Home Study Council. Request the "DETC Directory of Accredited Institutions" from:

The Distance Education and Training Council
1601 18th Street, NW.
Washington, DC 20009-2529
(202) 234-5100

Some publications profiling nontraditional college programs include addresses and descriptions of several high school correspondence ones. See the Resources section at the end of this article for more information.

Getting College Credit For What You Know

Adults can receive college credit for prior coursework, by passing examinations, and documenting experiential learning. With help from a college advisor, nontraditional students should assess their skills, establish their educational goals, and determine the number of college credits they might be eligible for.

Even before you meet with a college advisor, you should collect all your school and training records. Then, make a list of all knowledge and abilities acquired through experience, no matter how irrelevant they seem to your chosen field. Next, determine your educational goals: What specific field do you wish to study? What kind of a degree do you want? Finally, determine how your past work fits into the field of study. Later on, you will evaluate educational programs to find one that's right for you.

People who have complex educational or experiential learning histories might want to have their learning evaluated by the Regents Credit Bank. The Credit Bank, operated by Regents College of the University of the State of New York, allows people to consolidate credits earned through college, experience, or other methods. Special assessments are available for Regents College enrollees whose knowledge in a specific field cannot be adequately evaluated by standardized exams. For more information, contact the Regents Credit Bank at:

Regents College
7 Columbia Circle
Albany, NY 12203-5159
(518) 464-8500

Credit For Prior College Coursework

When Lynette was in college during the 1970s, she attended several different schools and took a variety of courses. She did well in some classes and poorly in others. Now that she is a successful business owner and has more focus, Lynette thinks she should forget about her previous coursework and start from scratch. Instead, she should start from where she is.

Lynette should have all her transcripts sent to the colleges or universities of her choice and let an admissions officer determine which classes are applicable toward a degree. A few credits here and there may not seem like much, but they add up. Even if the subjects do not seem relevant to any major, they might be counted as elective credits toward a degree. And comparing the cost of transcripts with the cost of college courses, it makes sense to spend a few dollars per transcript for a chance to save hundreds, and perhaps thousands, of dollars in books and tuition.

Rules for transferring credits apply to all prior coursework at accredited colleges and universities, whether done on campus or off. Courses completed off campus, often called extended learning, include those available to students through independent study and correspondence. Many schools have extended learning programs; Brigham Young University, for example, offers more than 300 courses through its Department of Independent Study. One type of extended learning is distance learning, a form of correspondence study by technological means such as television, video and audio, CD-ROM, electronic mail, and computer tutorials. See the Resources section at the end of this article for more information about publications available from the National University Continuing Education Association.

Any previously earned college credits should be considered for transfer, no matter what the subject or the grade received. Many schools do not accept the transfer of courses graded below a C or ones taken more than a designated number of years ago. Some colleges and universities also have limits on the number of credits that can be transferred and applied toward a degree. But not all do. For example, Thomas Edison State College, New Jersey's State college for adults, accepts the transfer of all 120 hours of credit required for a baccalaureate degree – provided all the credits are transferred from regionally accredited schools, no more than 80 are at the junior college level, and the student's grades overall and in the field of study average out to C.

To assign credit for prior coursework, most schools require original transcripts. This means you must complete a form or send a written, signed request to have your transcripts released directly to a college or university. Once you have chosen the schools you want to apply to, contact the schools you attended before. Find out how much each transcript costs, and ask them to send your transcripts to the ones you are applying to. Write a letter that includes your name (and names used during attendance, if different) and dates of attendance, along with the names and addresses of the schools to which your transcripts should be sent. Include payment and mail to the registrar at the schools you have attended. The registrar's office will process your request and send an official transcript of your coursework to the colleges or universities you have designated.

Credit For Noncollege Courses

Colleges and universities are not the only ones that offer classes. Volunteer organizations and employers often provide formal training worth college credit. The American Council on Education has two programs that assess thousands of specific courses and make recommendations on the amount of college credit they are worth. Colleges and universities accept the recommendations or use them as guidelines.

One program evaluates educational courses sponsored by government agencies, business and industry, labor unions, and professional and voluntary organizations. It is the Program on Noncollegiate Sponsored Instruction (PONSI). Some of the training seminars Alice has participated in covered topics such as food preparation, kitchen safety, and nutrition. Although she has not yet earned her GED, Alice can earn college credit because of her completion of these formal job-training seminars. The number of credits each seminar is worth does not hinge on Alice's current eligibility for college enrollment.

The other program evaluates courses offered by the Army, Navy, Air Force, Marines, Coast Guard, and Department of Defense. It is the Military Evaluations Program. Jorge has never attended college, but the engineering technology classes he completed as part of his military training are worth college credit. And as an Army veteran, Jorge is eligible for a service that takes the evaluations one step further. The Army/American Council on Education Registry Transcript System (AARTS) will provide Jorge with an individualized transcript of American Council on Education credit recommendations for all courses he completed, the military occupational specialties (MOS's) he held, and examinations he passed while in the Army. All Army and National Guard enlisted personnel and veterans who enlisted after October 1981 are eligible for the transcript. Similar services are being considered by the Navy and Marine Corps.

To obtain a free transcript, see your Army Education Center for a 5454R transcript request form. Include your name, Social Security number, basic active service date, and complete address where you want the transcript sent. Mail your request to:
AARTS Operations Center
415 McPherson Ave.
Fort Leavenworth, KS 66027-1373

Recommendations for PONSI are published in *The National Guide to Educational Credit for Training Programs;* military program recommendations are in *The Guide to the Evaluation of Educational Experiences in the Armed Forces.* See the Resources section at the end of this article for more information about these publications.

Former military personnel who took a foreign language course through the Defense Language Institute may request course transcripts by sending their name, Social Security number, course title, duration of the course, and graduation date to:

Commandant, Defense Language Institute
Attn: ATFL-DAA-AR
Transcripts
Presidio of Monterey
Monterey, CA 93944-5006

Not all of Jorge's and Alice's courses have been assessed by the American Council on Education. Training courses that have no Council credit recommendation should still be assessed by an advisor at the schools they want to attend. Course descriptions, class notes, test scores, and other documentation may be helpful for comparing training courses to their college equivalents. An oral examination or other demonstration of competency might also be required.

There is no guarantee you will receive all the credits you are seeking – but you certainly won't if you make no attempt.

Credit By Examination

Standardized tests are the best-known method of receiving college credit without taking courses. These exams are often taken by high school students seeking advanced placement for college, but they are also available to adult learners. Testing programs and colleges and universities offer exams in a number of subjects. Two U.S. Government institutes have foreign language exams for employees that also may be worth college credit.

It is important to understand that receiving a passing score on these exams does not mean you get college credit automatically. Each school determines which test results it will accept, minimum scores required, how scores are converted for credit, and the amount of credit, if any, to be assigned. Most colleges and universities accept the American Council on Education credit recommendations, published every other year in the 250-page *Guide to Educational Credit by Examination*. For more information, contact:

The American Council on Education
Credit by Examination Program
One Dupont Circle, Suite 250
Washington, DC 20036-1193
(202) 939-9434

Testing programs:

You might know some of the five national testing programs by their acronyms or initials: CLEP, ACT PEP: RCE, DANTES, AP, and NOCTI. (The meanings of these initialisms are explained below.) There is some overlap among programs; for example, four of them have introductory accounting exams. Since you will not be awarded credit more than once for a specific subject, you should carefully evaluate each program for the subject exams you wish to take. And before taking an exam, make sure you will be awarded credit by the college or university you plan to attend.

CLEP (College-Level Examination Program), administered by the College Board, is the most widely accepted of the national testing programs; more than 2,800 accredited schools award credit for passing exam scores. Each test covers material taught in basic undergraduate courses. There are five general exams – English composition, humanities, college mathematics, natural sciences, and social sciences and history – and many subject exams. Most exams are entirely multiple-choice, but English composition exams may include an essay section. For more information, contact:

    CLEP
    P.O. Box 6600
    Princeton, NJ 08541-6600
    (609) 771-7865

ACT PEP: RCE (American College Testing Proficiency Exam Program: Regents College Examinations) tests are given in 38 subjects within arts and sciences, business, education, and nursing. Each exam is recommended for either lower- or upper-level credit. Exams contain either objective or extended response questions, and are graded according to a standard score, letter grade, or pass/fail. Fees vary, depending on the subject and type of exam. For more information or to request free study guides, contact:

    ACT PEP: Regents College Examinations
    P.O. Box 4014
    Iowa City, IA 52243
    (319) 337-1387
    (New York State residents must contact Regents College directly.)

DANTES (Defense Activity for Nontraditional Education Support) standardized tests are developed by the Educational Testing Service for the Department of Defense. Originally administered only to military personnel, the exams have been available to the public since 1983. About 50 subject tests cover business, mathematics, social science, physical science, humanities, foreign languages, and applied technology. Most of the tests consist entirely of multiple-choice questions. Schools determine their own administering fees and testing schedules. For more information or to request free study sheets, contact:

    DANTES Program Office
    Mail Stop 31-X
    Educational Testing Service
    Princeton, NJ 08541
    1(800) 257-9484

The AP (Advanced Placement) Program is a cooperative effort between secondary schools and colleges and universities. AP exams are developed each year by committees of college and high school faculty appointed by the College Board and assisted by consultants from the Educational Testing Service. Subjects include arts and languages, natural sciences, computer science, social sciences, history, and mathematics. Most tests are 2 or 3 hours long and include both multiple-choice and essay questions. AP courses are available to help students prepare for exams, which are offered in the spring. For more information about the Advanced Placement Program, contact:

    Advanced Placement Services
    P.O. Box 6671
    Princeton, NJ 08541-6671
    (609) 771-7300

NOCTI (National Occupational Competency Testing Institute) assessments are designed for people like Alice, who have vocational-technical skills that cannot be evaluated by other tests. NOCTI assesses competency at two levels: Student/job ready and teacher/experienced worker. Standardized evaluations are available for occupations such as auto-body repair, electronics, mechanical drafting, quantity food preparation, and upholstering. The tests consist of multiple-choice questions and a performance component. Other services include workshops, customized assessments, and pre-testing. For more information, contact:

NOCTI
500 N. Bronson Ave.
Ferris State University
Big Rapids, MI 49307
(616) 796-4699

Colleges and universities:

Many colleges and universities have credit-by-exam programs, through which students earn credit by passing a comprehensive exam for a course offered by the institution. Among the most widely recognized are the programs at Ohio University, the University of North Carolina, Thomas Edison State College, and New York University.

Ohio University offers about 150 examinations for credit. In addition, you may sometimes arrange to take special examinations in non-laboratory courses offered at Ohio University. To take a test for credit, you must enroll in the course. If you plan to transfer the credit earned, you also need written permission from an official at your school. Books and study materials are available, for a cost, through the university. Exams must be taken within 6 months of the enrollment date; most last 3 hours. You may arrange to take the exam off campus if you do not live near the university.

Ohio University is on the quarter-hour system; most courses are worth 4 quarter hours, the equivalent of 3 semester hours. For more information, contact:

Independent Study
Tupper Hall 302
Ohio University
Athens, OH 45701-2979
1(800) 444-2910
(614) 593-2910

The University of North Carolina offers a credit-by-examination option for 140 independent study (correspondence) courses in foreign languages, humanities, social sciences, mathematics, business administration, education, electrical and computer engineering, health administration, and natural sciences. To take an exam, you must request and receive approval from both the course instructor and the independent studies department. Exams must be taken within six months of enrollment, and you may register for no more than two at a time. If you are not near the University's Chapel Hill campus, you may take your exam under supervision at an accredited college, university, community college, or technical institute. For more information, contact:

Independent Studies
CB #1020, The Friday Center
UNC-Chapel Hill
Chapel Hill, NC 27599-1020
1(800) 862-5669 / (919) 962-1134

The Thomas Edison College Examination Program offers more than 50 exams in liberal arts, business, and professional areas. Thomas Edison State College administers tests twice a month in Trenton, New Jersey; however, students may arrange to take their tests with a proctor at any accredited American college or university or U.S. military base. Most of the tests are multiple choice; some also include short answer or essay questions. Time limits range from 90 minutes to 4 hours, depending on the exam. For more information, contact:

Thomas Edison State College
TECEP, Office of Testing and Assessment
101 W. State Street
Trenton, NJ 08608-1176
(609) 633-2844

New York University's Foreign Language Program offers proficiency exams in more than 40 languages, from Albanian to Yiddish. Two exams are available in each language: The 12-point test is equivalent to 4 undergraduate semesters, and the 16-point exam may lead to upper level credit. The tests are given at the university's Foreign Language Department throughout the year.

Proof of foreign language proficiency does not guarantee college credit. Some colleges and universities accept transcripts only for languages commonly taught, such as French and Spanish. Nontraditional programs are more likely than traditional ones to grant credit for proficiency in other languages.

For an informational brochure and registration form for NYU's foreign language proficiency exams, contact:

New York University
Foreign Language Department
48 Cooper Square, Room 107
New York, NY 10003
(212) 998-7030

Government institutes:
The Defense Language Institute and Foreign Service Institute administer foreign language proficiency exams for personnel stationed abroad. Usually, the tests are given at the end of intensive language courses or upon completion of service overseas. But some people – like Jorge, who knows Spanish – speak another language fluently and may be allowed to take a proficiency exam in that language before completing their tour of duty. Contact one of the offices listed below to obtain transcripts of those scores. Proof of proficiency does not guarantee college credit, however, as discussed above.

To request score reports from the Defense Language Institute for Defense Language Proficiency Tests, send your name, Social Security number, language for which you were tested, and, most importantly, when and where you took the exam to:

Commandant, Defense Language Institute
Attn: ATFL-ES-T
DLPT Score Report Request
Presidio of Monterey
Monterey, CA 93944-5006

To request transcripts of scores for Foreign Service Institute exams, send your name, Social Security number, language for which you were tested, and dates or year of exams to:

Foreign Service Institute
Arlington Hall
4020 Arlington Boulevard
Rosslyn, VA 22204-1500
Attn: Testing Office (Send your request to the attention of the testing office of the foreign language in which you were tested)

Credit For Experience

Experiential learning credit may be given for knowledge gained through job responsibilities, personal hobbies, volunteer opportunities, homemaking, and other experiences. Colleges and universities base credit awards on the knowledge you have attained, not for the experience alone. In addition, the knowledge must be college level; not just any learning will do. Throwing horseshoes as a hobby is not likely to be worth college credit. But if you've done research on how and where the sport originated, visited blacksmiths, organized tournaments, and written a column for a trade journal – well, that's a horseshoe of a different color.

Adults attempting to get credit for their experience should be forewarned: Having your experience evaluated for college credit is time-consuming, tedious work – not an easy shortcut for people who want quick-fix college credits. And not all experience, no matter how valuable, is the equivalent of college courses.

Requesting college credit for your experiential learning can be tricky. You should get assistance from a credit evaluations officer at the school you plan to attend, but you should also have a general idea of what your knowledge is worth. A common method for converting knowledge into credit is to use a college catalog. Find course titles and descriptions that match what you have learned through experience, and request the number of credits offered for those courses.

Once you know what credit to ask for, you must usually present your case in writing to officials at the college you plan to attend. The most common form of presenting experiential learning for credit is the portfolio. A portfolio is a written record of your knowledge along with a request for equivalent college credit. It includes an identification and description of the knowledge for which you are requesting credit, an explanatory essay of how the knowledge was gained and how it fits into your educational plans, documentation that you have acquired such knowledge, and a request for college credit. Required elements of a portfolio vary by schools but generally follow those guidelines.

In identifying knowledge you have gained, be specific about exactly what you have learned. For example, it is not enough for Lynette to say she runs a business. She must identify the knowledge she has gained from running it, such as personnel management, tax law, marketing strategy, and inventory review. She must also include brief descriptions about her knowledge of each to support her claims of having those skills.

The essay gives you a chance to relay something about who you are. It should address your educational goals, include relevant autobiographical details, and be well organized, neat, and convey confidence. In his essay, Jorge might first state his goal of becoming an engineer. Then he would explain why he joined the Army, where he got hands-on training and experience in developing and servicing electronic equipment.

This, he would say, led to his hobby of creating remote-controlled model cars, of which he has built 20. His conclusion would highlight his accomplishments and tie them to his desire to become an electronic engineer.

Documentation is evidence that you've learned what you claim to have learned. You can show proof of knowledge in a variety of ways, including audio or video recordings, letters from current or former employers describing your specific duties and job performance, blueprints, photographs or artwork, and transcripts of certifying exams for professional licenses and certification – such as Alice's certification from the American Culinary Federation. Although documentation can take many forms, written proof alone is not always enough. If it is impossible to document your knowledge in writing, find out if your experiential learning can be assessed through supplemental oral exams by a faculty expert.

Earning a College Degree

Nontraditional students often have work, family, and financial obligations that prevent them from quitting their jobs to attend school full time. Can they still meet their educational goals? Yes.

More than 150 accredited colleges and universities have nontraditional bachelor's degree programs that require students to spend little or no time on campus; over 300 others have nontraditional campus-based degree programs. Some of those schools, as well as most junior and community colleges, offer associate's degrees nontraditionally. Each school with a nontraditional course of study determines its own rules for awarding credit for prior coursework, exams, or experience, as discussed previously. Most have charges on top of tuition for providing these special services.

Several publications profile nontraditional degree programs; see the Resources section at the end of this article for more information. To determine which school best fits your academic profile and educational goals, first list your criteria. Then, evaluate nontraditional programs based on their accreditation, features, residency requirements, and expenses. Once you have chosen several schools to explore further, write to them for more information. Detailed explanations of school policies should help you decide which ones you want to apply to.

Get beyond the printed word – especially the glowing words each school writes about itself. Check out the schools you are considering with higher education authorities, alumni, employers, family members, and friends. If possible, visit the campus to talk to students and instructors and sit in on a few classes, even if you will be completing most or all of your work off campus. Ask school officials questions about such things as enrollment numbers, graduation rate, faculty qualifications, and confusing details about the application process or academic policies. After you have thoroughly investigated each prospective college or university, you can make an informed decision about which is right for you.

Accreditation

Accreditation is a process colleges and universities submit to voluntarily for getting their credentials. An accredited school has been investigated and visited by teams of observers and has periodic inspections by a private accrediting agency. The initial review can take two years or more.

Regional agencies accredit entire schools, and professional agencies accredit either specialized schools or departments within schools. Although there are no national accrediting standards, not just any accreditation will do. Countless "accreditation associations" have been invented by schools, many of which have no academic programs and sell phony degrees, to accredit themselves. But 6 regional and about 80 professional accrediting associations in the United States are recognized by the U.S. Department of Education or the Commission on Recognition of Postsecondary Accreditation. When checking accreditation, these are the names to look for. For more information about accreditation and accrediting agencies, contact:

> Institutional Participation Oversight Service Accreditation and State Liaison Division
> U.S. Department of Education
> ROB 3, Room 3915
> 600 Independence Ave., SW
> Washington, DC 20202-5244
> (202) 708-7417

Because accreditation is not mandatory, lack of accreditation does not necessarily mean a school or program is bad. Some schools choose not to apply for accreditation, are in the process of applying, or have educational methods too unconventional for an accrediting association's standards. For the nontraditional student, however, earning a degree from a college or university with recognized accreditation is an especially important consideration. Although nontraditional education is becoming more widely accepted, it is not yet mainstream. Employers skeptical of a degree earned in a nontraditional manner are likely to be even less accepting of one from an unaccredited school.

Program Features

Because nontraditional students have diverse educational objectives, nontraditional schools are diverse in what they offer. Some programs are geared toward helping students organize their scattered educational credits to get a degree as quickly as possible. Others cater to those who may have specific credits or experience but need assistance in completing requirements. Whatever your educational profile, you should look for a program that works with you in obtaining your educational goals.

A few nontraditional programs have special admissions policies for adult learners like Alice, who plan to earn their GEDs but want to enroll in college in the meantime. Other features of nontraditional programs include individualized learning agreements, intensive academic counseling, cooperative learning and internship placement, and waiver of some prerequisites or other requirements – as well as college credit for prior coursework, examinations, and experiential learning, all discussed previously.

Lynette, whose primary goal is to finish her degree, wants to earn maximum credits for her business experience. She will look for programs that do not limit the number of credits awarded for equivalency exams and experiential learning. And since well-documented proof of knowledge is essential for earning experiential learning credits, Lynette should make sure the program she chooses provides assistance to students submitting a portfolio.

Jorge, on the other hand, has more credits than he needs in certain areas and is willing to forego some. To become an engineer, he must have a bachelor's degree; but because he is accustomed to hands-on learning, Jorge is interested in getting experience as he gains more technical skills. He will concentrate on finding schools with strong cooperative education, supervised fieldwork, or internship programs.

Residency Requirements

Programs are sometimes deemed nontraditional because of their residency requirements. Many people think of residency for colleges and universities in terms of tuition, with in-state students paying less than out-of-state ones. Residency also may refer to where a student lives, either on or off campus, while attending school.

But in nontraditional education, residency usually refers to how much time students must spend on campus, regardless of whether they attend classes there. In some nontraditional programs, students need not ever step foot on campus. Others require only a very short residency, such as one day or a few weeks. Many schools have standard residency requirements of several semesters but schedule classes for evenings or weekends to accommodate working adults.

Lynette, who previously took courses by independent study, prefers to earn credits by distance study. She will focus on schools that have no residency requirement. Several colleges and universities have nonresident degree completion programs for adults with some college credit. Under the direction of a faculty advisor, students devise a plan for earning their remaining credits. Methods for earning credits include independent study, distance learning, seminars, supervised fieldwork, and group study at arranged sites. Students may have to earn a certain number of credits through the degree-granting institution. But many programs allow students to take courses at accredited schools of their choice for transfer toward their degree.

Alice wants to attend lectures but has an unpredictable schedule. Her best course of action will be to seek out short residency programs that require students to attend seminars once or twice a semester. She can take courses that are televised and videotape them to watch when her schedule permits, with the seminars helping to ensure that she properly completes her coursework. Many colleges and universities with short residency requirements also permit students to earn some credits elsewhere, by whatever means the student chooses.

Some fields of study require classroom instruction. As Jorge will discover, few colleges and universities allow students to earn a bachelor's degree in engineering entirely through independent study. Nontraditional residency programs are designed to accommodate adults' daytime work schedules. Jorge should look for programs offering evening, weekend, summer, and accelerated courses.

Tuition and Other Expenses

The final decisions about which schools Alice, Jorge, and Lynette attend may hinge in large part on a single issue: Cost. And rising tuition is only part of the equation. Beginning with application fees and continuing through graduation fees, college expenses add up.

Traditional and nontraditional students have some expenses in common, such as the cost of books and other materials. Tuition might even be the same for some courses, especially for colleges and universities offering standard ones at unusual times. But for nontraditional programs, students may also pay fees for services such as credit or transcript review, evaluation, advisement, and portfolio assessment.

Students are also responsible for postage and handling or setup expenses for independent study courses, as well as for all examination and transcript fees for transferring credits. Usually, the more nontraditional the program, the more detailed the fees. Some schools charge a yearly enrollment fee rather than tuition for degree completion candidates who want their files to remain active.

Although tuition and fees might seem expensive, most educators tell you not to let money come between you and your educational goals. Talk to someone in the financial aid department of the school you plan to attend or check your library for publications about financial aid sources. The U.S. Department of Education publishes a guide to Federal aid programs such as Pell Grants, student loans, and work-study. To order the free 74-page booklet, *The Student Guide: Financial Aid from the U.S. Department of Education,* contact:

Federal Student Aid Information Center
P.O. Box 84
Washington, DC 20044
1 (800) 4FED-AID (433-3243)

Resources

Information on how to earn a high school diploma or college degree without following the usual routes is available from several organizations and in numerous publications. Information on nontraditional graduate degree programs, available for master's through doctoral level, though not discussed in this article, can usually be obtained from the same resources that detail bachelor's degree programs.

National Learning Corporation publishes study guides for all of these exams, for both general examinations and tests in specific subject areas. To order study guides, or to browse their catalog featuring more than 5,000 titles, visit NLC online at www.passbooks.com, or contact them by phone at (800) 632-8888.

Organizations

Adult learners should always contact their local school system, community college, or university to learn about programs that are readily available. The following national organizations can also supply information:

American Council on Education
One Dupont Circle
Washington, DC 20036-1193
(202) 939-9300

Within the American Council on Education, the Center for Adult Learning and Educational Credentials administers the National External Diploma Program, the GED Program, the Program on Noncollegiate Sponsored Instruction, the Credit by Examination Program, and the Military Evaluations Program.

College-Level Examination Program (CLEP)

1. WHAT IS CLEP?

CLEP stands for the College-Level Examination Program, sponsored by the College Board. It is a national program of credit-by-examination that offers you the opportunity to obtain recognition for college-level achievement. No matter when, where, or how you have learned – by means of formal or informal study – you can take CLEP tests. If the results are acceptable to your college, you can receive credit.

You may not realize it, but you probably know more than your academic record reveals. Each day you, like most people, have an opportunity to learn. In private industry and business, as well as at all levels of government, learning opportunities continually occur. If you read widely or intensively in a particular field, think about what you read, discuss it with your family and friends, you are learning. Or you may be learning on a more formal basis by taking a correspondence course, a television or radio course, a course recorded on tape or cassettes, a course assembled into programmed tests, or a course taught in your community adult school or high school.

No matter how, where, or when you gained your knowledge, you may have the opportunity to receive academic credit for your achievement that can be counted toward an undergraduate degree. The College-Level Examination Program (CLEP) enables colleges to evaluate your achievement and give you credit. A wide range of college-level examinations are offered by CLEP to anyone who wishes to take them. Scores on the tests are reported to you and, if you wish, to a college, employer, or individual.

2. WHAT ARE THE PURPOSES OF THE COLLEGE-LEVEL EXAMINATION PROGRAM?

The basic purpose of the College-Level Examination Program is to enable individuals who have acquired their education in nontraditional ways to demonstrate their academic achievement. It is also intended for use by those in higher education, business, industry, government, and other fields who need a reliable method of assessing a person's educational level.

Recognizing that the real issue is not how a person has acquired his education but what education he has, the College Level Examination Program has been designed to serve a variety of purposes. The basic purpose, as listed above, is to enable those who have reached the college level of education in nontraditional ways to assess the level of their achievement and to use the test results in seeking college credit or placement.

In addition, scores on the tests can be used to validate educational experience obtained at a nonaccredited institution or through noncredit college courses.

Some colleges and universities may use the tests to measure the level of educational achievement of their students, and for various institutional research purposes.

Other colleges and universities may wish to use the tests in the admission, placement, and guidance of students who wish to transfer from one institution to another.

Businesses, industries, governmental agencies, and professional groups now accept the results of these tests as a basis for advancement, eligibility for further training, or professional or semi-professional certification.

Many people are interested in the examination simply to assess their own educational progress and attainment.

The college, university, business, industry, or government agency that adopts the tests in the College-Level Examination Program makes its own decision about how it will use and interpret the test scores. The College Board will provide the tests, score them, and report the results either to the individuals who took the tests or the college or agency that administered them. It does NOT, and cannot, award college credit, certify college equivalency, or make recommendations regarding the standards these institutions should establish for the use of the test results.

Therefore, if you are taking the tests to secure credit from an institution, you should FIRST ascertain whether the college or agency involved will accept the scores. Each institution determines which CLEP tests it will accept for credit and the amount of credit it will award. If you want to take tests for college credit, first call, write, or visit the college you wish to attend to inquire about its policy on CLEP scores, as well as its other admission requirements.

The services of the program are also available to people who have been requested to take the tests by an employer, a professional licensing agency, a certifying agency, or by other groups that recognize college equivalency on the basis of satisfactory CLEP scores. You may, of course, take the tests SOLELY for your own information. If you do, your scores will be reported only to you.

While neither CLEP nor the College Board can evaluate previous credentials or award college credit, you will receive, with your scores, basic information to help you interpret your performance on the tests you have taken.

3. WHAT ARE THE COLLEGE-LEVEL EXAMINATIONS?

In order to meet different kinds of curricular organization and testing needs at colleges and universities, the College-Level Examination Program offers 35 different subject tests falling under five separate general categories: Composition and Literature, Foreign Languages, History and Social Sciences, Science and Mathematics, and Business.

4. WHAT ARE THE SUBJECT EXAMINATIONS?

The 35 CLEP tests offered by the College Board are listed below:

COMPOSITION AND LITERATURE:
- American Literature
- Analyzing and Interpreting Literature
- English Composition
- English Composition with Essay
- English Literature
- Freshman College Composition
- Humanities

FOREIGN LANGUAGES
- French
- German
- Spanish

HISTORY AND SOCIAL SCIENCES
- American Government
- Introduction to Educational Psychology
- History of the United States I: Early Colonization to 1877
- History of the United States II: 1865 to the Present
- Human Growth and Development
- Principles of Macroeconomics
- Principles of Microeconomics
- Introductory Psychology
- Social Sciences and History
- Introductory Sociology
- Western Civilization I: Ancient Near East to 1648
- Western Civilization II: 1648 to the Present

SCIENCE AND MATHEMATICS
- College Algebra
- College Algebra-Trigonometry
- Biology
- Calculus
- Chemistry
- College Mathematics
- Natural Sciences
- Trigonometry
- Precalculus

BUSINESS
- Financial Accounting
- Introductory Business Law
- Information Systems and Computer Applications
- Principles of Management
- Principles of Marketing

CLEP Examinations cover material taught in courses that most students take as requirements in the first two years of college. A college usually grants the same amount of credit to students earning satisfactory scores on the CLEP examination as it grants to students successfully completing the equivalent course.

Many examinations are designed to correspond to one-semester courses; some, however, correspond to full-year or two-year courses.

Each exam is 90 minutes long and, except for English Composition with Essay, is made up primarily of multiple-choice questions. Some tests have several other types of questions besides multiple choice. To see a more detailed description of a particular CLEP exam, visit www.collegeboard.com/clep.

The English Composition with Essay exam is the only exam that includes a required essay. This essay is scored by college English faculty designated by CLEP and does not require an additional fee. However, other Composition and Literature tests offer optional essays, which some college and universities require and some do not. These essays are graded by faculty at the individual institutions that require them and require an additional $10 fee. Contact the particular institution to ask about essay requirements, and check with your test center for further details.

All 35 CLEP examinations are administered on computer. If you are unfamiliar with taking a test on a computer, consult the CLEP Sampler online at www.collegeboard.com/clep. The Sampler contains the same tutorials as the actual exams and helps familiarize you with navigation and how to answer different types of questions.

Points are not deducted for wrong or skipped answers – you receive one point for every correct answer. Therefore it is best that an answer is supplied for each exam question, whether it is a guess or not. The number of correct answers is then converted to a formula score. This formula, or "scaled," score is determined by a statistical process called *equating*, which adjusts for slight differences in difficulty between test forms and ensures that your score does not depend on the specific test form you took or how well others did on the same form. The scaled scores range from 20 to 80 – this is the number that will appear on your score report.

To ensure that you complete all questions in the time allotted, you would probably be wise to skip the more difficult or perplexing questions and return to them later. Although the multiple-choice items in these tests are carefully designed so as not to be tricky, misleading, or ambiguous, on the other hand, they are not all direct questions of factual information. They attempt, in their way, to elicit a response that indicates your knowledge or lack of knowledge of the material in question or your ability or inability to use or interpret a fact or idea. Thus, you should concentrate on answering the questions as they appear to be without attempting to out-guess the testmakers.

5. WHAT ARE THE FEES?

The fee for all CLEP examinations is $55. Optional essays required by some institutions are an additional $10.

6. WHEN ARE THE TESTS GIVEN?

CLEP tests are administered year-round. Consult the CLEP website (www.collegeboard.com/clep) and individual test centers for specific information.

7. WHERE ARE THE TESTS GIVEN?

More than 1,300 test centers are located on college and university campuses throughout the country, and additional centers are being established to meet increased needs. Any accredited collegiate institution with an explicit and publicly available policy of credit by examination can become a CLEP test center. To obtain a list of these centers, visit the CLEP website at www.collegeboard.com/clep.

8. HOW DO I REGISTER FOR THE COLLEGE-LEVEL EXAMINATION PROGRAM?

Contact an individual test center for information regarding registration, scheduling and fees. Registration/admission forms can also be obtained on the CLEP website.

9. MAY I REPEAT THE COLLEGE-LEVEL EXAMINATIONS?

You may repeat any examination providing at least six months have passed since you were last administered this test. If you repeat a test within a period of time less than six months, your scores will be cancelled and your fees forfeited. To repeat a test, check the appropriate space on the registration form.

10. WHEN MAY I EXPECT MY SCORE REPORTS?

With the exception of the English Composition with Essay exam, you should receive your score report instantly once the test is complete.

11. HOW SHOULD I PREPARE FOR THE COLLEGE-LEVEL EXAMINATIONS?

This book has been specifically designed to prepare candidates for these examinations. It will help you to consider, study, and review important content, principles, practices, procedures, problems, and techniques in the form of varied and concrete applications.

12. QUESTIONS AND ANSWERS APPEARING IN THIS PUBLICATION

The College-Level Examinations are offered by the College Board. Since copies of past examinations have not been made available, we have used equivalent materials, including questions and answers, which are highly recommended by us as an appropriate means of preparing for these examinations.

If you need additional information about CLEP Examinations, visit www.collegeboard.com/clep.

THE COLLEGE-LEVEL EXAMINATION PROGRAM

How The Program Works

CLEP examinations are administered at many colleges and universities across the country, and most institutions award college credit to those who do well on them. The examinations provide people who have acquired knowledge outside the usual educational settings the opportunity to show that they have learned college-level material without taking certain college courses.

The CLEP examinations cover material that is taught in introductory-level courses at many colleges and universities. Faculties at individual colleges review the tests to ensure that they cover the important material taught in their courses. Colleges differ in the examinations they accept; some colleges accept only two or three of the examinations while others accept nearly all of them.

Although CLEP is sponsored by the College Board and the examinations are scored by Educational Testing Service (ETS), neither of these organizations can award college credit. Only accredited colleges may grant credit toward a degree. When you take a CLEP examination, you may request that a copy of your score report be sent to the college you are attending or plan to attend. After evaluating your scores, the college will decide whether or not to award you credit for a certain course or courses, or to exempt you from them. If the college gives you credit, it will record the number of credits on your permanent record, thereby indicating that you have completed work equivalent to a course in that subject. If the college decides to grant exemption without giving you credit for a course, you will be permitted to omit a course that would normally be required of you and to take a course of your choice instead.

What the Examinations Are Like

The examinations consist mostly of multiple-choice questions to be answered within a 90-minute time limit. Additional information about each CLEP examination is given in the examination guide and on the CLEP website.

Where To Take the Examinations

CLEP examinations are administered throughout the year at the test centers of approximately 1,300 colleges and universities. On the CLEP website, you will find a list of institutions that award credit for satisfactory scores on CLEP examinations. Some colleges administer CLEP examinations to their own students only. Other institutions administer the tests to anyone who registers to take them. If your college does not administer the tests, contact the test centers in your area for information about its testing schedule.

Once you have been tested, your score report will be available instantly. CLEP scores are kept on file at ETS for 20 years; and during this period, for a small fee, you may have your transcript sent to another college or to anyone else you specify. (Your scores will never be sent to anyone without your approval.)

APPROACHING A COLLEGE ABOUT CLEP

The following sections provide a step-by-step approach to learning about the CLEP policy at a particular college or university. The person or office that can best assist students desiring CLEP credit may have a different title at each institution, but the following guidelines will lead you to information about CLEP at any institution.

Adults returning to college often benefit from special assistance when they approach a college. Opportunities for adults to return to formal learning in the classroom are now widespread, and colleges and universities have worked hard to make this a smooth process for older students. Many colleges have established special service offices that are staffed with trained professionals who understand the kinds of problems facing adults returning to college. If you think you might benefit from such assistance, be sure to find out whether these services are available at your college.

How to Apply for College Credit

STEP 1. Obtain the General Information Catalog and a copy of the CLEP policy from the colleges you are considering. If you have not yet applied for admission, ask for an admissions application form too.

Information about admissions and CLEP policies can be obtained by contacting college admissions offices or finding admissions information on the school websites. Tell the admissions officer that you are a prospective student and that you are interested in applying for admission and CLEP credit. Ask for a copy of the publication in which the college's complete CLEP policy is explained. Also get the name and the telephone number of the person to contact in case you have further questions about CLEP.

At this step, you may wish to obtain information from external degree colleges. Many adults find that such colleges suit their needs exceptionally well.

STEP 2. If you have not already been admitted to the college you are considering, look at its admission requirements for undergraduate students to see if you can qualify.

This is an important step because if you can't get into college, you can't get college credit for CLEP. Nearly all colleges require students to be admitted and to enroll in one or more courses before granting the students CLEP credit.

Virtually all public community colleges and a number of four-year state colleges have open admission policies for in-state students. This usually means that they admit anyone who has graduated from high school or has earned a high school equivalency diploma.

If you think you do not meet the admission requirements, contact the admissions office for an interview with a counselor. Colleges do sometimes make exceptions, particularly for adult applicants. State why you want the interview and ask what documents you should bring with you or send in advance. (These materials may include a high school transcript, transcript of previous college work, completed application for admission, etc.) Make an extra effort to have all the information requested in time for the interview.

During the interview, relax and be yourself. Be prepared to state honestly why you think you are ready and able to do college work. If you have already taken CLEP examinations and scored high enough to earn credit, you have shown that you are able to do college work. Mention this achievement to the admissions counselor because it may increase your chances of being accepted. If you have not taken a CLEP examination, you can still improve your chances of being accepted by describing how your job training or independent study has helped prepare you for college-level work. Tell the counselor what you have learned from your work and personal experiences.

STEP 3. Evaluate the college's CLEP policy.

Typically, a college lists all its academic policies, including CLEP policies, in its general catalog. You will probably find the CLEP policy statement under a heading such as Credit-by-Examination, Advanced Standing, Advanced Placement, or External Degree Program. These sections can usually be found in the front of the catalog.

Many colleges publish their credit-by-examination policies in a separate brochure, which is distributed through the campus testing office, counseling center, admissions office, or registrar's office. If you find a very general policy statement in the college catalog, seek clarification from one of these offices.

Review the material in the section of this guide entitled Questions to Ask About a College's CLEP Policy. Use these guidelines to evaluate the college's CLEP policy. If you have not yet taken a CLEP examination, this evaluation will help you decide which examinations to take and whether or not to take the free-response or essay portion. Because individual colleges have different CLEP policies, a review of several policies may help you decide which college to attend.

STEP 4. If you have not yet applied for admission, do so early.

Most colleges expect you to apply for admission several months before you enroll, and it is essential that you meet the published application deadlines. It takes time to process your application for admission; and if you have yet to take a CLEP examination, it will be some time before the college receives and reviews your score report. You will probably want to take some, if not all, of the CLEP examinations you are interested in before you enroll so you know which courses you need not register for. In fact, some colleges require that all CLEP scores be submitted before a student registers.

Complete all forms and include all documents requested with your application(s) for admission. Normally, an admissions decision cannot be reached until all documents have been submitted and evaluated. Unless told to do so, do not send your CLEP scores until you have been officially admitted.

STEP 5. Arrange to take CLEP examination(s) or to submit your CLEP score(s).

You may want to wait to take your CLEP examinations until you know definitely which college you will be attending. Then you can make sure you are taking tests your college will accept for credit. You will also be able to request that your scores be sent to the college, free of charge, when you take the tests.

If you have already taken CLEP examinations, but did not have a copy of your score report sent to your college, you may request the College Board to send an official transcript at any time for a small fee. Use the Transcript Request Form that was sent to you with your score report. If you do not have the form, you may find it online at www.collegeboard.com/clep.

Your CLEP scores will be evaluated, probably by someone in the admissions office, and sent to the registrar's office to be posted on your permanent record once you are enrolled. Procedures vary from college to college, but the process usually begins in the admissions office.

STEP 6. Ask to receive a written notice of the credit you receive for your CLEP score(s).

A written notice may save you problems later, when you submit your degree plan or file for graduation. In the event that there is a question about whether or not you earned CLEP credit, you will have an official record of what credit was awarded. You may also need this verification of course credit if you go for academic counseling before the credit is posted on your permanent record.

STEP 7. Before you register for courses, seek academic counseling.

A discussion with your academic advisor can prevent you from taking unnecessary courses and can tell you specifically what your CLEP credit will mean to you. This step may be accomplished at the time you enroll. Most colleges have orientation sessions for new students prior to each enrollment period. During orientation, students are usually assigned an academic advisor who then gives them individual help in developing long-range plans and a course schedule for the next semester. In conjunction with this counseling, you may be asked to take some additional tests so that you can be placed at the proper course level.

External Degree Programs

If you have acquired a considerable amount of college-level knowledge through job experience, reading, or noncredit courses, if you have accumulated college credits at a variety of colleges over a period of years, or if you prefer studying on your own rather than in a classroom setting, you may want to investigate the possibility of enrolling in an external degree program. Many colleges offer external degree programs that allow you to earn a degree by passing examinations (including CLEP), transferring credit from other colleges, and demonstrating in other ways that you have satisfied the educational requirements. No classroom attendance is required, and the programs are open to out-of-state candidates as well as residents. Thomas A. Edison State College in New Jersey and Charter Oaks College in Connecticut are fully accredited independent state colleges; the New York program is part of the state university system and is also fully accredited. If you are interested in exploring an external degree, you can write for more information to:

Charter Oak College
The Exchange, Suite 171
270 Farmington Avenue
Farmington, CT 06032-1909

Regents External Degree Program
Cultural Education Center
Empire State Plaza
Albany, New York 12230

Thomas A. Edison State College
101 West State Street
Trenton, New Jersey 08608

Many other colleges also have external degree or weekend programs. While they often require that a number of courses be taken on campus, the external degree programs tend to be more flexible in transferring credit, granting credit-by-examination, and allowing independent study than other traditional programs. When applying to a college, you may wish to ask whether it has an external degree or weekend program.

Questions to Ask About a College's CLEP Policy

Before taking CLEP examinations for the purpose of earning college credit, try to find the answers to these questions:

1. Which CLEP examinations are accepted by this college?

A college may accept some CLEP examinations for credit and not others - possibly not the one you are considering. The English faculty may decide to grant college English credit based on the CLEP English Composition examination, but not on the Freshman College Composition examination. Or, the mathematics faculty may decide to grant credit based on the College Mathematics to non-mathematics majors only, requiring majors to take an examination in algebra, trigonometry, or calculus to earn credit. For these reasons, it is important that you know the specific CLEP tests for which you can receive credit.

2. Does the college require the optional free-response (essay) section as well as the objective portion of the CLEP examination you are considering?

Knowing the answer to this question ahead of time will permit you to schedule the optional essay examination when you register to take your CLEP examination.

3. Is credit granted for specific courses? If so, which ones?

You are likely to find that credit will be granted for specific courses and the course titles will be designated in the college's CLEP policy. It is not necessary, however, that credit be granted for a specific course in order for you to benefit from your CLEP credit. For instance, at many liberal arts colleges, all students must take certain types of courses; these courses may be labeled the core curriculum, general education requirements, distribution requirements, or liberal arts requirements. The requirements are often expressed in terms of credit hours. For example, all students may be required to take at least six hours of humanities, six hours of English, three hours of mathematics, six hours of natural science, and six hours of social science, with no particular courses in these disciplines specified. In these instances, CLEP credit may be given as 6 hrs. English credit or 3 hrs. Math credit without specifying for which English or mathematics courses credit has been awarded. In order to avoid possible disappointment, you should know before taking a CLEP examination what type of credit you can receive and whether you will only be exempted from a required course but receive no credit.

4. How much credit is granted for each examination you are considering, and does the college place a limit on the total amount of CLEP credit you can earn toward your degree?

Not all colleges that grant CLEP credit award the same amount for individual tests. Furthermore, some colleges place a limit on the total amount of credit you can earn through CLEP or other examinations. Other colleges may grant you exemption but no credit toward your degree. Knowing several colleges' policies concerning these issues may help you decide which college you will attend. If you think you are capable of passing a number of CLEP examinations, you may want to attend a college that will allow you to earn credit for all or most of them. For example, the state external degree programs grant credit for most CLEP examinations (and other tests as well).

5. What is the required score for earning CLEP credit for each test you are considering?

Most colleges publish the required scores or percentile ranks for earning CLEP credit in their general catalog or in a brochure. The required score may vary from test to test, so find out the required score for each test you are considering.

6. What is the college's policy regarding prior course work in the subject in which you are considering taking a CLEP test?

Some colleges will not grant credit for a CLEP test if the student has already attempted a college-level course closely aligned with that test. For example, if you successfully completed English 101 or a comparable course on another campus, you will probably not be permitted to receive CLEP credit in that subject, too. Some colleges will not permit you to earn CLEP credit for a course that you failed.

7. Does the college make additional stipulations before credit will be granted?

It is common practice for colleges to award CLEP credit only to their enrolled students. There are other stipulations, however, that vary from college to college. For example, does the college require you to formally apply for or accept CLEP credit by completing and signing a form? Or does the college require you to validate your CLEP score by successfully completing a more advanced course in the subject? Answers to these and other questions will help to smooth the process of earning college credit through CLEP.

The above questions and the discussions that follow them indicate some of the ways in which colleges' CLEP policies can vary. Find out as much as possible about the CLEP policies at the colleges you are interested in so you can choose a college with a policy that is compatible with your educational goals. Once you have selected the college you will attend, you can find out which CLEP examinations your college recognizes and the requirements for earning CLEP credit.

DECIDING WHICH EXAMINATIONS TO TAKE

If You're Taking the Examinations for College Credit or Career Advancement:

Most people who take CLEP examinations do so in order to earn credit for college courses. Others take the examinations in order to qualify for job promotions or for professional certification or licensing. It is vital to most candidates who are taking the tests for any of these reasons that they be well prepared for the tests they are taking so that they can advance as rapidly as possible toward their educational or career goals.

It is usually advisable that those who have limited knowledge in the subjects covered by the tests they are considering enroll in the college courses in which that material is taught. Those who are uncertain about whether or not they know enough about a subject to do well on a particular CLEP test will find the following guidelines helpful.

There is no way to predict if you will pass a particular CLEP examination, but answers to the questions under the seven headings below should give you an indication of whether or not you are likely to succeed.

1. Test Descriptions

Read the description of the test provided. Are you familiar with most of the topics and terminology in the outline?

2. Textbooks

Examine the suggested textbooks and other resource materials following the test descriptions in this guide. Have you recently read one or more of these books, or have you read similar college-level books on this subject? If you have not, read through one or more of the textbooks listed, or through the textbook used for this course at your college. Are you familiar with most of the topics and terminology in the book?

3. Sample Questions

The sample questions provided are intended to be typical of the content and difficulty of the questions on the test. Although they are not an exact miniature of the test, the proportion of the sample questions you can answer correctly should be a rough estimate of the proportion of questions you will be able to answer correctly on the test.

Answer as many of the sample questions for this test as you can. Check your answers against the correct answers. Did you answer more than half the questions correctly?

Because of variations in course content at different institutions, and because questions on CLEP tests vary from easy to difficult - with most being of moderate difficulty - the average student who passes a course in a subject can usually answer correctly about half the questions on the corresponding CLEP examination. Most colleges set their passing scores near this level, but some set them higher. If your college has set its required score above the level required by most colleges, you may need to answer a larger proportion of questions on the test correctly.

4. Previous Study

Have you taken noncredit courses in this subject offered by an adult school or a private school, through correspondence, or in connection with your job? Did you do exceptionally well in this subject in high school, or did you take an honors course in this subject?

5. Experience

Have you learned or used the knowledge or skills included in this test in your job or life experience? For example, if you lived in a Spanish-speaking country and spoke the language for a year or more, you might consider taking the Spanish examination. Or, if you have worked at a job in which you used accounting and finance skills, Principles of Accounting would be a likely test for you to take. Or, if you have read a considerable amount of literature and attended many art exhibits, concerts, and plays, you might expect to do well on the Humanities exam.

6. Other Examinations

Have you done well on other standardized tests in subjects related to the one you want to take? For example, did you score well above average on a portion of a college entrance examination covering similar skills, or did you obtain an exceptionally high score on a high school equivalency test or a licensing examination in this subject? Although such tests do not cover exactly the same material as the CLEP examinations and may be easier, persons who do well on these tests often do well on CLEP examinations, too.

7. Advice

Has a college counselor, professor, or some other professional person familiar with your ability advised you to take a CLEP examination?

If your answer was yes to questions under several of the above headings, you probably have a good chance of passing the CLEP examination you are considering. It is unlikely that you would have acquired sufficient background from experience alone. Learning gained through reading and study is essential, and you will probably find some additional study helpful before taking a CLEP examination.

If You're Taking the Examinations to Prepare for College

Many people entering college, particularly adults returning to college after several years away from formal education, are uncertain about their ability to compete with other college students. They wonder whether they have sufficient background for college study, and those who have been away from formal study for some time wonder whether they have forgotten how to study, how to take tests, and how to write papers. Such people may wish to improve their test-taking and study skills prior to enrolling in courses.

One way to assess your ability to perform at the college level and to improve your test-taking and study skills at the same time is to prepare for and take one or more CLEP examinations. You need not be enrolled in a college to take a CLEP examination, and you may have your scores sent only to yourself and later request that a transcript be sent to a college if you then decide to apply for credit. By reviewing the test descriptions and sample questions, you may find one or several subject areas in which you think you have substantial knowledge. Select one examination, or more if you like, and carefully read at least one of the textbooks listed in the bibliography for the test. By doing this, you will get a better idea of how much you know of what is usually taught in a college-level course in that subject. Study as much material as you can, until you think you have a good grasp of the subject matter. Then take the test at a college in your area. It will be several weeks before you receive your results, and you may wish to begin reviewing for another test in the meantime.

To find out if you are eligible for credit for your CLEP score, you must compare your score with the score required by the college you plan to attend. If you are not yet sure which college you will attend, or whether you will enroll in college at all, you should begin to follow the steps outlined. It is best that you do this before taking a CLEP test, but if you are taking the test only for the experience and to familiarize yourself with college-level material and requirements, you might take the test before you approach a college. Even if the college you decide to attend does not accept the test you took, the experience of taking such a test will enable you to meet with greater confidence the requirements of courses you will take.

You will find information about how to interpret your scores in WHAT YOUR SCORES MEAN, which you will receive with your score report, and which can also be found online at the CLEP website. Many colleges follow the recommendations of the American Council on Education (ACE) for setting their required scores, so you can use this information as a guide in determining how well you did. The ACE recommendations are included in the booklet.

If you do not do well enough on the test to earn college credit, don't be discouraged. Usually, it is the best college students who are exempted from courses or receive credit-by-examination. The fact that you cannot get credit for your score means that you should probably enroll in a college course to learn the material. However, if your score was close to the required score, or if you feel you could do better on a second try or after some additional study, you may retake the test after six months. Do not take it sooner or your score will not be reported and your fee will be forfeited.

If you do earn the score required to earn credit, you will have demonstrated that you already have some college-level knowledge. You will also have a better idea whether you should take additional CLEP examinations. And, what is most important, you can enroll in college with confidence, knowing that you do have the ability to succeed.

PREPARING TO TAKE CLEP EXAMINATIONS

Having made the decision to take one or more CLEP examinations, most people then want to know if it is worthwhile to prepare for them - how much, how long, when, and how should they go about it? The precise answers to these questions vary greatly from individual to individual. However, most candidates find that some type of test preparation is helpful.

Most people who take CLEP examinations do so to show that they have already learned the important material that is taught in a college course. Many of them need only a quick review to assure themselves that they have not forgotten some of what they once studied, and to fill in some of the gaps in their knowledge of the subject. Others feel that they need a thorough review and spend several weeks studying for a test. A few wish to take a CLEP examination as a kind of final examination for independent study of a subject instead of the college course. This last group requires significantly more study than those who only need to review, and they may need some guidance from professors of the subjects they are studying.

The key to how you prepare for CLEP examinations often lies in locating those skills and areas of prior learning in which you are strong and deciding where to focus your energies. Some people may know a great deal about a certain subject area, but may not test well. These individuals would probably be just as concerned about strengthening their test-taking skills as they are about studying for a specific test. Many mental and physical skills are used in preparing for a test. It is important not only to review or study for the examinations, but to make certain that you are alert, relatively free of anxiety, and aware of how to approach standardized tests. Suggestions on developing test-taking skills and preparing psychologically and physically for a test are given. The following section suggests ways of assessing your knowledge of the content of a test and then reviewing and studying the material.

Using This Study Guide

Begin by carefully reading the test description and outline of knowledge and skills required for the examination, if given. As you read through the topics listed there, ask yourself how much you know about each one. Also note the terms, names, and symbols that are mentioned, and ask yourself whether you are familiar with them. This will give you a quick overview of how much you know about the subject. If you are familiar with nearly all the material, you will probably need a minimum of review; however, if less than half of it is familiar, you will probably require substantial study to do well on the test.

If, after reviewing the test description, you find that you need extensive review, delay answering the sample question until you have done some reading in the subject. If you complete them before reviewing the material, you will probably look for the answers as you study, and then they will not be a good assessment of your ability at a later date.

If you think you are familiar with most of the test material, try to answer the sample questions.

Apply the test-taking strategies given. Keeping within the time limit suggested will give you a rough idea of how quickly you should work in order to complete the actual test.

Check your answers against the answer key. If you answered nearly all the questions correctly, you probably do not need to study the subject extensively. If you got about half the questions correct, you ought o review at least one textbook or other suggested materials on the subject. If you answered less than half the questions correctly, you will probably benefit from more extensive reading in the subject and thorough study of one or more textbooks. The textbooks listed are used at many colleges but they are not the only good texts. You will find helpful almost any standard text available to you., such as the textbook used at your college, or earlier editions of texts listed. For some examinations, topic outlines and textbooks may not be available. Take the sample tests in this book and check your answers at the end of each test. Check wrong answers.

Suggestions for Studying

The following suggestions have been gathered from people who have prepared for CLEP examinations or other college-level tests.

1. Define your goals and locate study materials

First, determine your study goals. Set aside a block of time to review the material provided in this book, and then decide which test(s) you will take. Using the suggestions, locate suitable resource materials. If a preparation course is offered by an adult school or college in your area, you might find it helpful to enroll.

2. Find a good place to study

To determine what kind of place you need for studying, ask yourself questions such as: Do I need a quiet place? Does the telephone distract me? Do objects I see in this place remind me of things I should do? Is it too warm? Is it well lit? Am I too comfortable here? Do I have space to spread out my materials? You may find the library more conducive to studying than your home. If you decide to study at home, you might prevent interruptions by other household members by putting a sign on the door of your study room to indicate when you will be available.

3. Schedule time to study

To help you determine where studying best fits into your schedule, try this exercise: Make a list of your daily activities (for example, sleeping, working, and eating) and estimate how many hours per day you spend on each activity. Now, rate all the activities on your list in order of their importance and evaluate your use of time. Often people are astonished at how an average day appears from this perspective. They may discover that they were unaware how large portions of time are spent, or they learn their time can be scheduled in alternative ways. For example, they can remove the least important activities from their day and devote that time to studying or another important activity.

4. Establish a study routine and a set of goals

In order to study effectively, you should establish specific goals and a schedule for accomplishing them. Some people find it helpful to write out a weekly schedule and cross out each study period when it is completed. Others maintain their concentration better by writing down the time when they expect to complete a study task. Most people find short periods of intense study more productive than long stretches of time. For example, they may follow a regular schedule of several 20- or 30-minute study periods with short breaks between them. Some people like to allow themselves rewards as they complete each study goal. It is not essential that you accomplish every goal exactly within your schedule; the point is to be committed to your task.

5. Learn how to take an active role in studying.

If you have not done much studying for some time, you may find it difficult to concentrate at first. Try a method of studying, such as the one outlined below, that will help you concentrate on and remember what you read.

    a. First, read the chapter summary and the introduction. Then you will know what to look for in your reading.

    b. Next, convert the section or paragraph headlines into questions. For example, if you are reading a section entitled, The Causes of the American Revolution, ask yourself: *What were the causes of the American Revolution?* Compose the answer as you read the paragraph. Reading and answering questions aloud will help you understand and remember the material.

c. Take notes on key ideas or concepts as you read. Writing will also help you fix concepts more firmly in your mind. Underlining key ideas or writing notes in your book can be helpful and will be useful for review. Underline only important points. If you underline more than a third of each paragraph, you are probably underlining too much.

d. If there are questions or problems at the end of a chapter, answer or solve them on paper as if you were asked to do them for homework. Mathematics textbooks (and some other books) sometimes include answers to some or all of the exercises. If you have such a book, write your answers before looking at the ones given. When problem-solving is involved, work enough problems to master the required methods and concepts. If you have difficulty with problems, review any sample problems or explanations in the chapter.

e. To retain knowledge, most people have to review the material periodically. If you are preparing for a test over an extended period of time, review key concepts and notes each week or so. Do not wait for weeks to review the material or you will need to relearn much of it.

Psychological and Physical Preparation

Most people feel at least some nervousness before taking a test. Adults who are returning to college may not have taken a test in many years or they may have had little experience with standardized tests. Some younger students, as well, are uncomfortable with testing situations. People who received their education in countries outside the United States may find that many tests given in this country are quite different from the ones they are accustomed to taking.

Not only might candidates find the types of tests and the kinds of questions on them unfamiliar, but other aspects of the testing environment may be strange as well. The physical and mental stress that results from meeting this new experience can hinder a candidate's ability to demonstrate his or her true degree of knowledge in the subject area being tested. For this reason, it is important to go to the test center well prepared, both mentally and physically, for taking the test. You may find the following suggestions helpful.

1. Familiarize yourself, as much as possible, with the test and the test situation before the day of the examination. It will be helpful for you to know ahead of time:

a. How much time will be allowed for the test and whether there are timed subsections.

b. What types of questions and directions appear on the examination.

c. How your test score will be computed.

d. How to properly answer the questions on the computer (See the CLEP Sample on the CLEP website)

e. In which building and room the examination will be administered. If you don't know where the building is, locate it or get directions ahead of time.

f. The time of the test administration. You might wish to confirm this information a day or two before the examination and find out what time the building and room will be open so that you can plan to arrive early.

g. Where to park your car or, if you wish to take public transportation, which bus or train to take and the location of the nearest stop.

h. Whether smoking will be permitted during the test.

i. Whether there will be a break between examinations (if you will be taking more than one on the same day), and whether there is a place nearby where you can get something to eat or drink.

2. Go to the test situation relaxed and alert. In order to prepare for the test:

a. Get a good night's sleep. Last minute cramming, particularly late the night before, is usually counterproductive.

b. Eat normally. It is usually not wise to skip breakfast or lunch on the day of the test or to eat a big meal just before the test.

c. Avoid tranquilizers and stimulants. If you follow the other directions in this book, you won't need artificial aids. It's better to be a little tense than to be drowsy, but stimulants such as coffee and cola can make you nervous and interfere with your concentration.

d. Don't drink a lot of liquids before the test. Having to leave the room during the test will disturb your concentration and take valuable time away from the test.

e. If you are inclined to be nervous or tense, learn some relaxation exercises and use them before and perhaps during the test.

3. Arrive for the test early and prepared. Be sure to:

a. Arrive early enough so that you can find a parking place, locate the test center, and get settled comfortably before testing begins. Allow some extra time in case you are delayed unexpectedly.

b. Take the following with you:

- Your completed Registration/Admission Form
- Two forms of identification – one being a government-issued photo ID with signature, such as a driver's license or passport
- Non-mechanical pencil
- A watch so that you can time your progress (digital watches are prohibited)
- Your glasses if you need them for reading or seeing the chalkboard or wall clock

c. Leave all books, papers, and notes outside the test center. You will not be permitted to use your own scratch paper; it will be provided. Also prohibited are calculators, cell phones, beepers, pagers, photo/copy devices, radios, headphones, food, beverages, and several other items.

d. Be prepared for any temperature in the testing room. Wear layers of clothing that can be removed if the room is too hot but will keep you warm if it is too cold.

4. When you enter the test room:

a. Sit in a seat that provides a maximum of comfort and freedom from distraction.

b. Read directions carefully, and listen to all instructions given by the test administrator. If you don't understand the directions, ask for help before test timing begins. If you must ask a question after the test has begun, raise your hand and a proctor will assist you. The proctor can answer certain kinds of questions but cannot help you with the test.

c. Know your rights as a test taker. You can expect to be given the full working time allowed for the test(s) and a reasonably quiet and comfortable place in which to work. If a poor test situation is preventing you from doing your best, ask if the situation can be remedied. If bad test conditions cannot be remedied, ask the person in charge to report the problem in the Irregularity Report that will be sent to ETS with the answer sheets. You may also wish to contact CLEP. Describe the exact circumstances as completely as you can. Be sure to include the test date and name(s) of the test(s) you took. ETS will investigate the problem to make sure it does not happen again, and, if the problem is serious enough, may arrange for you to retake the test without charge.

TAKING THE EXAMINATIONS

A person may know a great deal about the subject being tested, but not do as well as he or she is capable of on the test. Knowing how to approach a test is an important part of the testing process. While a command of test-taking skills cannot substitute for knowledge of the subject matter, it can be a significant factor in successful testing.

Test-taking skills enable a person to use all available information to earn a score that truly reflects his or her ability. There are different strategies for approaching different kinds of test questions. For example, free-response questions require a very different tack than do multiple-choice questions. Other factors, such as how the test will be graded, may also influence your approach to the test and your use of test time. Thus, your preparation for a test should include finding out all you can about the test so that you can use the most effective test-taking strategies.

Before taking a test, you should know approximately how many questions are on the test, how much time you will be allowed, how the test will be scored or graded, what types of questions and directions are on the test, and how you will be required to record your answers.

Taking Multiple-Choice Tests

1. Listen carefully to the instructions given by the test administrator and read carefully all directions before you begin to answer the questions.

2. Note the time that the test administrator starts timing the test. As you proceed, make sure that you are not working too slowly. You should have answered at least half the questions in a section when half the time for that section has passed. If you have not reached that point in the section, speed up your pace on the remaining questions.

3. Before answering a question, read the entire question, including all the answer choices. Don't think that because the first or second answer choice looks good to you, it isn't necessary to read the remaining options. Instructions usually tell you to select the best answer. Sometimes one answer choice is partially correct, but another option is better; therefore, it is usually a good idea to read all the answers before you choose one.

4. Read and consider every question. Questions that look complicated at first glance may not actually be so difficult once you have read them carefully.

5. Do not puzzle too long over any one question. If you don't know the answer after you've considered it briefly, go on to the next question. Make sure you return to the question later.

6. Make sure you record your response properly.

7. In trying to determine the correct answer, you may find it helpful to cross out those options that you know are incorrect, and to make marks next to those you think might be correct. If you decide to skip the question and come back to it later, you will save yourself the time of reconsidering all the options.

8. Watch for the following key words in test questions:

all	generally	never	perhaps
always	however	none	rarely
but	may	not	seldom
except	must	often	sometimes
every	necessary	only	usually

When a question or answer option contains words such as always, every, only, never, and none, there can be no exceptions to the answer you choose. Use of words such as often, rarely, sometimes, and generally indicates that there may be some exceptions to the answer.

9. Do not waste your time looking for clues to right answers based on flaws in question wording or patterns in correct answers. Professionals at the College Board and ETS put

a great deal of effort into developing valid, reliable, fair tests. CLEP test development committees are composed of college faculty who are experts in the subject covered by the test and are appointed by the College Board to write test questions and to scrutinize each question that is included on a CLEP test. Committee members make every effort to ensure that the questions are not ambiguous, that they have only one correct answer, and that they cover college-level topics. These committees do not intentionally include trick questions. If you think a question is flawed, ask the test administrator to report it, or contact CLEP immediately.

Taking Free-Response or Essay Tests

If your college requires the optional free-response or essay portion of a CLEP Composition and Literature exams, you should do some additional preparation for your CLEP test. Taking an essay test is very different from taking a multiple-choice test, so you will need to use some other strategies.

The essay written as part of the English Composition and Essay exam is graded by English professors from a variety of colleges and universities. A process called holistic scoring is used to rate your writing ability.

The optional free-response essays, on the other hand, are graded by the faculty of the college you designate as a score recipient. Guidelines and criteria for grading essays are not specified by the College Board or ETS. You may find it helpful, therefore, to talk with someone at your college to find out what criteria will be used to determine whether you will get credit. If the test requires essay responses, ask how much emphasis will be placed on your writing ability and your ability to organize your thoughts as opposed to your knowledge of subject matter. Find out how much weight will be given to your multiple-choice test score in comparison with your free-response grade in determining whether you will get credit. This will give you an idea where you should expend the greatest effort in preparing for and taking the test.

Here are some strategies you will find useful in taking any essay test:

1. Before you begin to write, read all questions carefully and take a few minutes to jot down some ideas you might include in each answer.

2. If you are given a choice of questions to answer, choose the questions you think you can answer most clearly and knowledgeably.

3. Determine in what order you will answer the questions. Answer those you find the easiest first so that any extra time can be spent on the more difficult questions.

4. When you know which questions you will answer and in what order, determine how much testing time remains and estimate how many minutes you will devote to each question. Unless suggested times are given for the questions or one question appears to require more or less time than the others, allot an equal amount of time to each question.

5. Before answering each question, indicate the number of the question as it is given in the test book. You need not copy the entire question from the question sheet, but it will be helpful to you and to the person grading your test if you indicate briefly the topic you are addressing – particularly if you are not answering the questions in the order in which they appear on the test.

6. Before answering each question, read it again carefully to make sure you are interpreting it correctly. Underline key words, such as those listed below, that often appear in free-response questions. Be sure you know the exact meaning of these words before taking the test.

analyze	demonstrate	enumerate	list
apply	derive	explain	outline
assess	describe	generalize	prove
compare	determine	illustrate	rank
contrast	discuss	interpret	show
define	distinguish	justify	summarize

If a question asks you to outline, define, or summarize, do not write a detailed explanation; if a question asks you to analyze, explain, illustrate, interpret, or show, you must do more than briefly describe the topic.

For a current listing of CLEP Colleges

where you can get credit and be tested, write:

CLEP, P.O. Box 6600, Princeton, NJ 08541-6600

Or e-mail: clep@ets.org, or call: (609) 771-7865

CHEMISTRY

Description of the Examination

The Chemistry examination covers material that is usually taught in a one-year college course in general chemistry. Understanding of the structure and states of matter, reaction types, equations and stoichiometry, equilibrium, kinetics, thermodynamics, and descriptive and experimental chemistry is required, as is the ability to interpret and apply this material to new and unfamiliar problems. During this examination, an online scientific calculator function and a periodic table are available as part of the testing software.

The examination contains approximately 75 questions to be answered in 90 minutes. Some of these are pretest questions that will not be scored. Any time spent on tutorials and providing personal information is in addition to the actual testing time.

Knowledge and Skills Required

Questions on the Chemistry examination require candidates to demonstrate one or more of the following abilities.

- **Recall** - remember specific facts; demonstrate straightforward knowledge of information and familiarity with terminology

- **Application** - understand concepts and reformulate information into other equivalent terms; apply knowledge to unfamiliar and/or practical situations; use mathematics to solve chemistry problems

- **Interpretation** - infer and deduce from data available and integrate information to form conclusions; recognize unstated assumptions

The subject matter of the Chemistry examination is drawn from the following topics. The percentages next to the main topics indicate the approximate percentage of exam questions on that topic.

20%   Structure of Matter

Atomic theory and atomic structure

- Evidence for the atomic theory
- Atomic masses; determination by chemical and physical means
- Atomic number and mass number; isotopes and mass spectroscopy
- Electron energy levels: atomic spectra, quantum numbers, atomic orbitals
- Periodic relationships, including, for example, atomic radii, ionization energies, electron affinities, oxidation states

Chemical bonding

- Binding forces
    - Types: covalent, ionic, metallic, macromolecular (or network), dispersion, hydrogen bonding
    - Relationships to structure and to properties
    - Polarity of bonds, electronegativities

- Geometry of molecules, ions, and coordination complexes: structural isomerism, dipole moments of molecules, relation of properties to structure

- Molecular models
    - Valence bond theory; hybridization of orbitals, resonance, sigma and pi bonds
    - Other models, for example, molecular orbital

- Nuclear chemistry: nuclear equations, half-lives, and radioactivity; chemical applications

19%   States of Matter

Gases
- Laws of ideal gases; equations of state for an ideal gas

- Kinetic-molecular theory
    - Interpretation of ideal gas laws on the basis of this theory
    - The mole concept; Avogadro's number
    - Dependence of kinetic energy of molecules on temperature: Boltzmann distribution
    - Deviations from ideal gas laws

Liquids and solids

- Liquids and solids from the kineticmolecular viewpoint

- Phase diagrams of one-component systems

- Changes of state, critical phenomena

- Crystal structure

Solutions

- Types of solutions and factors affecting solubility

- Methods of expressing concentration

- Colligative properties; for example, Raoult's law

- Effect of interionic attraction on colligative properties and solubility

12%   Reaction Types
Formation and cleavage of covalent bonds

- Acid-base reactions; concepts of Arrhenius, Bronsted-Lowry, and Lewis; amphoterism

- Reactions involving coordination complexes

Precipitation reactions

Oxidation-reduction reactions

- Oxidation number

- The role of the electron in oxidation-reduction

- Electrochemistry; electrolytic cells, standard half-cell potentials, prediction of the direction of redox reactions, effect of concentration changes

10% **Equations and Stoichiometry**

Ionic and molecular species present in chemical systems; net-ionic equations
Stoichiometry: mass and volume relations with emphasis on the mole concept
Balancing of equations, including those for redox reactions

7% **Equilibrium**

Concept of dynamic equilibrium, physical and chemical; LeChâtelier's principle; equilibrium constants

Quantitative treatment

- Equilibrium constants for gaseous reactions in terms of both molar concentrations and partial pressure (K_c, K_p)
- Equilibrium constants for reactions in solutions
    - Constants for acids and bases; pK; pH
    - Solubility-product constants and their application to precipitation and the dissolution of slightly soluble compounds - Constants for complex ions
    - Common ion effect; buffers

4% **Kinetics**

Concept of rate of reaction

Order of reaction and rate constant: their determination from experimental data

Effect of temperature change on rates

Energy of activation; the role of catalysts

The relationship between the rate-determining step and a mechanism

5% **Thermodynamics**

State functions

First law: heat of formation; heat of reaction; change in enthalpy, Hess's law; heat capacity; heats of vaporization and fusion

Second law: free energy of formation; free energy of reaction; dependence of change in free energy on enthalpy and entropy changes

Relationship of change in free energy to equilibrium constants and electrode potentials

14% **Descriptive Chemistry**

The accumulation of certain specific facts of chemistry is essential to enable students to comprehend the development of principles and concepts, to demonstrate applications of principles, to relate fact to theory and properties to structure, and to develop an understanding of systematic nomenclature that facilitates communication. The following areas are normally included on the examination:

- Chemical reactivity and products of chemical reactions

- Relationships in the periodic table: horizontal, vertical, and diagonal

- Chemistry of the main groups and transition elements, including typical examples of each

- Organic chemistry, including such topics as functional groups and isomerism (may be treated as a separate unit or as exemplary material in other areas, such as bonding)

9% Experimental Chemistry

Some experiments are based on laboratory experiments widely performed in general chemistry and ask about the equipment used, observations made, calculations performed, and interpretation of the results. The questions are designed to provide a measure of understanding of the basic tools of chemistry and their applications to simple chemical systems.

HOW TO TAKE A TEST

You have studied long, hard and conscientiously.

With your official admission card in hand, and your heart pounding, you have been admitted to the examination room.

You note that there are several hundred other applicants in the examination room waiting to take the same test.

They all appear to be equally well prepared.

You know that nothing but your best effort will suffice. The "moment of truth" is at hand: you now have to demonstrate objectively, in writing, your knowledge of content and your understanding of subject matter.

You are fighting the most important battle of your life—to pass and/or score high on an examination which will determine your career and provide the economic basis for your livelihood.

What extra, special things should you know and should you do in taking the examination?

I. YOU MUST PASS AN EXAMINATION

A. WHAT EVERY CANDIDATE SHOULD KNOW
Examination applicants often ask us for help in preparing for the written test. What can I study in advance? What kinds of questions will be asked? How will the test be given? How will the papers be graded?

B. HOW ARE EXAMS DEVELOPED?
Examinations are carefully written by trained technicians who are specialists in the field known as "psychological measurement," in consultation with recognized authorities in the field of work that the test will cover. These experts recommend the subject matter areas or skills to be tested; only those knowledges or skills important to your success on the job are included. The most reliable books and source materials available are used as references. Together, the experts and technicians judge the difficulty level of the questions.
Test technicians know how to phrase questions so that the problem is clearly stated. Their ethics do not permit "trick" or "catch" questions. Questions may have been tried out on sample groups, or subjected to statistical analysis, to determine their usefulness.
Written tests are often used in combination with performance tests, ratings of training and experience, and oral interviews. All of these measures combine to form the best-known means of finding the right person for the right job.

II. HOW TO PASS THE WRITTEN TEST

A. BASIC STEPS

1) Study the announcement

How, then, can you know what subjects to study? Our best answer is: "Learn as much as possible about the class of positions for which you've applied." The exam will test the knowledge, skills and abilities needed to do the work.

Your most valuable source of information about the position you want is the official exam announcement. This announcement lists the training and experience qualifications. Check these standards and apply only if you come reasonably close to meeting them. Many jurisdictions preview the written test in the exam announcement by including a section called "Knowledge and Abilities Required," "Scope of the Examination," or some similar heading. Here you will find out specifically what fields will be tested.

2) Choose appropriate study materials

If the position for which you are applying is technical or advanced, you will read more advanced, specialized material. If you are already familiar with the basic principles of your field, elementary textbooks would waste your time. Concentrate on advanced textbooks and technical periodicals. Think through the concepts and review difficult problems in your field.

These are all general sources. You can get more ideas on your own initiative, following these leads. For example, training manuals and publications of the government agency which employs workers in your field can be useful, particularly for technical and professional positions. A letter or visit to the government department involved may result in more specific study suggestions, and certainly will provide you with a more definite idea of the exact nature of the position you are seeking.

3) Study this book!

III. KINDS OF TESTS

Tests are used for purposes other than measuring knowledge and ability to perform specified duties. For some positions, it is equally important to test ability to make adjustments to new situations or to profit from training. In others, basic mental abilities not dependent on information are essential. Questions which test these things may not appear as pertinent to the duties of the position as those which test for knowledge and information. Yet they are often highly important parts of a fair examination. For very general questions, it is almost impossible to help you direct your study efforts. What we can do is to point out some of the more common of these general abilities needed in public service positions and describe some typical questions.

1) General information

Broad, general information has been found useful for predicting job success in some kinds of work. This is tested in a variety of ways, from vocabulary lists to questions about current events. Basic background in some field of work, such as sociology or economics, may be sampled in a group of questions. Often these are principles which have become familiar to most persons through exposure rather than through formal training. It is difficult to advise you how to study for these questions; being alert to the world around you is our best suggestion.

2) Verbal ability

An example of an ability needed in many positions is verbal or language ability. Verbal ability is, in brief, the ability to use and understand words. Vocabulary and grammar tests are typical measures of this ability. Reading comprehension or paragraph interpretation questions are common in many kinds of civil service tests. You are given a paragraph of written material and asked to find its central meaning.

IV. KINDS OF QUESTIONS

1. Multiple-choice Questions

Most popular of the short-answer questions is the "multiple choice" or "best answer" question. It can be used, for example, to test for factual knowledge, ability to solve problems or judgment in meeting situations found at work.

A multiple-choice question is normally one of three types:
- It can begin with an incomplete statement followed by several possible endings. You are to find the one ending which best completes the statement, although some of the others may not be entirely wrong.
- It can also be a complete statement in the form of a question which is answered by choosing one of the statements listed.
- It can be in the form of a problem – again you select the best answer.

Here is an example of a multiple-choice question with a discussion which should give you some clues as to the method for choosing the right answer:

When an employee has a complaint about his assignment, the action which will best help him overcome his difficulty is to
    A. discuss his difficulty with his coworkers
    B. take the problem to the head of the organization
    C. take the problem to the person who gave him the assignment
    D. say nothing to anyone about his complaint

In answering this question, you should study each of the choices to find which is best. Consider choice "A" – Certainly an employee may discuss his complaint with fellow employees, but no change or improvement can result, and the complaint remains unresolved. Choice "B" is a poor choice since the head of the organization probably does not know what assignment you have been given, and taking your problem to him is known as "going over the head" of the supervisor. The supervisor, or person who made the assignment, is the person who can clarify it or correct any injustice. Choice "C" is, therefore, correct. To say nothing, as in choice "D," is unwise. Supervisors have and interest in knowing the problems employees are facing, and the employee is seeking a solution to his problem.

2. True/False

3. Matching Questions

Matching an answer from a column of choices within another column.

V. RECORDING YOUR ANSWERS

Computer terminals are used more and more today for many different kinds of exams.

For an examination with very few applicants, you may be told to record your answers in the test booklet itself. Separate answer sheets are much more common. If this separate answer sheet is to be scored by machine – and this is often the case – it is highly important that you mark your answers correctly in order to get credit.

VI. BEFORE THE TEST

YOUR PHYSICAL CONDITION IS IMPORTANT

If you are not well, you can't do your best work on tests. If you are half asleep, you can't do your best either. Here are some tips:

1) Get about the same amount of sleep you usually get. Don't stay up all night before the test, either partying or worrying—DON'T DO IT!
2) If you wear glasses, be sure to wear them when you go to take the test. This goes for hearing aids, too.
3) If you have any physical problems that may keep you from doing your best, be sure to tell the person giving the test. If you are sick or in poor health, you relay cannot do your best on any test. You can always come back and take the test some other time.

Common sense will help you find procedures to follow to get ready for an examination. Too many of us, however, overlook these sensible measures. Indeed, nervousness and fatigue have been found to be the most serious reasons why applicants fail to do their best on civil service tests. Here is a list of reminders:

- Begin your preparation early – Don't wait until the last minute to go scurrying around for books and materials or to find out what the position is all about.
- Prepare continuously – An hour a night for a week is better than an all-night cram session. This has been definitely established. What is more, a night a week for a month will return better dividends than crowding your study into a shorter period of time.
- Locate the place of the exam – You have been sent a notice telling you when and where to report for the examination. If the location is in a different town or otherwise unfamiliar to you, it would be well to inquire the best route and learn something about the building.
- Relax the night before the test – Allow your mind to rest. Do not study at all that night. Plan some mild recreation or diversion; then go to bed early and get a good night's sleep.
- Get up early enough to make a leisurely trip to the place for the test – This way unforeseen events, traffic snarls, unfamiliar buildings, etc. will not upset you.
- Dress comfortably – A written test is not a fashion show. You will be known by number and not by name, so wear something comfortable.
- Leave excess paraphernalia at home – Shopping bags and odd bundles will get in your way. You need bring only the items mentioned in the official notice you received; usually everything you need is provided. Do not bring reference books to the exam. They will only confuse those last minutes and be taken away from you when in the test room.

- Arrive somewhat ahead of time – If because of transportation schedules you must get there very early, bring a newspaper or magazine to take your mind off yourself while waiting.
- Locate the examination room – When you have found the proper room, you will be directed to the seat or part of the room where you will sit. Sometimes you are given a sheet of instructions to read while you are waiting. Do not fill out any forms until you are told to do so; just read them and be prepared.
- Relax and prepare to listen to the instructions
- If you have any physical problem that may keep you from doing your best, be sure to tell the test administrator. If you are sick or in poor health, you really cannot do your best on the exam. You can come back and take the test some other time.

VII. AT THE TEST

The day of the test is here and you have the test booklet in your hand. The temptation to get going is very strong. Caution! There is more to success than knowing the right answers. You must know how to identify your papers and understand variations in the type of short-answer question used in this particular examination. Follow these suggestions for maximum results from your efforts:

1) Cooperate with the monitor

The test administrator has a duty to create a situation in which you can be as much at ease as possible. He will give instructions, tell you when to begin, check to see that you are marking your answer sheet correctly, and so on. He is not there to guard you, although he will see that your competitors do not take unfair advantage. He wants to help you do your best.

2) Listen to all instructions

Don't jump the gun! Wait until you understand all directions. In most civil service tests you get more time than you need to answer the questions. So don't be in a hurry. Read each word of instructions until you clearly understand the meaning. Study the examples, listen to all announcements and follow directions. Ask questions if you do not understand what to do.

3) Identify your papers

Civil service exams are usually identified by number only. You will be assigned a number; you must not put your name on your test papers. Be sure to copy your number correctly. Since more than one exam may be given, copy your exact examination title.

4) Plan your time

Unless you are told that a test is a "speed" or "rate of work" test, speed itself is usually not important. Time enough to answer all the questions will be provided, but this does not mean that you have all day. An overall time limit has been set. Divide the total time (in minutes) by the number of questions to determine the approximate time you have for each question.

5) Do not linger over difficult questions

If you come across a difficult question, mark it with a paper clip (useful to have along) and come back to it when you have been through the booklet. One caution if you do this – be sure to skip a number on your answer sheet as well. Check often to be sure that you have not lost your place and that you are marking in the row numbered the same as the question you are answering.

6) Read the questions

Be sure you know what the question asks! Many capable people are unsuccessful because they failed to read the questions correctly.

7) Answer all questions

Unless you have been instructed that a penalty will be deducted for incorrect answers, it is better to guess than to omit a question.

8) Speed tests

It is often better NOT to guess on speed tests. It has been found that on timed tests people are tempted to spend the last few seconds before time is called in marking answers at random – without even reading them – in the hope of picking up a few extra points. To discourage this practice, the instructions may warn you that your score will be "corrected" for guessing. That is, a penalty will be applied. The incorrect answers will be deducted from the correct ones, or some other penalty formula will be used.

9) Review your answers

If you finish before time is called, go back to the questions you guessed or omitted to give them further thought. Review other answers if you have time.

10) Return your test materials

If you are ready to leave before others have finished or time is called, take ALL your materials to the monitor and leave quietly. Never take any test material with you. The monitor can discover whose papers are not complete, and taking a test booklet may be grounds for disqualification.

VIII. EXAMINATION TECHNIQUES

1) Read the general instructions carefully. These are usually printed on the first page of the exam booklet. As a rule, these instructions refer to the timing of the examination; the fact that you should not start work until the signal and must stop work at a signal, etc. If there are any special instructions, such as a choice of questions to be answered, make sure that you note this instruction carefully.

2) When you are ready to start work on the examination, that is as soon as the signal has been given, read the instructions to each question booklet, underline any key words or phrases, such as least, best, outline, describe and the like. In this way you will tend to answer as requested rather than discover on reviewing your paper that you listed without describing, that you selected the worst choice rather than the best choice, etc.

3) If the examination is of the objective or multiple-choice type – that is, each question will also give a series of possible answers: A, B, C or D, and you are called upon to select the best answer and write the letter next to that answer on your answer paper – it is advisable to start answering each question in turn. There may be anywhere from 50 to 100 such questions in the three or four hours allotted and you can see how much time would be taken if you read through all the questions before beginning to answer any. Furthermore, if you

come across a question or group of questions which you know would be difficult to answer, it would undoubtedly affect your handling of all the other questions.

4) If the examination is of the essay type and contains but a few questions, it is a moot point as to whether you should read all the questions before starting to answer any one. Of course, if you are given a choice – say five out of seven and the like – then it is essential to read all the questions so you can eliminate the two that are most difficult. If, however, you are asked to answer all the questions, there may be danger in trying to answer the easiest one first because you may find that you will spend too much time on it. The best technique is to answer the first question, then proceed to the second, etc.

5) Time your answers. Before the exam begins, write down the time it started, then add the time allowed for the examination and write down the time it must be completed, then divide the time available somewhat as follows:
    - If 3-1/2 hours are allowed, that would be 210 minutes. If you have 80 objective-type questions, that would be an average of 2-1/2 minutes per question. Allow yourself no more than 2 minutes per question, or a total of 160 minutes, which will permit about 50 minutes to review.
    - If for the time allotment of 210 minutes there are 7 essay questions to answer, that would average about 30 minutes a question. Give yourself only 25 minutes per question so that you have about 35 minutes to review.

6) The most important instruction is to read each question and make sure you know what is wanted. The second most important instruction is to time yourself properly so that you answer every question. The third most important instruction is to answer every question. Guess if you have to but include something for each question. Remember that you will receive no credit for a blank and will probably receive some credit if you write something in answer to an essay question. If you guess a letter – say "B" for a multiple-choice question – you may have guessed right. If you leave a blank as an answer to a multiple-choice question, the examiners may respect your feelings but it will not add a point to your score. Some exams may penalize you for wrong answers, so in such cases only, you may not want to guess unless you have some basis for your answer.

7) Suggestions
    a. Objective-type questions
        1. Examine the question booklet for proper sequence of pages and questions
        2. Read all instructions carefully
        3. Skip any question which seems too difficult; return to it after all other questions have been answered
        4. Apportion your time properly; do not spend too much time on any single question or group of questions
        5. Note and underline key words – all, most, fewest, least, best, worst, same, opposite, etc.
        6. Pay particular attention to negatives
        7. Note unusual option, e.g., unduly long, short, complex, different or similar in content to the body of the question
        8. Observe the use of "hedging" words – probably, may, most likely, etc.

9. Make sure that your answer is put next to the same number as the question
10. Do not second-guess unless you have good reason to believe the second answer is definitely more correct
11. Cross out original answer if you decide another answer is more accurate; do not erase until you are ready to hand your paper in
12. Answer all questions; guess unless instructed otherwise
13. Leave time for review

b. Essay questions
   1. Read each question carefully
   2. Determine exactly what is wanted. Underline key words or phrases.
   3. Decide on outline or paragraph answer
   4. Include many different points and elements unless asked to develop any one or two points or elements
   5. Show impartiality by giving pros and cons unless directed to select one side only
   6. Make and write down any assumptions you find necessary to answer the questions
   7. Watch your English, grammar, punctuation and choice of words
   8. Time your answers; don't crowd material

8) Answering the essay question

Most essay questions can be answered by framing the specific response around several key words or ideas. Here are a few such key words or ideas:

M's: manpower, materials, methods, money, management
P's: purpose, program, policy, plan, procedure, practice, problems, pitfalls, personnel, public relations

a. Six basic steps in handling problems:
   1. Preliminary plan and background development
   2. Collect information, data and facts
   3. Analyze and interpret information, data and facts
   4. Analyze and develop solutions as well as make recommendations
   5. Prepare report and sell recommendations
   6. Install recommendations and follow up effectiveness

b. Pitfalls to avoid
   1. Taking things for granted – A statement of the situation does not necessarily imply that each of the elements is necessarily true; for example, a complaint may be invalid and biased so that all that can be taken for granted is that a complaint has been registered
   2. Considering only one side of a situation – Wherever possible, indicate several alternatives and then point out the reasons you selected the best one
   3. Failing to indicate follow up – Whenever your answer indicates action on your part, make certain that you will take proper follow-up action to see how successful your recommendations, procedures or actions turn out to be
   4. Taking too long in answering any single question – Remember to time your answers properly

EXAMINATION SECTION

EXAMINATION SECTION
TEST 1

DIRECTIONS: Each question or incomplete statement is followed by several suggested answers or completions. Select the one that BEST answers the question or completes the statement. *PRINT THE LETTER OF THE CORRECT ANSWER IN THE SPACE AT THE RIGHT.*

The following list of atomic weights may be referred to in solving problems involving computations:

Aluminum	27.0	Hydrogen	1.0	Phosphorous	31.0		
Bromine	79.9	Iodine	126.9	Silver	107.9		
Calcium	40.1	Iron	55.9	Sodium	23.0		
Carbon	12.0	Lead	207.2	Sulfur	32.0		
Chlorine	35.5	Nitrogen	14.0	Tin	118.7		
Copper	63.5	Oxygen	16.0	Zinc	65.4		

1. A solution of 0.02 M HCl has a pH of

   A. 1.7   B. 2.0   C. 2.3   D. 2.7

2. The pH of a saturated solution of CO_2 in water at 25 °C is MOST NEARLY

   A. 3   B. 5   C. 7   D. 9

3. An aqueous solution containing 100 grams of HCl per liter of solution is APPROXIMATELY _____ N.

   A. 1.0   B. 2.8   C. 3.2   D. 12.0

4. The volume of 12 N HCl which must be taken and made up to 100 ml with distilled water in order to make 100 ml of 1 N HCl is _____ ml.

   A. 1.2   B. 6.5   C. 8.3   D. 12

5. Of the following, the one which has the HIGHEST melting point is

   A. benzoic acid
   B. lead
   C. sodium chloride
   D. sulfur

6. Of the following, the one which has the LOWEST boiling point is

   A. $CH_3\text{-}CH_3$
   B. $CH_3\text{-}CO\text{-}CH_3$
   C. $CH_3\text{-}CH_2\text{-}O\text{-}CH_2\text{-}CH_3$
   D. CCl_4

7. Of the following, the one which has the HIGHEST boiling point is

   A. CH_3COOH B. HCl   C. HNO_3 D. H_2SO_4

8. Of the following, the STRONGEST oxidizing agent is

   A. $CrCl_3$ B. I_2 C. $KMnO_4$ D. $SnCl_2$

9. Of the following, the STRONGEST reducing agent is

   A. $BaCl_2$ B. $FeCl_3$ C. $Na_2S_2O_3$ D. $Na_2S_4O_6$

10. Of the following substances, the one with the HIGHEST softening point is

    A. Pyrex
    B. quartz
    C. soda-lime glass
    D. Vycor

11. The purpose of annealing glass is to

    A. give a shiny finish
    B. increase the ductility
    C. relieve strains
    D. remove fogging

12. Of the following reagents, the one which is NOT corrosive to chemical glassware is hot

    A. 12 M HCl
    B. 16 M HNO$_3$
    C. conc. HCl + conc. HNO$_3$
    D. saturated NaOH

13. Of the following reagents, the one which is MOST corrosive to a platinum crucible is

    A. a mixture of conc. HCl and conc. HNO$_3$
    B. boiling H$_2$SO$_4$
    C. fused NaOH
    D. hot 12 M NH$_3$

14. Of the following metals, the one which is MOST active chemically is

    A. copper
    B. iron
    C. mercury
    D. zinc

15. Of the following gases, the one which is MOST soluble in water is

    A. CO$_2$
    B. HCl
    C. H$_2$S
    D. N$_2$

16. Of the following, the gas with the GREATEST density at standard temperature and pressure is

    A. air
    B. carbon dioxide
    C. hydrogen sulfide
    D. methane

17. Water is at its GREATEST density at a temperature of

    A. 0° C
    B. 4° C
    C. 20° C
    D. 37° C

18. The term Ostwald refers to a type of apparatus GENERALLY used to determine

    A. color
    B. refractive index
    C. temperature
    D. viscosity

19. The term Beilstein refers to a chemical

    A. reference book
    B. society
    C. technique
    D. unit of radioactivity

20. The term Westphal refers to a type of apparatus GENERALLY used to determine

    A. boiling point elevation
    B. freezing point
    C. refractive index
    D. specific gravity

21. The recommended solder for ordinary electrical connections is

   A. Babbitt metal
   B. resin-core solder
   C. silver solder
   D. soft solder with an acid flux

22. Soft solder is composed PRINCIPALLY of lead and

   A. antimony   B. bismuth   C. cadmium   D. tin

23. Solid Na_2CO_3 is BEST removed from a saturated solution of NaOH by

   A. distillation
   B. filtration through ashless filter paper
   C. filtration through a Gooch crucible with asbestos
   D. filtration through a sintered glass funnel

24. A Type K potentiometer is USUALLY used for measuring

   A. amount of electrical charge
   B. parachor
   C. refractive index
   D. voltage

25. A Wheatstone bridge is FREQUENTLY used to

   A. calibrate photographic developer
   B. determine optical rotation
   C. measure electrical resistance
   D. support electrodes

26. The McLeod gauge is used to measure

   A. amperage   B. humidity
   C. low pressures   D. low temperatures

27. The minimum amount of liquid needed for an accurate pyknometric determination of its density is MOST NEARLY

   A. 0.1 liter   B. 1.0 liter
   C. 0.1 ml   D. 10 ml

28. The minimum volume of liquid needed for routine measurement of its refractive index is MOST NEARLY _____ ml.

   A. 0.1   B. 1.0   C. 10   D. 100

29. Of the following, the one which is NOT intended for measuring temperature is the

   A. iron-contstantan thermocouple
   B. mercury thermoregulator
   C. nickel resistance thermometer
   D. optical pyrometer

30. The only one of the following substances which is SAFE to heat is   30.____

    A. ammonium nitrate   B. lead azide
    C. perchloric acid   D. potassium persulfate

31. The PRINCIPAL function of the *fix* in photographic processing is to   31.____

    A. dissolve the unreacted gelatine
    B. dissolve the unreacted silver
    C. dissolve the unreacted silver halide
    D. tan the emulsion

32. The temperature of an incandescent object which is glowing cherry red is APPROXI-   32.____
    MATELY _____ °C.

    A. 250   B. 400   C. 700   D. 1300

33. Chromatography is used PRINCIPALLY for   33.____

    A. carbon and hydrogen analysis of organic compounds
    B. purification of industrial water supplies
    C. quantitative inorganic analysis
    D. separation of small amounts of organic compounds from mixtures

34. A unit of radioactivity is the   34.____

    A. microcurie   B. microlumen
    C. microradian   D. microwave

35. Of the following substances, the one with the LOWEST solubility in water (measured in   35.____
    grams per liter) is

    A. barium chloride   B. calcium nitrate
    C. ferrous sulfate   D. mercurous chloride

36. The solubility product of AgCl is 10^{-10}.   36.____
    The solubility of AgCl in a 0.1 M NaCl solution is MOST NEARLY _____ moles/liter.

    A. 10^{-11} B. 10^{-9} C. 10^{-5} D. 10^{-1}

37. A violet color in a flame test indicates the presence of   37.____

    A. lithium   B. potassium   C. sodium   D. strontium

38. The one of the following which will dissolve 10 gms of AgI is 100 ml of   38.____

    A. 1 M HNO_3 B. 1 M NH^3 C. 6 M HCl   D. 6 M NaCN

39. The one of the following substances which is NOT white is   39.____

    A. aluminum hydroxide   B. cuprous chloride
    C. mercuric iodide   D. zinc sulfate

40. An unknown white solid dissolves in 6 M NH_3 to give a clear colorless solution.   40.____
    It, therefore, CANNOT contain _____ ions.

    A. magnesium   B. mercuric   C. silver   D. zinc

KEY (CORRECT ANSWERS)

1. A	11. C	21. B	31. C
2. B	12. D	22. D	32. C
3. B	13. A	23. C	33. D
4. C	14. D	24. D	34. A
5. C	15. B	25. C	35. D
6. A	16. B	26. C	36. B
7. D	17. B	27. D	37. B
8. C	18. D	28. A	38. D
9. C	19. A	29. B	39. C
10. B	20. D	30. D	40. B

TEST 2

DIRECTIONS: Each question or incomplete statement is followed by several suggested answers or completions. Select the one that BEST answers the question or completes the statement. *PRINT THE LETTER OF THE CORRECT ANSWER IN THE SPACE AT THE RIGHT.*

1. In titrating 0.1 M acetic acid with 0.1 M NaOH, the CORRECT endpoint will be at a pH of APPROXIMATELY

    A. 2   B. 5   C. 9   D. 11

2. Potassium thiocyanate gives a reddish color with aqueous solutions of _____ ions.

    A. cuprous   B. ferric   C. lead   D. magnesium

3. Of the following, the one used in the colorimetric test for low concentrations of ammonia in water is

    A. Fehling's Solution
    B. Karl Fischer Reagent
    C. Nessler Reagent
    D. Ringer's Solution

4. Dimethylglyoxime is a reagent used to detect the presence of

    A. chlorine   B. lead   C. nickel   D. tin

5. In the gravimetric analysis of a chloride, the weighing form is NORMALLY

    A. AgCl   B. $BaCl_2$ C. Hg_2Cl_2 D. NaCl

6. Of the following salts, the one which is MOST soluble in water at room temperature is

    A. Ag_2SO_4 B. $BaSO_4$ C. CaC_2O_4 D. $MgSO_4$

7. The one of the following solids which is MOST soluble in 8 M NaOH is

    A. $BaSO_4$
    B. $Fe(OH)_3$
    C. hydrated aluminum hydroxide
    D. hydrated silver hydroxide

8. Of the following, the one which is the amide group is

    A. $-\overset{O}{\underset{}{C}}-NH_2$ B. $-N(CH_3)(CH_3)$ C. $-NH_2$ D. $-N=O$

9. The linkage between the amino acid units of a protein is called

    A. ether linkage
    B. hydrogen bond
    C. oxazole linkage
    D. peptide linkage

10. Of the following compounds, the one which will react MOST vigorously with sodium at room temperature is

A. CH₃CH₂OH

B. CH₃-C(=O)-O-CH₃

C. CH₃CH₂-O-CH₂CH₃

D. [benzene ring structure]

11. Of the following compounds, the one which possesses geometrical isomers is   11._____
    A. CCl₂=CCl₂   B. CH₂=CCl₂   C. CH₂=CHCl   D. CHCl=CHCl

12. Of the following, the one which is the STRONGEST acid is   12._____
    A. CCl₃COOH   B. CHCl₂COOH   C. CH₂ClCOOH   D. CH₃COOH

13. Glucose is a   13._____
    A. disaccharide   B. monosaccharide
    C. polysaccharide   D. starch

14. Of the following, the one which is an example of an amino acid is   14._____
    A. cellulose   B. diastase   C. maltose   D. tyrosine

15. Of the following acids, the one with the LARGEST acid constant is   15._____
    A. acetic acid   B. carbonic acid
    C. hydrocyanic acid   D. hydrogen sulfide

16. A water solution of calcium oxide is   16._____
    A. acid   B. alkaline   C. neutral   D. a base

17. A water solution of aluminum chloride is   17._____
    A. acid   B. alkaline   C. neutral   D. a base

18. The vapor pressure of mercury at room temperature is APPROXIMATELY _____ mm Hg.   18._____
    A. 10^{-6} B. 10^{-3} C. 1   D. 760

19. Of the following elements, the ONLY one which is ferromagnetic is   19._____
    A. aluminum   B. boron   C. nickel   D. tungsten

20. Mixing gelatine with water gives a(n)   20._____
    A. emulsion   B. lyophilic colloid
    C. lyophobic colloid   D. suspension

21. In the reaction $Ra_{226}^{90} \rightarrow Th_{222}^{88} + X$, X is a(n)   21._____
    A. alpha particle   B. beta particle
    C. gamma ray   D. meson

22. Of the following, the one with the LEAST mass is the

   A. deuteron   B. electron   C. neutron   D. proton

23. Beer's law refers to the

   A. absorption of light in solutions
   B. boiling point of non-associated liquids
   C. surface tension of a homologous series of fatty acids
   D. vapor pressure of binary liquid mixtures

24. A spectrophotometer working in the ultraviolet and visible regions of the spectrum is PARTICULARLY useful in

   A. colorimetric analysis
   B. distinguishing the components of gasoline
   C. distinguishing optical isomers
   D. qualitative analysis of inorganic salts

25. The addition of a neutron to a nucleus

   A. raises the atomic number by one without changing the atomic weight
   B. raises the atomic weight by one without changing atomic weight
   C. raises both the atomic number and the atomic weight by one
   D. always causes nuclear fission to occur

26. Of the following elements, the only one which CANNOT be tested for on an emission spectrograph is

   A. copper   B. iron   C. mercury   D. oxygen

27. A gas which is LIGHTER than air has the formula

   A. C_2H_2 B. C_2H_6 C. N_2O D. NO_2

28. The kinetic theory of gases predicts that the viscosity of gases will _____ density.

   A. decrease with decreased
   B. vary with the square root of the
   C. increase with decreased
   D. be independent of

29. The specific resistance of a 0.1 N NaCl solution was found to be 93.6 ohms at 25°C. Its SPECIFIC conductance will be _____ ohms.

   A. 0.936   B. 6.4 reciprocal
   C. 0.011 reciprocal   D. 93.6

30. Pure carbon monoxide may be prepared in the laboratory by

   A. adding dilute sulfuric acid to marble chips
   B. adding concentrated sulfuric acid to formic acid
   C. burning coke in a limited supply of air
   D. adding dilute hydrochloric acid to limestone

31. Pound for pound, sodium carbonate, when compared with sodium bicarbonate, will provide _____ sodium ions and _____ carbon dioxide.

    A. fewer; less
    B. more; less
    C. more; more
    D. fewer; more

32. Water gas (synthesis gas) is MAINLY a mixture of

    A. CO and N_2
    B. CO and H_2
    C. CO_2 and H_2O
    D. CO and O_2

33. The anhydride of nitrous acid is

    A. NO
    B. N_2O_3
    C. N_2O_5
    D. NO_2

34. The percent of gold in 14-carat gold is APPROXIMATELY

    A. 58
    B. 78
    C. 83
    D. 70

35. Three of the following are ores of iron. The one which is NOT is

    A. siderite
    B. hematite
    C. limonite
    D. spiegeleisen

36. The symbol of the element with the GREATEST tendency to gain electrons is

    A. F
    B. Bi
    C. At
    D. O

37. The Kroll process is used for extracting

    A. geramium
    B. molybdenum
    C. titanium
    D. wolfram

38. Waste rock material in an ore is called

    A. gangue
    B. slag
    C. flux
    D. iroth

39. Cementite is of fundamental importance in iron alloys. Its formula is

    A. FeC
    B. Fe_2C
    C. Fe_3C
    D. Fe_4C_3

40. Lead is dissolved MOST readily in dilute _____ acid.

    A. acetic
    B. sulfuric
    C. hydrochloric
    D. phosphoric

KEY (CORRECT ANSWERS)

1. C	11. D	21. A	31. D
2. B	12. A	22. B	32. A
3. C	13. B	23. A	33. A
4. C	14. D	24. A	34. B
5. A	15. A	25. D	35. C
6. D	16. B	26. D	36. A
7. C	17. A	27. A	37. B
8. A	18. B	28. C	38. A
9. D	19. C	29. A	39. A
10. A	20. B	30. D	40. A

EXAMINATION SECTION
TEST 1

DIRECTIONS: Each question or incomplete statement is followed by several suggested answers or completions. Select the one that BEST answers the question or completes the statement. *PRINT THE LETTER OF THE CORRECT ANSWER IN THE SPACE AT THE RIGHT.*

1. The industrial preparation of methanol from wood is an example of 1.____
    A. crystallization B. destructive distillation
    C. hydrogenation D. organic fermentation

2. An emulsion is a dispersion of a 2.____
    A. gas in a liquid B. liquid in a liquid
    C. liquid in a solid D. solid in a liquid

3. In volumetric analysis, it is NOT recommended to titrate a 3.____
    A. strong acid with a strong base
    B. weak acid with a strong base
    C. weak base with a strong acid
    D. weak base with a weak acid

4. Of the following, the element which forms an amphoteric oxide is 4.____
    A. arsenic B. chlorine C. silver D. sulfur

5. The term used to indicate water-free chemicals is 5.____
    A. abs. B. anhyd. C. C.P. D. "technical"

6. X-rays are MOST similar to 6.____
    A. alpha rays B. beta rays
    C. electrons D. gamma rays

7. Of the following atoms, the one with the LOWEST atomic weight is 7.____
    A. lead B. radium C. radon D. uranium

8. Of the following atomic particles, the one with the GREATEST mass is the 8.____
    A. alpha particle B. beta particle
    C. neutron D. proton

9. The *angstrom* is a unit of 9.____
    A. length B. mass C. volume D. weight

10. The chemical symbol for plutonium is 10.____
    A. Pn B. Pt C. Pu D. Pv

11. Of the following, the metal of GREATEST chemical activity is 11.____
    A. calcium B. copper C. mercury D. nickel

12. Of the following, the chemical which is COMMONLY used as an oxidizing agent in analytical work is

    A. $H_2C_2O_4$　　B. Iron　　C. Na_2SO_3　　D. PbO_2

13. Sodium stannite is used in the confirmatory qualitative test for

    A. bismuth　　B. calcium　　C. chromium　　D. silver

14. An acid solution is one in which the $[H^+]$ is

    A. equal to 10^{-7} mole/liter
    B. greater than 10^{-7} mole/liter
    C. less than 10^{-7} mole/liter
    D. less than 10^{-14} mole/liter

15. Beer's law is the BASIS of calculations in

    A. acidimetry
    B. calorimetry
    C. oxidation-reduction reactions
    D. photometry

16. Charles' law states: At constant

    A. pressure, the volume of a given mass of gas varies directly with the absolute temperature
    B. temperature, the volume of a given mass of gas varies inversely with the pressure
    C. volume, the pressure of a given mass of gas varies directly with the absolute temperature
    D. volume, the pressure of a given mass of gas varies inversely with the absolute temperature

17. According to LeChatelier's law, if the pressure is increased in the system $H_2 + I_2 \rightleftarrows 2\,HI$ (assume that the system is in equilibrium and that all substances are in the gaseous state), the reaction would

    A. go farther to the left
    B. go farther to the right
    C. go farther to the center
    D. not be affected

18. According to Van't Hoff's law, if the temperature is raised in the system $CO + 2\,H_2 \rightleftarrows CH_3OH + 24{,}000$ calories (assume that the system is in equilibrium and that all substances are in the gaseous state), the reaction would

    A. go farther to the left
    B. go farther to the right
    C. go farther to the center
    D. not be affected

19. The term *Thiele* refers to a type of   19.____

    A. balance   B. thermometer
    C. tube   D. viscosimeter

20. The term *Abbé* refers to a type of apparatus generally used to determine   20.____

    A. boiling point elevation   B. density
    C. refractive index   D. surface tension

21. The pycnometer is GENERALLY used to determine   21.____

    A. density   B. mass
    C. melting point   D. viscosity

22. The cryoscope is GENERALLY used to determine the   22.____

    A. boiling point   B. density
    C. freezing point   D. surface tension

23. Of the following carbohydrates, the one which is NOT classified as a polysaccharide is   23.____

    A. cellulose   B. inulin   C. invertose   D. starch

24. Aliphatic means, *most nearly*,   24.____

    A. acidic   B. cyclic
    C. nitrogen-containing   D. non-cyclic

25. Ethyl alcohol is often made UNSUITABLE for drinking by the addition of   25.____

    A. copper sulphate   B. methyl alcohol
    C. sodium chloride   D. water

KEY (CORRECT ANSWERS)

1. B   11. A
2. B   12. D
3. D   13. A
4. A   14. B
5. B   15. D

6. D   16. A
7. A   17. C
8. A   18. A
9. A   19. C
10. C   20. C

21. A
22. C
23. C
24. D
25. B

TEST 2

DIRECTIONS: Each question or incomplete statement is followed by several suggested answers or completions. Select the one that BEST answers the question or completes the statement. *PRINT THE LETTER OF THE CORRECT ANSWER IN THE SPACE AT THE RIGHT.*

1. The industrial process of transforming vegetable oils into solid fats is an example of   1.___
   A. halogenation   B. homogenization   C. hydrogenation   D. hydrolysis

2. Substances which are INTERMEDIATE between proteins and amino acids are called   2.___
   A. albumins   B. caseins   C. gelatines   D. peptones

3. The enzyme which hydrolyzes proteins into amino acids is   3.___
   A. amylase   B. emulsin   C. trypsin   D. saccharase

4. Hydrolysis of an ester in basic solution is GENERALLY termed   4.___
   A. fermentation   B. halogenation   C. hydrogenation   D. saponification

5. TEMPORARY hardness of water is generally removed by the addition of   5.___
   A. bicarbonates   B. carbonates   C. chlorides   D. hydroxides

6. PERMANENT hardness of water is generally removed by   6.___
   A. aeration   B. decantation   C. evaporation   D. precipitation

Questions 7-16.

DIRECTIONS: Column I lists terms, each of which can be properly matched with the laboratory apparatus in Column II. For each item of Column I, write in the answer space the letter in front of the option in Column II with which it is generally associated.

Column I

7. Arnold
8. Beckmann
9. Duboscq
10. Jackson
11. Kipp
12. Meker
13. Nessler
14. Ostwals
15. Westphal
16. Woulff

Column II

A. balance
B. beaker
C. bottle
D. burner
E. candle turbidimeter
F. colorimeter
G. funnel
H. gas generator
J. steam sterilizer
K. thermometer
L. tube
M. viscosimeter

7.___
8.___
9.___
10.___
11.___
12.___
13.___
14.___
15.___
16.___

Questions 17-25.

DIRECTIONS: Column I lists the names of metallic ions, each of which can be placed with one of the analytical groups in Column II. For each item of Column I, write in the answer space the letter in front of the group in Column II to which it belongs. (Where ions belong to more than one group, so indicate.)

17.	Aluminum	A.	Hydrochloric Acid Group	17.	____
18.	Ammonium	B.	Hydrogen Sulfide Group	18.	____
19.	Bismuth	A.	Ammonium Sulfide Group	19.	____
20.	Iron	D.	Ammonium Carbonate Group	20.	____
21.	Lead	E.	Soluble Group	21.	____
22.	Mercury			22.	____
23.	Strontium			23.	____
24.	Tin			24.	____
25.	Zinc			25.	____

KEY (CORRECT ANSWERS)

1.	C		11.	H
2.	D		12.	D
3.	C		13.	L
4.	D		14.	M
5.	D		15.	A
6.	D		16.	C
7.	J		17.	C
8.	K		18.	E
9.	F		19.	B
10.	E		20.	C

21. A, B
22. A, B
23. D
24. B
25. C

EXAMINATION SECTION
TEST 1

DIRECTIONS: Each question or incomplete statement is followed by several suggested answers or completions. Select the one that BEST answers the question or completes the statement. *PRINT THE LETTER OF THE CORRECT ANSWER IN THE SPACE AT THE RIGHT.*

1. The HOTTEST portion in a flame from a bunsen burner is located _____ of the flame. 1.____
   A. at the top of the outer yellow cone
   B. at the top of the inner blue cone
   C. at the middle of the inner blue cone
   D. about 1 cm above the very top

2. In which one of the following ways should a piece of small glass tubing be cut? 2.____
   A. Hold the tubing in a flame and pull the two ends apart
   B. Scratch the tubing with a file and bend the tube toward the scratch
   C. Scratch the tubing with a file and bend the tubing away from the scratch
   D. Heat the tubing in a flame and allow a drop of cold water to fall where you want the cut

3. Which one of the following materials is *transparent* in infrared light? 3.____
   A. NaCl crystals
   B. Glass
   C. Quartz
   D. Pyrex

4. Which one of the following solids will *dissolve* in concentrated aqueous NH_3? 4.____
   A. $Al(OH)_3$
   B. $Fe(OH)_3$
   C. $Cu(OH)_2$
   D. $Pb(OH)_2$

5. The one of the following ions which will cause a yellow color in a flame test is 5.____
   A. K^+
   B. Cu^{++}
   C. Na^+
   D. Ca^{++}

6. Which one of the following ions can NOT be precipitated in the presence of excess NaOH? 6.____
   A. Fe^{+++}
   B. Ni^{+++}
   C. Co^{+++}
   D. Al^{+++}

7. The one of the following poisonous gases which has no odor is 7.____
   A. CO
   B. HCN
   C. NH_3
   D. H_2S

8. Which one of the following indicators is *colorless* in acid and *red* in very basic solutions? 8.____
   A. Litmus
   B. Methyl violet
   C. Bromethymol blue
   D. Phenolphthalein

9. The one of the following compounds which is known as vitamin C is 9.____
   A. cyanocobalamin
   B. ascorbic acid
   C. boric acid
   D. arginine

10. The reaction between a conjugated diene and an alkene to form a six-membered ring compound is called

    A. esterification
    B. a Diels-Adler reaction
    C. an Aldol condensation
    D. a Markownikoff addition

11. The chemical name for aspirin is

    A. methylanthranilate
    B. acetylsalicyclic acid
    C. phenacetin
    D. methylsalicylate

12. Which one of the following compounds is NOT an organic base?

    A. Aniline
    B. Pyridine
    C. Trimethyamine
    D. Tetramethyammonium iodide

13. Which one of the following instruments is SUITABLE for the determination of ethanol in benzene?
    A(n)

    A. pH meter
    B. gas chromatograph
    C. atomic absorption spectrometer
    D. visible spectrometer

14. How many colloidal suspensions often be caused to coagulate and precipitate?
    By

    A. treatment with cold water
    B. occulusion
    C. addition of NH_4Cl
    D. centrifugation

15. The addition of $CaCl_2$ to water causes this compound to become

    A. hard   B. acidic   C. soft   D. basic

16. The Mohr and Volhard methods are used to determine the presence of

    A. acid
    B. chloride
    C. density
    D. molecular weight

17. The mean deviation of the three values of 2, 6, and 7 is

    A. 0   B. 2   C. 5   D. 6

18. A cation exchange resin can be used to remove _____ from water.

    A. Cl⁻   B. OH⁻   C. Na^+ D. alcohol

19. Which one of the following groups contains solvents which are all separately miscible with water at room temperature?

    A. Acetone, benzene, sulfuric acid
    B. Acetone, methanol, acetic acid
    C. Ether, methanol, ethanol
    D. Chloroform, carbontetrachloride, petroleum ether

20. The absorption of organic compounds on alumina followed by separation by elution with different solvents is called   20._____

    A. filtration
    C. crystallization
    B. distillation
    D. chromatography

KEY (CORRECT ANSWERS)

1. B
2. C
3. A
4. C
5. C
6. D
7. A
8. D
9. B
10. B

11. B
12. D
13. B
14. C
15. A
16. B
17. B
18. C
19. B
20. D

TEST 2

DIRECTIONS: Each question or incomplete statement is followed by several suggested answers or completions. Select the one that BEST answers the question or completes the statement. *PRINT THE LETTER OF THE CORRECT ANSWER IN THE SPACE AT THE RIGHT.*

1. The Fisher reagent (I_2 + SO_2 + C_5H_5N in CH_3OH) is used for

    A. the identification of amines
    B. the determination of the presence of H_2O in organic solvents
    C. the separation of amino acids
    D. testing for chloride ion

2. Which one of the following is an analytical method for the determination of the presence of nitrogen in organic compounds?

    A. The Kjeldahl method
    B. Treatment by the Versene (EDTA) method
    C. Iodometry
    D. X-ray diffraction method

3. Racemization of d-Tartaric acid will produce _____ tartaric acid.

    A. meso-   B. 1-   C. d, 1-   D. d-

4. Which one of the following reagents is used for the detection of amino acids by thin layer chromatography?

    A. Aniline phthalate   B. Bromothymol blue
    C. Benzene   D. Ninhydrin

5. What is the molar concentration of a material in solution in a 1 cm cell, if the optical density is 1.0 at a wave length where the solvent is transparent and the solute has an extinction coefficient of 10 liters/mole cm?

    A. 0.1M   B. 1.0M   C. 10M   D. 100M

6. What is the measurement of a standard taper 24/40 stopper? _____ mm at the top and _____ mm _____.

    A. 24; 40; at the bottom   B. 40; 24; at the bottom
    C. 24; 40; long   D. 40; 24; long

7. To what extent should a mercury thermometer calibrated for total immersion be immersed in a test solution?

    A. Totally
    B. Only 76 mm
    C. Sufficiently to reach the mercury column
    D. Only to totally cover the bulb of mercury at the bottom of the thermometer

8. The white precipitate formed when sodium thiosulfate ($Na_2S_2O_3$) solution is treated with acid is

    A. $H_2S_2O_3$ B. SO_3 C. S   D. Na_2SO_4

9. The one of the following atoms which possesses the GREATEST electronegativity is

   A. Na   B. C   C. O   D. Al

10. The oxidation states of cobalt in water solutions are

    A. +1 and +2
    C. +3 and +4
    B. +2 and +3
    D. +2 and +4

11. Which one of the following is an example of a reactive hydride?

    A. CH_4 B. SiH_4 C. NH_3 D. NaH

12. The infrared absorption indicative of an organic ketone is found at about _____ cm^{-1}.

    A. 1000   B. 1700   C. 3000   D. 10000

13. Which one of the following compounds does NOT show any NMR spectrum at 60 megacycles?

    A. CH_3OH B. CCl_4 C. C_6H_6 D. SiH_4

14. At which one of the following temperatures is the density of water GREATEST?

    A. -4° C   B. 0° C   C. 4° C   D. 100° C

15. Which one of the following forms of mercury offers the GREATEST environmental threat?

    A. Hg metal   B. CH_3HgCH_3 C. $HgCl_2$ D. Hg_2Cl_2

16. What is the APPROXIMATE melting point for a mixture of 99% benzoic acid (mp 122° C) and 1% succinic acid (mp 185° C)?

    A. Below 122° C
    C. Above 130° C
    B. Between 122° and 185° C
    D. 185°

17. The number of grams in 1 pound (avdp) is

    A. 3.3   B. 62.5   C. 100   D. 453

18. A water solution contains either Na_2SO_4 or Na_2CO_3 and nothing else. To determine which salt is present, you should

    A. use a flame test
    B. make the solution acid with HC1 and add a BaCl2 solution
    C. make the solution basic with NaOH and add a BaCl2 solution
    D. add a $BaCl_2$ solution only

19. Ignition of ferric hydroxide in air produces

    A. iron metal
    C. Fe_2O_3
    B. FeO
    D. Fe_3O_4

20. Coulometry is a technique which involves measurement of

    A. density
    C. current flow
    B. gas volume
    D. color shading

KEY (CORRECT ANSWERS)

1. B
2. A
3. C
4. D
5. A

6. C
7. A
8. C
9. C
10. B

11. D
12. B
13. B
14. C
15. B

16. A
17. D
18. B
19. C
20. C

EXAMINATION SECTION
TEST 1

DIRECTIONS: Each question or incomplete statement is followed by several suggested answers or completions. Select the one that BEST answers the question or completes the statement. *PRINT THE LETTER OF THE CORRECT ANSWER IN THE SPACE AT THE RIGHT.*

1. The valence of an element tells

    A. its atomic weight
    B. the solubility of its compounds
    C. its stability
    D. how many electrons its atom lends, borrows, or shares
    E. how many compounds can be formed

1.____

2. One way in which compounds differ from mixtures is that compounds have

    A. more elements
    C. greater activity
    E. physical properties
    B. fewer elements
    D. a definite composition

2.____

3. Sugar is a compound because it

    A. is granular
    B. gives off water when heated
    C. blackens when heated
    D. has a definite composition
    E. is sweet

3.____

4. Argon and neon are inert elements because their atoms have

    A. complete outermost rings
    C. chemical reactivity
    E. no neutrons
    B. no electrons
    D. no protons

4.____

5. Any solution which conducts an electric current is called a (n)

    A. ion
    C. non-electrolyte
    E. catalyst
    B. electrolyte
    D. electrode

5.____

6. Hydrogen is contained in all

    A. liquids
    C. salts
    E. acids
    B. oxides
    D. compounds

6.____

7. Plants give off oxygen during the day because

    A. the body of the plant needs to breathe oxygen to live
    B. oxygen is one of the products of photosynthesis
    C. oxygen is one of the products of respiration
    D. burning of food produces energy
    E. the extra warmth acts as a catalytic agent

7.____

8. A manufacturing city is relatively free from smoke. 8._____
This is often due to

   A. the use of acids in manufacturing
   B. an inventor who has found a new use of by-products
   C. the process of collecting carbon by charged electrodes
   D. the exclusive use of steam boilers in all manufacturing establishments
   E. the fact that the city is in a region of high-pressure areas

9. The substance used in etching glass is 9._____

   A. sulfuric acid   B. tincture of iodine
   C. hydrobromic acid   D. aqua regia
   E. hydrofluoric acid

10. Burning of wood is an example of 10._____

    A. an endothermic reaction   B. reduction
    C. chemical change   D. physical change
    E. catalysis

11. A gas collected in a bottle was allowed to mix with a small amount of air. A burning splint 11._____
applied to the mouth of the bottle caused a sharp explosion.
The gas collected was

    A. oxygen   B. chlorine
    C. hydrogen   D. nitrogen
    E. sulfur dioxide

12. Diamond is a (n) 12._____

    A. alloy   B. metal
    C. crystal   D. ore
    E. inorganic compound

13. If water is saturated with salt (sodium chloride), the freezing point is 13._____

    A. the same as for distilled water
    B. lower than for pure water
    C. higher than for pure water
    D. zero degrees Centigrade
    E. plus four degrees Centigrade

14. If a relatively small amount of solute is dissolved in a relatively large amount of solvent, 14._____
the solution is called

    A. dilute   B. saturated
    C. ionic   D. concentrated
    E. none of the above

15. In a Bunsen burner, luminous flames result when the 15._____

    A. gas is turned too low
    B. gas carbon dioxide is formed
    C. barrel of the burner is too long
    D. spud is closed
    E. air openings are closed

16. Sodium hydroxide is a (n)

    A. acid
    B. salt
    C. oxide
    D. base
    E. carbohydrate

17. Which of the following molecules contains five atoms?

    A. $Ca_3(PO_4)_2$
    B. Na_2CO_3
    C. Al_2O_3
    D. $CaSO_4$
    E. NH_4OH

18. Neutralization reactions usually form water and

    A. acids
    B. bases
    C. oxides
    D. salts
    E. absorbing agents

19. Why do chemical reactions of the body take place so much faster within the body than they do outside the body?
    Because

    A. the body is active
    B. the reactions are those of the body and designed to go on in the body
    C. the reactions of the body are organic reactions
    D. there are enzymes in the body which speed up reactions
    E. the blood is a good solvent

20. The study of carbon compounds is known as _____ chemistry.

    A. inorganic
    B. organic
    C. qualitative
    D. analytical
    E. physical

21. Sodium compounds, when heated in a flame, produce the color

    A. red
    B. yellow
    C. green
    D. violet
    E. pink

22. Substances which dissociate into ions when in solution are called

    A. electrolytes
    B. non-electrolytes
    C. hydrates
    D. aqueous
    E. catalysts

23. A hydrocarbon with the formula CH_4 is

    A. methylene
    B. acetylene
    C. ethane
    D. propane
    E. methane

24. Cotton is MOST often bleached by use of

    A. ozone
    B. hydrogen peroxide
    C. chlorine
    D. sulfur dioxide
    E. hydrochloric acid

25. The formula for milk of magnesia is

   A. $Mg(OH)_2$
   B. MgO
   C. $MgSO_4$
   D. $MgCl_2$
   E. $Mg_3(PO_4)2$

26. Natural gas is composed MAINLY of

   A. methane
   B. carbon monoxide
   C. hydrogen
   D. acetylene
   E. carbon dioxide

27. What gas in the atmosphere is necessary for the operation of an automobile engine?

   A. Carbon dioxide
   B. Hydrogen
   C. Helium
   D. Carbon monoxide
   E. Oxygen

28. An element has an atomic weight of 20 and its atomic number is 10. The number of planetary electrons about the nucleus of the element is

   A. 0   B. 10   C. 20   D. 30   E. 40

29. Concentrated sulfuric acid is used in the preparation of hydrogen chloride because it

   A. reacts slowly
   B. is very concentrated
   C. is a heavy acid
   D. is a dehydrating agent
   E. has a high boiling point

30. A hydrocarbon with the formula C_2H_2 is

   A. methyl chloride
   B. methylene
   C. chloroform
   D. iodoform
   E. acetylene

31. When iron rusts, it

   A. gains in weight
   B. remains chemically unchanged
   C. loses weight
   D. combines with hydrogen
   E. is reduced

32. Equations are balanced by

   A. the use of exponents
   B. the use of subscripts
   C. the use of coefficients
   D. placing parentheses around radicals
   E. placing all products on the right side of the equation

33. Chlorine is obtained commercially CHIEFLY by

   A. action of acids on metals
   B. heating sodium chloride
   C. electrolysis of hydrochloric acid
   D. electrolysis of brine
   E. heating chlorides

34. Slow oxidation differs from burning in that 34.____

   A. no heat is given off B. more time is required
   C. oxides are formed D. dioxides are formed
   E. compounds are formed

35. Which one of the following does NOT produce a high degree of ionization when in solution? 35.____

   A. HCl B. H_2SO_4 C. NaOH D. KCl E. CH_3OH

36. The anhydride of H_2SO_3 is 36.____

   A. SO_3 B. SO_2 C. SO_4 D. H_2O E. S_2O_3

37. Acids whose names end in -ous have salts with names ending in 37.____

   A. -ide B. -ate C. -ite D. -ine E. -ous

38. The general formula for organic acids is 38.____

   A. RCOOH B. ROH C. RCHO D. ROR E. RCOOR

39. Which one of the following iron ores contains the GREATEST percentage of iron? 39.____
   (Atomic weights: Fe = 56, O = 16,
   C = 12, S = 32, H = 1.)

   A. $Fe_2O_3(H_2O)_3$ B. FeS_2
   C. $FeCO_3$ D. Fe_2O_3
   E. Fe_3O_4

40. Which is the CORRECT formula for magnesium nitride? 40.____

   A. MgN B. Mg_3N_2
   C. $Mg(NO_2)2$ D. $Mg(NO_3)_2$
   E. Mg_3N

KEY (CORRECT ANSWERS)

1. D	11. C	21. B	31. A
2. D	12. C	22. A	32. C
3. D	13. B	23. E	33. D
4. A	14. A	24. C	34. B
5. B	15. E	25. A	35. E
6. E	16. D	26. A	36. B
7. B	17. C	27. E	37. C
8. C	18. D	28. B	38. A
9. E	19. D	29. E	39. E
10. C	20. B	30. E	40. B

TEST 2

DIRECTIONS: Each question or incomplete statement is followed by several suggested answers or completions. Select the one that BEST answers the question or completes the statement. *PRINT THE LETTER OF THE CORRECT ANSWER IN THE SPACE AT THE RIGHT.*

Questions 1-14.

DIRECTIONS: Questions 1 through 14 contain 7 sets of 2 questions each. The first question in each set is an information question, and the second is a question on the chemical principle that best explains the answer to the preceding question. In each case, put the letter of your answer in the space at the right.

1. A storekeeper placed some calcium chloride between his sash and storm window during a severe cold spell. What happened?

    A. The windows became more heavily frosted than the nearby windows.
    B. The substance became dry and powder-like.
    C. The calcium chloride evaporated.
    D. The windows remained almost free of frost.
    E. Nothing happened.

2. Which one of the following statements gives the principle that BEST explains the answer to Question 1? Many

    A. gases such as water vapor and carbon dioxide can be solidified
    B. chemical reactions depend upon the lack of or presence of moisture
    C. solids such as dry ice and iodine pass directly from a solid to a gaseous state
    D. substances readily lose their water of hydration or crystallization on exposure to air
    E. substances have the property of absorbing or adsorbing moisture from air or other substances

3. If a positive and a negative electrode are introduced into a solution of copper chloride, the copper will be deposited on the negative electrode.
   This indicates

    A. that the copper particles in the solution had a positive charge
    B. that the copper particles had acquired a negative charge from the negative electrode
    C. that the copper particles were electrically neutral
    D. that the chloride particles were repelled by the copper particles
    E. nothing at all

4. Which one of the following statements gives the principle that BEST explains the answer to Question 3?

    A. Colloidal suspensions of different metals impart different colors to a solution.
    B. When salts ionize, the metal gives up electrons to the non-metal.
    C. In combining with other elements, metals gain electrons.
    D. Like charges repel each other and unlike charges attract.
    E. Basic metals are protected from corrosion by plating them with relatively non-corrosive metals.

1.____

2.____

3.____

4.____

28

5. Sodium chloride and sulfuric acid were placed in a flask and heated gently. The hydrochloric acid gas was passed over water and dissolved, thereby making a solution of hydrochloric acid.
Why is HCl the only product given off as a gas?

   A. The heat produces a chemical reaction.
   B. The sodium chloride furnishes the chloride ion.
   C. The acid furnishes the hydrogen ion necessary to make an acid.
   D. HCl is the only product volatile at the temperature of the reaction.
   E. The sodium sulfate is a precipitate.

6. Which one of the following statements gives the principle that BEST explains the answer to Question 5?

   A. Compounds possessing different boiling points may be separated by destructive distillation.
   B. Acids are produced only by double decomposition reaction
   C. All chemical reactions are speeded up by heat.
   D. Acids furnish the hydrogen ion in varying degrees of concentration.
   E. Acids with low boiling points may be prepared by using an acid with a high boiling point.

7. A boy placed some zinc in a flask with some dilute hydrochloric acid.
What happened?

   A. Hydrogen was given off.
   B. Chlorine was given off.
   C. Oxygen was given off.
   D. Zinc chloride was precipitated.
   E. Nothing happened.

8. Which one of the following statements gives the principle that BEST explains the answer to Question 7?

   A. Metals replace hydrogen from all acids.
   B. Gases are produced by simple replacement reactions.
   C. Elements are able to replace those below them in the electrochemical series.
   D. Chemical opposites, such as a metal and an acid, usually unite.
   E. Zinc is a very inactive metal.

9. Hydrogen gas was passed into a test tube containing copper oxide. Heat was then applied to the tube.
What probably happened?

   A. An explosion occurred.
   B. Water was formed in the tube.
   C. A reddish-colored gas was given off.
   D. A thin green coating appeared on the copper.
   E. Nothing happened.

10. Which one of the following statements gives the principle that BEST explains the answer to Question 9?   10._____

    A. Copper is a comparatively inactive metal.
    B. Metal oxides often combine with an acid to form a carbonate.
    C. Many oxygen compounds when heated with hydrogen will release oxygen.
    D. Noticeable heat and light occur in many chemical reactions.
    E. Some chemical compounds are able to absorb water from air.

11. One series of hydrocarbons contains these compounds: CH_4, C_2H_6, C_3H_8. What is the general formula for finding the formulas of additional members of this series?   11._____

    A. C_nH_{2n} B. C_nH_{2n+2}
    C. C_nH_{2n+4} D. C_nH_{2n-2}
    E. C_nH_{2n+6}

12. Which one of the following statements gives the principle that BEST explains the answer to Question 11?   12._____

    A. Unsaturated hydrocarbons are capable of taking on additional hydrogen.
    B. Saturated hydrocarbons are incapable of holding more hydrogen.
    C. Organic compounds are compounds in which the elements share electrons.
    D. Saturated hydrocarbons form what is known as substitution products.
    E. In a homologous series, each member differs from the next by the same group of elements.

13. A bottle was filled almost to the top with sulfuric acid and left unstoppered. What MOST likely happened?   13._____

    A. The amount of sulfuric acid was increased.
    B. The sulfuric acid became more concentrated.
    C. The bottle overflowed.
    D. Sulfur dioxide was given off.
    E. Nothing happened.

14. Which one of the following statements gives the principle that BEST explains the answer to Question 13?   14._____

    A. Evaporation takes place at the surface of the liquid.
    B. Unstable compounds often give off gases in decomposing.
    C. Dissociation or ionization has made possible the production of new elements.
    D. Most acids will expand in volume if exposed to the air.
    E. Some chemical compounds are able to absorb water from the air.

Questions 15-20.

DIRECTIONS: Each of Questions 15 through 20 consists of five terms, one of which does NOT belong with the other four. You are to select the term which does NOT belong. Mark its letter in the space at the right.

15. A. nitrogen   B. magnesium   C. tin   15.____
    D. antimony   E. bismuth

16. A. boiling point   B. inert   C. solubility   16.____
    D. specific gravity   E. density

17. A. aldehyde   B. ketone   C. nitride   D. ester   E. ether   17.____

18. A. dissolving   B. evaporating   C. freezing   18.____
    D. burning   E. solidifying

19. A. Bunsen   B. Cavendish   C. Einstein   19.____
    D. Frasch   E. Priestley

20. A. $CaCO_3$ B. $CaSO_4$ C. $Ca_3(PO_4)_2$ 20.____
    D. $CaCl_2$ E. $CaSiO_3$

Questions 21-24.

DIRECTIONS: Questions 21 through 24 are based on the following data:

RESULTS OF THREE EXPERIMENTS TO DETERMINE WHAT
FACTORS, IF ANY, AFFECT THE SOLUBILITY OF SOLIDS

Experiment	Kind and Amount of Solvent	Temperature of Solvent	Pressure	Kind of Solute	Amount of Solute Dissolved
I	100 cc CCl_4	10° C.	600 mm	Sulfur	15 grams
	100 cc CCl_4	10° C.	700 mm	Sulfur	15 grams
II	100 cc H_2O	100° C.	700 mm	Sulfur	15 grams
	100 cc H_2O	50° C.	800 mm	Sulfur	1 gram
III	100 cc H_2O	10° C.	700 mm	Sulfur	.1 gram
	100 cc CCl_4	10° C.	700 mm	Sulfur	15 grams

Constant factors are those which are kept the same in an experiment. Varied factors are those which are not kept the same. You are to assume that if a factor was found NOT to affect the solubility of solids in any one experiment, it would not do so in any other experiment. The number of grams of solute dissolved in the given volume of solvent produced saturation.

Read each question and study the table carefully. Decide which answer is best and mark its letter in the space at the right.

21. What factor or combination of factors was constant in Experiment I?   21.____

    A. Temperature of solvent
    B. Kind of solute; pressure
    C. Temperature of solvent; pressure; kind of solute
    D. Kind of solvent; pressure; kind of solute
    E. Kind of solvent; temperature of solvent; kind of solute

22. What factor or combination of factors was varied in Experiment II?

   A. Temperature of solvent
   B. Kind of solute; temperature of solvent
   C. Pressure; temperature of solvent
   D. Kind of solvent; pressure
   E. Kind of solute; kind of solvent

23. What factor in Experiment III produced the observed difference in the amount of solute dissolved?

   A. Kind of solvent
   B. Temperature of solvent
   C. Pressure
   D. Kind of solute
   E. None of the above

24. In these experiments, what factors definitely affect the solubility of solids?

   A. Kind of solute; pressure
   B. Kind of solvent; kind of solute
   C. Temperature of solvent; pressure
   D. Pressure; temperature of solvent; kind of solvent
   E. Temperature of solvent; kind of solvent

Questions 25-29.

DIRECTIONS: Questions 25 through 29 are based on the figure below. Study the figure and read each question carefully. Then, in the space at the right, mark the letter of the BEST answer

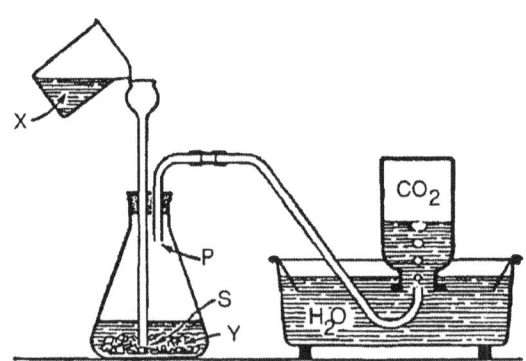

25. If this reaction is to work successfully, Beaker X should contain

   A. sodium hydroxide
   B. copper sulfate
   C. hydrochloric acid
   D. carbon tetrachloride
   E. sodium chloride

26. If this reaction is to work successfully, Flask Y should contain

   A. calcium sulfate
   B. calcium hydroxide
   C. zinc sulfate
   D. calcium carbonate
   E. calcium oxide

27. The MOST common chemical test for the presence of carbon dioxide makes use of   27._____

   A. sodium hydroxide
   B. hydrochloric acid
   C. ammonium hydroxide
   D. calcium sulfate
   E. calcium hydroxide

28. The ends of the glass tubing, S and P,   28._____

   A. are in correct position
   B. should be reversed in their respective positions
   C. should both be just above the liquid
   D. should both be near the top of the flask
   E. should both be in the liquid

29. Which of the following substances should NOT be used at Y?   29._____

   A. Limestone
   B. Coral
   C. Gypsum
   D. Chalk
   E. Marble

Questions 30-31.

DIRECTIONS: Questions 30 and 31 are based on the equation for the preparation of oxygen by heating potassium chlorate. (Atomic weights: K = 39, Cl = 35.5, O = 16.)

30. To balance the equation, the coefficient of the potassium chlorate is   30._____

   A. 1   B. 2   C. 3   D. 4   E. E. 5

31. To obtain 67.2 liters of oxygen, how many grams of potassium chlorate will be required?   31._____

   A. 74   B. 122.5   C. 200   D. 245   E. E. 367.5

Questions 32-33.

DIRECTIONS: Questions 32 and 33 are based on the equation for the preparation of hydrogen using zinc and hydrochloric acid. (Atomic weights: Zn = 65, H = 1, Cl = 35.5.)

32. What is the equation or reacting weight of zinc chloride?   32._____

   A. 65   B. 100.5   C. 125   D. 136   E. E. 165.5

33. If 65 grams of zinc are used, how many grams of hydrogen will be formed?   33._____

   A. 1   B. 2   C. 4   D. 6   E. E. 8

34. What will be one of the ions in the ionic equation for the formation of $CuSO_4$?   34._____

   A. Cu^+ B. Cu^{++} C. SO_3^{--} D. SO_4^- E. E. SO_4^{---}

35. Which is the CORRECT formula for aluminum oxide?   35._____

   A. Al_2O_3 B. AlO C. Al_3O_2 D. Al_3O_4 E. E. Al_2O_5

36. How many electrons will the iron lose when $FeCl_2$ is changed to $FeCl_3$?

    A. 1   B. 2   C. 3   D. 4   E. E. 6

37. Which is the CORRECT formula for silver bromide?

    A. AgBr   B. Ag_2Br C. Ag_2BrO_3 D. $Ag_2(Br)_3$ E. E.Ag_3Br_2

38. What is one of the products in the completely balanced equation Na2SO3 + H2SO4 (dilute) $\rightarrow$?

    A. Na_2SO_3 B. SO_3 C. Na_2SO_4 D. $NaHSO_3$ E. E.H_2S

39. The electrolysis of water represents which one of the following chemical changes?

    A. Synthesis
    B. Simple decomposition
    C. Simple replacement
    D. Double replacement
    E. Hydrolysis

40. Which is the CORRECT formula for ammonium sulfate?

    A. NH_4SO_4 B. NH_4SO_3 C. NH_4S D. $(NH_4)_2SO_4$ E. $(NH_4)_2SO_3$

KEY (CORRECT ANSWERS)

1. D	11. B	21. E	31. D
2. E	12. E	22. C	32. D
3. A	13. C	23. A	33. B
4. D	14. E	24. E	34. B
5. D	15. A	25. C	35. A
6. E	16. B	26. D	36. A
7. A	17. C	27. E	37. A
8. C	18. D	28. A	38. C
9. B	19. C	29. C	39. B
10. C	20. D	30. B	40. D

EXAMINATION SECTION
TEST 1

DIRECTIONS: Each question or incomplete statement is followed by several suggested answers or completions. Select the one that BEST answers the question or completes the statement. *PRINT THE LETTER OF THE CORRECT ANSWER IN THE SPACE AT THE RIGHT.*

Questions 1-4.

DIRECTIONS: Questions 1 through 4 are based upon the following equation representing the principal method of producing methyl alcohol: $CO + 2H_2 = CH_3OH$. As the alcohol is a gas under conditions of the reaction, the reaction takes place entirely in the gaseous state.

1. The presence of a catalyst will

   A. *increase* the yield of methyl alcohol
   B. *increase* the rate of the reaction and increase the yield of methyl alcohol
   C. *decrease* the time required to reach equilibrium but have no effect on the equilibrium concentrations
   D. *decrease* the time required to reach equilibrium and decrease the yield of methyl alcohol
   E. *increase* the amount of heat evolved during the reaction

2. As the temperature is raised, the yield of CH_3OH is decreased.
   This indicates

   A. an increase in temperature decreases the rate of a reaction
   B. the reaction as written absorbs heat
   C. the reaction as written evolves heat
   D. an increase in temperature increases the rate of reaction
   E. the catalyst is heat sensitive

3. If after the equilibrium is established, the pressure is increased, the yield of CH_3OH will

   A. be increased
   B. be decreased
   C. not be affected
   D. depend on the catalyst being used
   E. be 32 grams

4. For every 1000 cubic feet of hydrogen that react,

   A. 1000 cubic feet of carbon monoxide react
   B. 1000 cubic feet of methyl alcohol are formed
   C. 2000 cubic feet of methyl alcohol are formed
   D. 500 cubic feet of methyl alcohol are formed
   E. 1000 gallons of methyl alcohol are formed

Questions 5-13.

DIRECTIONS: Answer Questions 5 through 13 based upon the following atom. An assumed atom has the following structure: The nucleus contains 46 neutrons and 35 protons. The first three electron orbits contain 2, 8, 18 electrons.

5. The atomic weight is
   A. 28 B. 35 C. 46 D. 70 E. 81

6. The atomic number is
   A. 28 B. 35 C. 46 D. 70 E. 81

7. The negative oxidation number of the element would *probably* be
   A. -1 B. -2 C. -3 D. -4 E. -7

8. The MAXIMUM POSITIVE oxidation number of the element would *probably* be
   A. 1 B. 3 C. 5 D. 7 E. 8

9. In concentrated sulfuric acid, the bond between hydrogen and oxygen is BEST classified as a(n) _____ bond.
   A. ionic
   B. covalent
   C. hydrogen
   D. coordinate covalent
   E. ion-dipole

10. In sulfuric acid, the bond between sulfur and the oxygen to which no hydrogen is attached is a(n) _____ bond.
    A. ionic
    B. coordinate covalent
    C. double
    D. ion dipole
    E. nonpolar covalent

11. All normal solution of sulfuric acid, molecular weight 98, contains _____ grams solute per liter.
    A. 1 B. 2 C. 49 D. 98 E. 196

12. _____ will conduct an electric current.
    A. Carbon tetrachloride
    B. Hydrogen chloride dissolved in toluene
    C. Hydrogen chloride dissolved in water
    D. Sugar dissolved in water
    E. Glacial acetic acid

13. Solid iodine is heated, converted to a purple gas, and resolidified on the surface of the container.
    This process is known as
    A. precipitation
    B. condensation
    C. evaporation
    D. sublimation
    E. purification

Questions 14-19.

DIRECTIONS: Answer Questions 14 through 19 concerning the following reaction: $Cu + 2H_2SO_4 \rightarrow CuSO_4 + 2H_2O + SO_2$ using the atomic weights Cu = 63.5, H = 1, S = 32, O = 16.

14. The substance reduced is   14.____

    A. hydrogen   B. copper   C. sulfur
    D. oxygen   E. water

15. The reducing agent is   15.____

    A. copper   B. sulfuric acid   C. cupric sulfate
    D. water   E. sulfur dioxide

16. If 31.75 grams of copper are used, the volume of SO_2 gas produced at STP is _____ liters.   16.____

    A. 2   B. 11.2   C. 22.4   D. 32   E. 64

17. The substance which loses electrons is   17.____

    A. copper   B. hydrogen   C. sulfur
    D. oxygen   E. water

18. If an excess H_2SO_4 is present, the amount of copper needed to produce 3 gram moles of $CuSO_4$ is   18.____

    A. 3   B. 21.1
    C. 63.5   D. 254
    E. correct answer not given

19. _____ gram(s) of water are produced when 9.8 grams H_2SO_4 react with 7 grams of Cu.   19.____

    A. 1.0   B. 1.8   C. 2   D. 3.6   E. 4

20. The oxidation number of sulfur in Ag_2S is   20.____

    A. 2   B. 1   C. 0   D. -1   E. -2

21. The oxidation number of oxygen in Al_2O_3 is   21.____

    A. +3   B. +2   C. 0   D. -2   E. -6

22. For the reaction $4HCl(g) + O_2(g) = 2H_2O(g) + 2Cl_2(g) + 27$ Kcal, the equilibrium concentration of Cl_2 would be increased by   22.____

    A. increasing the temperature
    B. adding a catalyst
    C. adding water
    D. increasing the pressure
    E. all the preceding procedures would increase the equilibrium concentration of Cl_2

23. For the reaction $2SO_2(g) + O_2(g) = 2SO_3(g) + 23$ Kcal, the equilibrium concentration of SO_2 would be increased by

    A. an increase in temperature
    B. an increase in pressure
    C. removing SO_3
    D. addition of oxygen
    E. addition of catalyst

23. ____

24. A substance that exists *mainly* as molecules when dissolved in water is

    A. NaCl   B. NaOH   C. CH_3OH D. HCl   E. $CaBr_2$

24. ____

25. The solubility product for $PbCl_2$ is equal to

    A. $\{Pb^{++}\} + 2\{Cl^-\}$
    B. $\{Pb^{++}\} + \{Cl^-\}$
    C. $\{Pb^{++}\}\{Cl^-\}$
    D. $\{Pb^{++}\}\{Cl^-\}^2$
    E. $\{Pb^{++}\}\,2\{Cl^-\}^2$

25. ____

KEY (CORRECT ANSWERS)

1. C		11. C	
2. C		12. C	
3. A		13. D	
4. D		14. C	
5. E		15. A	
6. B		16. B	
7. A		17. A	
8. D		18. E	
9. B		19. B	
10. B		20. E	

21. D
22. D
23. A
24. C
25. D

TEST 2

DIRECTIONS: Each question or incomplete statement is followed by several suggested answers or completions. Select the one that BEST answers the question or completes the statement. *PRINT THE LETTER OF THE CORRECT ANSWER IN THE SPACE AT THE RIGHT.*

1. The oxidation number of chromium in $K_2Cr_2O_7$ is

    A. -2 B. 0 C. 2 D. 6 E. 12

    1.____

2. A metal that will react with acids to produce hydrogen gas is

    A. Ag
    B. Cu
    C. Hg
    D. Al
    E. all of listed metals

    2.____

3. A metal that will react with cold water to produce hydrogen gas is

    A. Al B. Zn C. Cu D. K E. Hg

    3.____

4. In general, nonmetals

    A. are electric conductors
    B. displace hydrogen from dilute acid solutions
    C. exist as positive ions
    D. are *malleable*
    E. exhibit both negative and positive oxidation numbers

    4.____

5. A water solution of _____ is classified as a base.

    A. CaO B. C_2H_5OH C. CO_2 D. CH_3COOH E. H_2O_2

    5.____

6. An oxidizing agent

    A. always contains oxygen
    B. is always reduced in a redox reaction
    C. always donates electrons
    D. is a catalyst
    E. is an electron donor

    6.____

7. An element forming an ion resembling the electronic structure of $_2He^4$ is

    A. $_3Li^6$ B. $_8O^{16}$ C. $_{11}Na^{23}$ D. $_{17}Cl^{35}$ E. $_{10}Ne^{20}$

    7.____

8. A Lewis base

    A. must contain hydroxide ion
    B. is an electron pair donor
    C. is a substance that yields hydronium ion
    D. is one classification of $AlCl_3$
    E. is a proton acceptor.

    8.____

9. An example of a nonpolar solvent is

    A. H_2O B. C_2H_5OH C. CH_3Cl D. CCl_4 E. CO_2

    9.____

10. Water is a good solvent for

   A. C_2H_5OH B. CH_4 C. CS_2 D. CCl_4 E. Br_2

11. An element in the same family as sodium and *more* electropositive than sodium is

   A. rubidium
   B. oxygen
   C. chlorine
   D. carbon
   E. fluorine

12. A strong acid that is *also* a strong oxidizing agent is

   A. acetic
   B. phosphoric
   C. hydrochloric
   D. nitric
   E. boric

13. Water has a *higher* boiling point than hydrogen sulfide because

   A. water has the higher molecular weight
   B. hydrogen sulfide ionizes
   C. water molecules form aggregates by hydrogen bonding
   D. water ionizes
   E. water expands on freezing

14. The position of an element in the periodic table is determined by

   A. electron configuration
   B. electronegativity
   C. atomic volume
   D. atomic mass
   E. number of neutrons

15. One mole of H_2SO_4 contains

   A. 2 grams of hydrogen
   B. Avogadros number of hydrogen atoms
   C. 3 moles of atoms
   D. 64 grams of sulfur
   E. 7 atoms

16. One molecule of gas A reacts with three molecules of gas B to form 2 molecules of gas C and no other substance. Gas C contains _____ atoms.

   A. 1
   B. 2
   C. 3
   D. 4
   E. all answers possible

17. Sodium perchlorate ($NaClO_4$) will decompose to give oxygen gas and sodium chloride. One mole sodium will yield _____ gram(s) oxygen.

   A. 1   B. 16   C. 32   D. 48   E. 64

18. A flask contained .32 grams of oxygen gas. The same flask filled with an unknown gas at the same temperature and pressure contained .18 grams of gas.
The molecular weight of the unknown gas is

   A. 2   B. 9   C. 18   D. 22   E. 32

19. Two grams of a gas occupies 2.24 liters at standard temperature and pressure. The molecular weight of the gas is

   A. 2.0   B. 16   C. 20   D. 22.4   E. 44.8

20. −218° C can be expressed as

    A. −218° F   B. 55° K   C. 218° K   D. 273° K   E. 491° K

21. Of the following substances, the one with the HIGHEST boiling point is

    A. He   B. H_2 C. O_2 D. SO_2 E. S

22. A solution of a salt gives a violet flame test and a white precipitate when treated with barium chloride. The solution could contain

    A. NaCl   B. KI   C. K_2SO_4
    D. $NH_4C_2H_3O_2$ E. KNO_3

23. An element that forms ionic solids with chlorine is

    A. carbon   B. calcium   C. aluminum
    D. phosphorus   E. hydrogen

24. When a liquid evaporates, one observes a cooling effect. This is accounted for by

    A. the liquid being wet
    B. energy being required to convert a liquid to a gas
    C. movement of air
    D. the conversion of liquid to gas being an exothermic process
    E. energy being liberated when a liquid is converted to a gas

25. Given $H_2 + Br_2 = 2HBr + 17.2$ kilocalories, the heat liberated when .5 mole hydrogen reacts with .5 mole bromine is _____ kilocalorie(s).

    A. .5   B. 1   C. 8.6   D. 17.2   E. 34.4

KEY (CORRECT ANSWERS)

1. D		11. A	
2. D		12. D	
3. D		13. C	
4. E		14. A	
5. A		15. A	
6. B		16. D	
7. A		17. E	
8. B		18. C	
9. D		19. C	
10. A		20. B	

21. E
22. C
23. B
24. B
25. C

TEST 3

DIRECTIONS: Each question or incomplete statement is followed by several suggested answers or completions. Select the one that BEST answers the question or completes the statement. *PRINT THE LETTER OF THE CORRECT ANSWER IN THE SPACE AT THE RIGHT.*

1. _____ is the STRONGEST acid.

   A. H_2S B. NH_4OH C. H_2SO_3 D. $HClO_4$ E. H_2PO_4

2. A substance which alters the speed of a chemical reaction but leaves the process unchanged is termed

   A. a cation
   B. a catalyst
   C. an activator
   D. a spectator ion
   E. nascent

3. The symbol CO represents

   A. carbon
   B. carbon monoxide
   C. cobalt
   D. cobalt oxide
   E. copper

4. A good example of a mixture is

   A. sodium perchlorate
   B. carbon monoxide
   C. hydrogen gas
   D. milk
   E. cane sugar

5. A compound containing only zinc and sulfur would be named zinc

   A. sulfide   B. disulfide   C. sulfite
   D. bisulfite   E. sulfate

6. The formula of nitrous acid is

   A. H_2HO_4 B. HNO_3 C. HNO_2 D. HNO E. NH_4OH

7. Which of these substances is a nonelectrolyte when dissolved in water?

   A. Sugar
   B. Hydrogen chloride
   C. Sodium chloride
   D. Ammonia
   E. Acetic acid

8. One of the following electron arrangements represents that of an active nonmetal.

   A. 2   B. 2 8   C. 2 8 1   D. 2 8 3   E. 2 8 7

9. Oxygen may be prepared by

   A. heating a carbonate
   B. reacting an acid with a metal
   C. heating sodium chloride
   D. electrolysis of water
   E. reacting a metal oxide with water

10. A crystal of solid solute is added to a solution. The crystal does NOT change in mass. The solution was

    A. unsaturated
    B. saturated
    C. supersaturated
    D. dilute
    E. normal

11. The oxidation number of chlorine in $KClO_4$ is

    A. -1   B. +1   C. +4   D. +5   E. +7

12. The valence of aluminum in $Al_2(SO_4)_3$ is

    A. +1   B. +2   C. +3   D. +4   E. +6

13. The formula of potassium sulfate is

    A. PSO_3 B. Po_2SO_3 C. KSO_4 D. K_2SO_4 E. KS

14. Barium, which is in the same family as calcium, would be predicted to exhibit a valence of

    A. +1   B. +2   C. +3   D. +4   E. +5

15. One of the following elements would be MOST likely to be found as components of compounds in nature:

    A. Helium
    B. Platinum
    C. Potassium
    D. Gold
    E. All of these occur naturally as components of compounds

16. An electron arrangement that represents an inert gas is

    A. 282   B. 24   C. 287   D. 288   E. 283

17. The class of compounds to which H_3PO_4 belongs is

    A. acid
    B. base
    C. salt
    D. anhydride
    E. phosphite

18. In gaseous hydrogen, the chemical bond is BEST classified as a(n) _____ bond.

    A. ionic
    B. polar covalent
    C. covalent
    D. hydrogen
    E. coordinate covalent

19. In solid potassium bromide, the chemical bond is BEST classified as a(n) _____ bond.

    A. ionic
    B. polar covalent
    C. covalent
    D. coordinate covalent
    E. bromine

20. A property that is characteristic of an electrovalent compound is

    A. low boiling point
    B. usually a gas at room temperature
    C. non-electrolyte

D. high heat of vaporization
E. all of these

21. A water would be classified as hard if it contained _____ ion.

    A. calcium   B. sodium   C. chloride
    D. potassium   E. bicarbonate

22. $_1H^1$, $_1H^2$, $_1H^3$ are

    A. isotopes   B. allotropes
    C. isomers   D. chemically unrelated
    E. hydrides

23. A base may be defined as

    A. any strong electrolyte
    B. a proton acceptor
    C. an electron acceptor
    D. any hydroxyl containing compound
    E. ammonia

24. A piece of copper is coated with CuO.
    A substance that would react with this compound without reacting with the copper is

    A. NaOH   B. CaSO$_4$ C. Na$_2$CO$_3$ D. HCl   E. KNO$_3$

25. When acid is spilled, a nonhazardous material that should be used to neutralize the acid is

    A. NaOH   B. NaHCO$_3$ C. NaCl   D. CH$_3$COOH   E. HCl

KEY (CORRECT ANSWERS)

1. D
2. B
3. B
4. D
5. A

6. C
7. A
8. E
9. D
10. B

11. E
12. C
13. D
14. B
15. C

16. D
17. A
18. C
19. A
20. D

21. A
22. A
23. B
24. D
25. B

TEST 4

DIRECTIONS: Each question or incomplete statement is followed by several suggested answers or completions. Select the one that BEST answers the question or completes the statement. *PRINT THE LETTER OF THE CORRECT ANSWER IN THE SPACE AT THE RIGHT.*

1. 65° centigrade is equivalent to _____ ° absolute.

   A. 97   B. 117   C. 149   D. 273   E. 338

2. A two molar solution of phosphoric acid, molecular weight 98, contains _____ grams solute per liter.

   A. 2   B. 49   C. 98   D. 196   E. 392

3. Carbon dioxide may be prepared by reacting sodium carbonate with

   A. sodium oxide
   B. hydrochloric acid
   C. water
   D. potassium hydroxide
   E. calcium chloride

4. A sugar solution is boiling.
   As the water boils away, the temperature

   A. is 100 degrees
   B. remains constant
   C. decreases
   D. increases
   E. depends on source of heat

5. A chemical reaction is started by heating the reacting substances. The reaction continues when the heat is removed.
   This indicates the reaction

   A. is exothermic
   B. is endothermic
   C. yields carbon dioxide
   D. is very slow
   E. is at equilibrium

6. The predicted compound of element number seven which we shall represent as Y with hydrogen would be

   A. HY
   B. H_2Y
   C. H_3Y
   D. H_4Y
   E. none of these

7. The predicted compound of element number eleven with chlorine would be

   A. an electric conductor in the molten state
   B. predicted to exist as individual molecules
   C. a gas at room temperature
   D. an acid
   E. a nonelectrolyte in aqueous solutions

8. The type of chemical bond that is considered to account for the unusual properties of water is a(n) _____ bond.

   A. ionic
   B. covalent
   C. hydrogen
   D. coordinate covalent
   E. ion dipole

9. Zinc metal is placed in concentrated sulfuric acid. It would

   A. react violently
   B. react at a very slow rate
   C. NOT react as sulfuric acid as an oxidizing acid
   D. react only at low temperatures
   E. react more rapidly than in 6 normal acid

Questions 10-14.

DIRECTIONS: For the reaction $2H_3PO_4 + 3Zn \rightarrow Zn_3(PO_4)_2 + 3H_2$ using the atomic weights H = 1, O = 16, P = 31, Zn = 65.4.

10. The molecular weight of H_3PO_4 phosphoric acid, is

    A. 2   B. 48   C. 96   D. 98   E. 196

11. Four gram atoms of zinc will yield

    A. four moles hydrogen
    B. four grams hydrogen
    C. four liters hydrogen at STP
    D. eight moles hydrogen
    E. eight liters hydrogen at STP

12. 196 grams phosphoric acid will yield

    A. 1 gram hydrogen
    B. 3 grams hydrogen
    C. 6 grams hydrogen
    D. 3 liters hydrogen at STP
    E. 6 liters hydrogen at STP

13. Four moles of phosphoric acid will yield

    A. 1 mole zinc phosphate
    B. 2 moles zinc phosphate
    C. 4 moles zinc phosphate
    D. 3 moles hydrogen
    E. 22.4 liters of hydrogen at STP

14. 392 grams phosphoric acid will yield _____ liter(s) hydrogen at STP.

    A. 1   B. 3   C. 22.4   D. 67.2   E. 134.4

Questions 15-18.

DIRECTIONS: For the reaction H₂ + Cl₂ → 2HCl using atomic weights H = 1 and Cl = 35.5.

15. Four liters of hydrogen would react with _____ liters chlorine.   15._____
    A. 2   B. 4   C. 35.5   D. 89.6   E. 142

16. 22.4 liters hydrogen at STP would yield _____ grams HCl.   16._____
    A. 2
    B. 36.5
    C. 73
    D. 877
    E. correct answer not given

17. 35.5 grams of chlorine would yield _____ grains HCl.   17._____
    A. 2   B. 35.5   C. 36.5   D. 71   E. 73

18. Two moles of HCl weigh _____ grams.   18._____
    A. 2   B. 4   C. 36.5   D. 73   E. 219

19. The weight of 2.24 liters of oxygen gas at STP is _____ grams.   19._____
    A. 2.24   B. 1.6   C. 3.2   D. 16.0   E. 32.0

20. The molecular weight of a gas that exhibits a density of 3.2 grams per liter at STP is   20._____
    A. 3.2   B. 2.24   C. 32   D. 71.5   E. 7.0

21. The *approximate* volume of 3 moles of methane gas (molecular weight 20) at STP is _____ liters.   21._____
    A. 3   B. 20   C. 22.4   D. 67   E. 213

22. The volume of a gas halves at constant pressure.   22._____
    The temperature

    A. remains constant
    B. doubles in degrees absolute
    C. is decreased to 1/2 the original value in degrees absolute
    D. was 273 degrees absolute
    E. increases to 4 times the original value in degrees centigrade

23. The numerical value of the vapor pressure of water at 100 centigrade is _____ mm. of Hg.   23._____
    A. 22.4   B. 100   C. 224   D. 760   E. 1000

24. 100 grams of ice at 0° C is melted and converted to liquid water at 20° C.   24._____
    It requires _____ calories.
    A. 20   B. 80   C. 2000   D. 8000   E. 10,000

25. A solid changes to a gas and then reforms solid. This represents   25.____

    A. precipitation   B. condensation
    C. evaporation   D. sublimation
    E. homogenization

KEY (CORRECT ANSWERS)

1.	E	11.	A
2.	D	12.	C
3.	B	13.	B
4.	D	14.	E
5.	A	15.	B
6.	C	16.	C
7.	A	17.	C
8.	C	18.	D
9.	B	19.	C
10.	D	20.	D

21.	D
22.	B
23.	D
24.	E
25.	D

EXAMINATION SECTION
TEST 1

DIRECTIONS: Each question or incomplete statement is followed by several suggested answers or completions. Select the one that BEST answers the question or completes the statement. *PRINT THE LETTER OF THE CORRECT ANSWER IN THE SPACE AT THE RIGHT.*

1. Analysis of 1 mg. samples is termed
   - A. microanalysis
   - B. macroanalysis
   - C. meganalysis
   - D. semimicroanalysis

2. Lambert's law is *generally* associated with _____ methods of analysis.
   - A. electrical
   - B. mechanical
   - C. optical
   - D. thermal

3. Of the following substances, the one classified as an aliphatic compound is _____ acid.
   - A. benzoic
   - B. oxalic
   - C. phthalic
   - D. salicylic

4. Of the following substances, the one classified as an aromatic compound is _____ acid.
   - A. acetic
   - B. carbolic
   - C. carbonic
   - D. citric

5. The one of the following carbohydrates classified as an polysaccharide is
   - A. cellulose
   - B. fructose
   - C. glucose
   - D. maltose

6. Of the following, the one classified as an amino acid is _____ acid.
   - A. glutamic
   - B. lactic
   - C. oleic
   - D. oxalic

7. Of the following compounds, the one which is a member of the paraffin series of hydrocarbons is
   - A. acetylene
   - B. cyclohexane
   - C. ethane
   - D. ethylene

8. The carbohydrate obtained from sugar cane is called
   - A. dextrose
   - B. lactose
   - C. starch
   - D. sucrose

9. The name of the enzyme that catalyzes the decomposition of starch into sugar is
   - A. amylase
   - B. lipase
   - C. pepsin
   - D. rennin

10. The one of the following which is a form of electromagnetic radiation is _____ rays.
    - A. alpha
    - B. beta
    - C. cathode
    - D. gamma

11. The unit of electric current is the
    - A. ampere
    - B. coulomb
    - C. joule
    - D. volt

12. In centrifuging, the rate of sedimentation varies inversely with the

    A. centrifugal force
    B. difference in density between the solid and that of the solution
    C. size of the particle
    D. viscosity of the solution

13. The symbol Å is used to designate a unit of

    A. charge
    B. length
    C. mass
    D. specific gravity

14. In the electrolysis of water, the gas liberated at the anode is

    A. CO
    B. CO_2
    C. H_2
    D. O_2

15. The use of a safety bottle is *generally* recommended in

    A. colorimetric determinations
    B. decantations of small volumes
    C. electrolytic precipitations
    D. filtrations by suction

16. In colimetry, the name of tubes frequently used for comparison of colors is _____ tubes.

    A. Inner
    B. Litmus
    C. Nessler
    D. Wolff

17. SO_2 is the anhydride of

    A. H_2SO_3
    B. H_2SO_4
    C. $H_2S_2O_3$
    D. $H_2S_2O_7$

18. Of the following types of glass, the one with the SMALLEST coefficient of thermal expansion is _____ glass.

    A. pyrex
    B. safety
    C. soda-lime
    D. soft

19. The product, volts x amperes, is equal to

    A. faradays
    B. joules
    C. ohms
    D. watts

20. The pH of a solution whose (H^+) is 1 x 10-4 mole per liter is

    A. 4
    B. 5
    C. 6
    D. 7

Questions 21-30.

DIRECTIONS: Column I lists terms, each of which can be properly matched with one of the pieces of laboratory equipment in Column II. For each item of Column I, write in the space at the right the letter in front of the option in Column II with which it is generally associated.

COLUMN I	COLUMN II	
21. Daniel	A. balance	21.____
22. Duboscq	B. beaker	22.____
23. Erlenmeyer	C. burner	23.____
24. Gooch	D. cell	24.____
25. Griffin	E. colorimeter	25.____
26. Jones	F. condenser	26.____
27. Liebig	G. crucible	27.____
28. Meker	H. flask	28.____
29. Plattner	I. mortar	29.____
30. Westphal	J. reductor	30.____
	K. tube	
	L. viscosimeter	

KEY (CORRECT ANSWERS)

1. A		16. C	
2. C		17. A	
3. B		18. A	
4. B		19. D	
5. A		20. A	
6. A		21. D	
7. C		22. E	
8. D		23. H	
9. A		24. G	
10. D		25. B	
11. A		26. J	
12. D		27. F	
13. B		28. C	
14. D		29. I	
15. D		30. A	

TEST 2

DIRECTIONS: Each question or incomplete statement is followed by several suggested answers or completions. Select the one that BEST answers the question or completes the statement. *PRINT THE LETTER OF THE CORRECT ANSWER IN THE SPACE AT THE RIGHT.*

1. Of the following, the substance whose water solution is acid is   1.____

    A. CH_3OH B. $NaHCO_3$ C. NH_3 D. $(NH_4)HSO_4$

2. The instrument *generally* used to measure electric current is the   2.____

    A. ammeter   B. coulometer
    C. potentiometer   D. voltmeter

3. Of the following substances, the one which is LEAST soluble in water is   3.____

    A. $CuSO_4$ B. K_2SO_4 C. $MgSO_4$ D. $SrSO_4$

4. In qualitative analysis, potassium thiocyanate is used to test for   4.____

    A. Al^{+++} B. Cu^{++} C. Fe^{+++} D. Ni^{++}

5. Dimethylglyoxime is used as a specific reagent for the detection of   5.____

    A. Ca^{++} B. Ni^{++} C. NO_3^- D. SO_4^{--}

6. One liter of a 2 M HCl solution will *readily* dissolve 10 grams of   6.____

    A. Ag_2S B. CuS C. S D. ZnS

7. A colorless solution is treated with dilute HCl giving a white precipitate. When the precipitate is treated with 6 M NH_3, the white precipitate turns black. The original solution must have contained   7.____

    A. Ag^+ B. Hg^{++} C. Hg_2^{++} D. Pb^{++}

8. A mixture of $BaCl_2$, LiCl, NaCl, and NH_4Cl is heated in an evaporating dish over a strong Bunsen flame.
    The cloud of white vapor which is observed is due to the   8.____

    A. $BaCl_2$ B. LiCl   C. NaCl   D. NH_4Cl

9. A violet color obtained in a flame test indicates the presence of   9.____

    A. copper   B. lead   C. potassium   D. sodium

10. A solution of $KMnO_4$ may be standardized by titration against   10.____

    A. oxalic acid   B. potassium acid phthalate
    C. sodium bicarbonate   D. sulfuric acid

11. A solution of sodium hydroxide may be standardized by titration against   11.____

    A. barium diphenylamine sulfonate   B. potassium acid phthalate
    C. sodium carbonate   D. sodium thiosulfate

12. Cellulose is a	12.____

    A. mineral deposit in plant cells
    B. mixture of proteins
    C. polysaccharide
    D. synthetic rubber

13. The heat of combustion of an organic compound is *generally* measured by means of a	13.____

    A. bomb calorimeter	B. Carius tube
    C. pyrometer	D. Victor Meyer apparatus

14. The amount of nitrogen in an organic compound may be measured by means of	14.____

    A. an emission spectroscope
    B. a polarimeter
    C. the Hell-Volhard-Zelinsky reaction
    D. the Kjeldahl method

15. Small amounts of soluble solid impurities in solutions of organic compounds are *frequently* removed by boiling with	15.____

    A. activated charcoal
    B. boiling stones
    C. glass beads
    D. small scraps of rubber tubing

16. Enzymes are	16.____

    A. an essential part of the diet
    B. biological catalysts
    C. hormones
    D. vitamins

17. In quantitative analysis, a precipitate of silver chloride is *generally* separated from the supernatant solution by	17.____

    A. a Gooch crucible
    B. a powder funnel
    C. a separatory funnel
    D. mixing with strong NH_3 solution and then decanting

18. The amount of rise of a liquid in a capillary is used to measure	18.____

    A. conductivity	B. diffusion coefficient
    C. surface tension	D. viscosity

19. The molecular weight of an *unknown* may be determined by dissolving a definite amount of *unknown* in a measured amount of solvent and determining the	19.____

    A. conductivity
    B. freezing point depression
    C. temperature coefficient of conductivity
    D. temperature coefficient of surface tension

20. A current of 10 amperes at 110 volts corresponds to _____ watts.   20.____

    A. 0.091   B. 11   C. 1100   D. 11,000

21. A diffusion pump is *generally* used   21.____

    A. for suction filtration
    B. to maintain the level of a water bath
    C. to obtain a high pressure
    D. to obtain a high vacuum

22. An endothermic reaction is one which   22.____

    A. absorbs heat
    B. liberates heat
    C. takes place only at low temperature
    D. takes place only at high temperature

23. A voltage of 110 volts flowing through a 110 ohm resistor produces   23.____

    A. 1 watt
    B. 110 watts
    C. 12,100 watts
    D. a wattage depending upon the time the current is allowed to flow

24. Stannous chloride is   24.____

    A. a reducing agent
    B. an oxidizing agent
    C. used for galvanizing iron
    D. very insoluble in water

25. The atomic weight of an element is determined by the   25.____

    A. number of neutrons in the nucleus
    B. number of planetary electrons
    C. number of protons in the nucleus
    D. sum of the number of protons and neutrons in the nucleus

KEY (CORRECT ANSWERS)

1. D
2. A
3. D
4. C
5. B

6. D
7. C
8. D
9. C
10. A

11. B
12. C
13. A
14. D
15. A

16. B
17. A
18. C
19. B
20. C

21. D
22. A
23. B
24. A
25. D

EXAMINATION SECTION
TEST 1

DIRECTIONS: Each question or incomplete statement is followed by several suggested answers or completions. Select the one that BEST answers the question or completes the statement. *PRINT THE LETTER OF THE CORRECT ANSWER IN THE SPACE AT THE RIGHT.*

The following list of atomic weights may be referred to in solving problems involving computations:

Calcium	40.1	Hydrogen	1.0	Potassium	39.1
Carbon	12.0	Iodine	126.9	Silver	107.9
Chlorine	35.5	Nitrogen	14.0	Sodium	23.0
Chromium	52.0	Oxygen	16.0	Sulfur	32.0

1. A catalyst is a substance which

    A. increases the rate of the reaction
    B. is made of platinum
    C. pushes the point of equilibrium farther towards the products
    D. slows up side reactions

2. One liter is APPROXIMATELY

    A. 1 pint   B. 2 pints   C. 2 quarts   D. 1 gallon

3. An electrolyte is a compound whose solution

    A. decomposes water
    B. has an electrical potential
    C. has the property of electrical conduction
    D. moves in an electrical field

4. Oxides of non-metals when dissolved in water

    A. evolve hydrogen   B. evolve oxygen
    C. form acids   D. form bases

5. Of the following metals, the one which is MOST active chemically is

    A. copper   B. iron   C. nickel   D. zinc

6. When the temperature is increased, the rate of a simple chemical reaction is

    A. decreased
    B. increased
    C. sometimes increased and sometimes decreased
    D. unaffected

7. The pressure in a freshly filled standard cylinder of oxygen is APPROXIMATELY

    A. 100 lbs/in^2 B. 400 lbs/in^2
    C. 2000 lbs/in^2 D. 400 atmospheres

8. Of the following substances, the one which is LEAST soluble in water at 25° C is

   A. ferric sulfate
   B. lead nitrate
   C. mercuric chloride
   D. silver iodide

9. Of the following solids, the one with the HIGHEST melting point is

   A. lead
   B. silver
   C. silver nitrate
   D. tungsten

10. An accurate estimate of the number of protons in an atomic nucleus is obtained by taking the atomic

    A. number
    B. number plus the atomic weight
    C. weight
    D. weight minus the atomic number

11. Of the following, the MOST electropositive element is

    A. arsenic   B. copper   C. mercury   D. rubidium

12. If 100 grams of a substance requires 100 calories to raise its temperature 10° C, the specific heat of the substance is

    A. .01   B. 0.1   C. 1.0   D. 10.0

13. The volume occupied by 200 grams of a solution whose density is 0.92 is MOST NEARLY _____ ml.

    A. 92   B. 109.5   C. 134   D. 217.5

14. Of the following, the one which would be the MOST appropriate for keeping a dry ice and acetone mixture for several hours is the _____ flask.

    A. Claisen
    B. Dewar
    C. Ehrlenmeyer
    D. Florence

15. A solution of KNO_3 containing 303 grams in one liter of solution is APPROXIMATELY _____ molar.

    A. 1   B. 3   C. 10   D. 12

16. A violet color obtained in a flame test indicates the presence of

    A. barium   B. mercury   C. potassium   D. sodium

17. One gram of an *unknown* metal reacts completely with dilute hydrochloric acid to release 112 ml of hydrogen (measured at STP). The equivalent weight of the metal is _____ gm.

    A. 50   B. 100   C. 200   D. 400

18. An unknown white solid dissolves in 0.3M HCl to give a clear solution. When H_2S is bubbled through this solution, no reaction is The solution, therefore, CANNOT contain

    A. NH_4^+ B. BA^{++} C. Hg^{++} D. $SO_4^=$

19. If 50 ml of a solution of H$_2$SO$_4$ exactly neutralizes 25 ml of a 1.00 N solution of NaOH, the normality of the H$_2$SO$_4$ solution is

    A. 0.50   B. .25   C. 1.0   D. 2.0

20. A Kjeldahl analysis can be used to determine the percentage of

    A. acetone in urine
    B. sugar in urine
    C. nitrogen in protein
    D. sulfate in water

21. Potassium thiocyanate solution gives an intense red solution with

    A. Fe^{++}
    B. Ag$^+$
    C. Mn^{++}
    D. none of the above

22. The concentration of silver chromate in a saturated solution is approximately 1.3 x 10^{-4} M. The solubility product of silver chromate is

    A. 9 x 10^{-12}
    B. 2.2 x 10^{-12}
    C. 1.7 x 10^{-8}
    D. 3.9 x 10^{-4}

23. Of the following, the STRONGEST oxidizing agent is sodium

    A. dichromate and sulfuric acid
    B. nitrate and sodium hydroxide
    C. thiocyanate and ammonia
    D. thiosulfate and hydrochloric acid

24. The name of the instrument used for the precise determination of electrical voltage is the

    A. ammeter
    B. ohmmeter
    C. potentiometer
    D. Wheatstone bridge

25. Which of the following will dissolve the MOST barium hydroxide?

    A. 2 ml of 1.0M nitric acid
    B. 10 ml of 0.2M perchloric acid
    C. 1.5 ml of 0.1M sulfuric acid
    D. 25 ml of 0.1M hydrochloric acid

26. An unknown white solid dissolves in 0.3M HCl to give a clear solution. It, therefore, CANNOT contain _____ ions.

    A. calcium   B. mercurous   C. arsenic   D. rubidium

27. Of the following solids, the one which is MOST readily soluble in 6M NaOH is

    A. barium sulfate
    B. ferric chloride
    C. hydrated zinc hydroxide
    D. mercuric chloride

28. An *unknown* metal dissolves readily in dilute nitric acid to give a colorless solution (ignore color due to nitric acid). This solution was evaporated to dryness, and the residue was then taken up in water. Treatment of this aqueous solution with thioacetamide (or hydrogen sulfide) gave a yellow
    The *unknown* metal was PROBABLY

    A. Cd   B. Ni   C. Pt   D. Zn

29. The one of the following titrations in which phenolphtha-lein is useful as an indicator is

    A. acetic acid with ammonia
    B. acetic acid with sodium hydroxide
    C. ammonia with hydrochloric acid
    D. sodium hydroxide with hydrochloric acid

30. The series in which each element will displace from aqueous solution those following it is

    A. Ag, Hg, H, N, Cu
    B. K, Fe, H, Hg, Pt
    C. K, Zn, Pb, Pt, H
    D. Na, H, Zn, Pb, Pt

31. A pH of 2 means that the H^+ is equal to

    A. 2   B. 10^2 C. 10^{-2} D. e^{-2}

32. Raoult's Law

    A. gives the vapor pressure of a liquid as a function of temperature
    B. relates the specific heat and atomic weight of certain solids
    C. relates the vapor pressure and concentration of one component of a binary solution
    D. tells which way an equilibrium changes with the temperature

33. A *perfect* gas is a gas which

    A. does not change pressure with a change in temperature if the volume is kept constant
    B. follows van der Waals equation exactly
    C. forms no chemical compounds
    D. has one equation of state, PV = NRT

34. The vapor pressure of liquids

    A. decreases with increasing temperature
    B. does not change with increasing temperature
    C. increases with increasing temperature
    D. sometimes increases and sometimes decreases with temperature

35. The nucleus of a chloride ion contains _____ the chlorine atom from which it is

    A. one more electron than
    B. one more neutron than
    C. one more proton than
    D. the same number of protons and neutrons as

36. Analysis of a compound gave 14.1%C, 2.4%H, and 83.5%Cl. The compound was PROBABLY

    A. carbon tetrachloride
    B. chloroform
    C. chloromethane
    D. dichloromethane

37. Optical isomers are also called

    A. allotropic forms
    B. enantiomorphs
    C. geometrical isomers
    D. peritectics

38. A soap solution in water foams readily because soap _____ of water.

   A. *lowers* the surface tension
   B. *raises* the viscosity
   C. *lowers* the viscosity
   D. *raises* the surface tension

39. The extraction of I_2 from 100 ml of a water solution is performed MOST efficiently by

   A. one 50 ml portion of CCl_4
   B. one 50 ml portion of ethanol
   C. five 10 ml portions of CCl_4
   D. five 10 ml portions of ethanol

40. A reliable way to construct a straight line through a set of experimentally obtained points on a graph is the

   A. latin square
   B. method of convergent slopes
   C. method of least squares
   D. method of random samples

KEY (CORRECT ANSWERS

1. A	11. D	21. D	31. C
2. B	12. B	22. A	32. C
3. C	13. D	23. A	33. D
4. C	14. B	24. C	34. C
5. D	15. B	25. D	35. D
6. B	16. C	26. B	36. D
7. C	17. B	27. C	37. B
8. D	18. C	28. A	38. A
9. D	19. A	29. B	39. C
10. A	20. C	30. B	40. C

TEST 2

DIRECTIONS: Each question or incomplete statement is followed by several suggested answers or completions. Select the one that BEST answers the question or completes the statement. *PRINT THE LETTER OF THE CORRECT ANSWER IN THE SPACE AT THE RIGHT.*

1. A temperature of 45°C is MOST readily measured with a

   A. iron-constantan thermocouple
   B. mercury thermometer
   C. adiabatic calorimeter
   D. spinthariscope

2. Of the following, the BEST drying agent is

   A. anhydrous potassium bromide
   B. concentrated HCl
   C. hydrated sodium sulfate
   D. P_2O_5

3. In order to make 50 ml of approximately 0.3M HCl, enough water to make 100 ml of solution should be added to

   A. 0.36 ml of 12M HCl
   B. 2.5 ml of 6M HCl
   C. 5.0 ml of 12M HCl
   D. 3.6 ml of 12M HCl

4. The purity of distilled water used in the laboratory may be estimated MOST readily by

   A. analyzing for likely impurities
   B. measuring the absorption spectrum
   C. measuring the boiling point
   D. measuring the electrical conductivity

5. The density of a liquid can be readily measured with a(n)

   A. densitometer
   B. galvanometer
   C. pycnometer
   D. isoteniscope

6. The average reading error on a standard 50 ml burette is APPROXIMATELY _____ ml.

   A. .002   B. .02   C. .2   D. 2

7. The average weighing error on the standard analytical balance is MOST NEARLY

   A. 0.2 milligrams
   B. 20 milligrams
   C. .02 grams
   D. 0.2 grams

8. In the preparation of potassium permanganate solution, a period of storage is recommended before standardization to allow time for

   A. diffusion of the permanganate through the solution
   B. escape of air from the solution
   C. oxidation of accidentally included organic impurities such as dust
   D. reduction of accidentally included organic impurities such as dust

9. The recommended method for drying ethanol is

   A. by fractional distillation
   B. in an oven
   C. over anhydrous Na_2SO_4
   D. over sodium

10. Indicators for pH are GENERALLY

    A. acid catalysts
    B. easily oxidizable compounds
    C. easily reducible compounds
    D. weak acids or bases

11. Of the following, the one with the LOWEST freezing point is

    A. acetic acid
    B. benzene
    C. mercury
    D. water

12. Of the following, the one with the HIGHEST melting point is

    A. Au
    B. Al_2O_3
    C. KCl
    D. Na

13. Of the following gases, the one with the HIGHEST boiling point is

    A. NH_3
    B. SO_2
    C. N_2
    D. He

14. As a lead storage battery is discharged,

    A. sulfuric acid should be added to the cell
    B. the density of the liquid in the cell decreases
    C. the density of the liquid in the cell increases
    D. the density of the liquid in the cell is unchanged

15. Of the following substances, the one which dissolves to the LEAST extent in 1M HCl at 25° C is

    A. copper sulfide
    B. silver carbonate
    C. sodium sulfate
    D. zinc hydroxide

16. The volumetric determination of copper USUALLY employs titration with

    A. ammonia
    B. potassium iodide
    C. sodium hydroxide
    D. sodium sulfide

17. A conductometric titration would be PARTICULARLY useful for determining

    A. the electrical properties of a transformer coil
    B. non-protein nitrogen in blood
    C. oxidizing strength of hydrogen peroxide
    D. total acidity of a highly colored solution

18. The unit in which viscosities are often reported is the

    A. millipoise
    B. coulomb
    C. dyne
    D. amagat

19. The component part of an instrument widely used for measuring pH is

    A. dropping mercury
    B. glass electrode
    C. protective electrode
    D. sacrificial electrode

20. The freezing point of a dilute solution of any salt in water is

    A. always 0° C
    B. always higher than 0° C
    C. always lower than 0° C
    D. sometimes higher and sometimes lower than 0° C

21. A protein consists of

    A. C and H *only*
    B. C, H, and N *only*
    C. C, H, and O *only*
    D. at least C, H, N, and O

22. An aldehyde may be produced by a mild oxidation of a

    A. phenol
    B. primary alcohol
    C. secondary alcohol
    D. tertiary alcohol

23. Amino acids are formed in the hydrolysis of

    A. carbohydrates
    B. fats
    C. hydrocarbons
    D. proteins

24. The one of the following elements which is NOT presently known to be usable as a fuel in a nuclear fission reactor is

    A. hydrogen   B. plutonium   C. thorium   D. uranium

25. Of the following compounds, the one which possesses optical isomers is

    A. $CH_2 = CH - CH_2 - CH_3$
    B. $CH_3 - CHCl - CH_2 - CH_3$
    C. $H - \overset{O}{\underset{\|}{C}} - NH_2$
    D. (biphenyl) $- O - CH_3$

26. A solution of one metal in another is termed a(n)

    A. alloy
    B. cermet
    C. double displacement
    D. twinned crystal

27. The molecular weight of a substance can be calculated from a measurement of its(the)

    A. density in the liquid state
    B. freezing point
    C. vapor pressure
    D. density of its vapor

28. Elements with the same number of protons in the nucleus but different numbers of neutrons are called

    A. isentropes
    B. isomers
    C. isomorphs
    D. isotopes

29. The quality of a precipitate for analytical purposes is often improved by

   A. co-precipitation
   B. digestion
   C. double filtration
   D. salting out

30. In order to make a bend in 20 mm pyrex tubing, one should use a(n)

   A. blue Bunsen flame
   B. oxygen-gas torch
   C. oxygen-hydrogen torch
   D. yellow Bunsen flame

31. If 1M NaOH is slowly poured into a beaker containing 0.1M AgNO$_3$,

   A. a brown precipitate is formed which then redissolves
   B. a light brown precipitate is formed which then turns black
   C. a light brown precipitate is formed which then turns red
   D. the solution gets very warm and evolves brown fumes which have a pungent odor

32. If a piece of Zn is dropped into a beaker containing 6M NaOH,

   A. a black film forms over the surface
   B. a white crust forms over the metal surface
   C. gas is evolved
   D. no significant change is seen

33. A crude instrument for measuring surface tension could be readily improvised from a(n)

   A. graduated cylinder and a manometer
   B. piece of capillary tubing and a ruler
   C. thermos bottle and a thermometer
   D. analytical balance and a pair of pliers

34. The condition of a small opaque fuse is readily checked with a(n)

   A. ammeter
   B. ohmmeter
   C. potentiometer
   D. voltmeter

35. A device often used to vary an electrical current is the

   A. coulometer
   B. polarograph
   C. rheostat
   D. vacuum tube voltmeter

36. A neutral solution will result upon mixing equal volumes of 0.1N solutions of

   A. hydrogen sulfide and sodium hydroxide
   B. nitric acid and calcium hydroxide
   C. phosphoric acid and sodium hydroxide
   D. sodium chloride and ammonium chloride

37. Potassium permanganate may be used in analytical chemistry for the direct determination of

   A. arsenious compounds, carbonates, and ferric chloride
   B. chloride, oxalate, and metals
   C. ferrocyanide, oxalate, and sulfite
   D. ferricyanide, sulfite, and thiosulfate

38. The refractive indices of liquids are GENERALLY between _____ and _____.   38._____

    A. 0; 0.1   B. 0; 1.0   C. 1; 10   D. 10; 100

39. A photographic developer is a   39._____

    A. mild oxidizing agent
    B. mild reducing agent
    C. solvent for silver
    D. solvent for silver halides

40. Comparing solution #1, containing exactly one mole of potassium bromide and one mole   40._____
    of calcium nitrate, with solution #2, containing one mole of calcium bromide and one
    mole of potassium nitrate, the solutions

    A. differ in bromide content
    B. differ in calcium content
    C. differ in potassium content
    D. are identical

KEY (CORRECT ANSWERS)

1.	A	11.	C	21.	D	31.	B
2.	D	12.	B	22.	B	32.	C
3.	B	13.	B	23.	D	33.	B
4.	D	14.	B	24.	A	34.	B
5.	C	15.	A	25.	B	35.	C
6.	B	16.	B	26.	A	36.	B
7.	A	17.	D	27.	D	37.	C
8.	C	18.	A	28.	D	38.	C
9.	C	19.	B	29.	B	39.	B
10.	D	20.	C	30.	B	40.	A

TEST 3

DIRECTIONS: Each question or incomplete statement is followed by several suggested answers or completions. Select the one that BEST answers the question or completes the statement. *PRINT THE LETTER OF THE CORRECT ANSWER IN THE SPACE AT THE RIGHT.*

1. The term synonymous with biological catalyst is   1._____

   A. enzyme B. hormone C. vaccine
   D. virus   E. vitamin

2. The name MOST closely associated with the Periodic Table is   2._____

   A. Arrhenius   B. Born   C. Einstein
   D. Mendelejeff E. Pauling

3. A solution of one metal in another is termed a(n)   3._____

   A. alloy   B. cermet
   C. double displacement D. solvolysis
   E. twinned crystal

4. The branch of chemistry that is PRIMARILY concerned with the rate of chemical reactions is called   4._____

   A. cryogenics   B. kinaesthetics   C. kinetics
   D. mechanics   E. thermodynamics

5. Isotopes are atoms of elements which differ in   5._____

   A. atomic weight and extranuclear charge
   B. atomic weight and nuclear charge
   C. atomic weight but not in nuclear charge
   D. nuclear charge but not in extranuclear charge
   E. valency

6. The one of the following elements which is NOT presently known to be usable as a fuel in a nuclear fission reactor is   6._____

   A. actinium   B. hydrogen   C. plutonium
   D. thorium   E. uranium

7. An electrolyte is a compound whose solution   7._____

   A. decomposes water
   B. does electrical work
   C. has an electrical potential
   D. has the property of electrical conduction
   E. moves in the electrical field

8. The *inert* gases do NOT form compounds because   8._____

   A. all of the electron shells are completed
   B. their kinetic energies are so great that they cannot approach any other atom
   C. their sizes are too great to form compounds

D. they have even numbers of electrons
E. they have equal numbers of protons and electrons in their structure

9. The number of positive charges in the nucleus of a neutral element and the number of electrons in the orbits about it differ by

    A. 0   B. 1   C. 2   D. 3   E. 4

10. A common unit of radioactivity is the

    A. angstrom   B. curie   C. geiger
    D. radian   E. standard rat unit

11. Water gas is a mixture of

    A. CO, H_2 and CH_4 B. CO and H_2O
    C. CO, H_2O and H_2 D. CO_2 and H_2
    E. CO_2 and H_2O

12. Ordinary soft solder is composed PRINCIPALLY of

    A. antimony and bismuth   B. antimony and tin
    C. bismuth and lead   D. bismuth and tin
    E. lead and tin

13. The MOST active halogen is

    A. astatine   B. bromine   C. chlorine
    D. fluorine   E. iodine

14. The elements F, Cl, Br, and I form compounds with all elements in groups I through VII of the periodic The compounds form less covalent and more electrovalent bonds as the group number of the other elements comes closer to

    A. I   B. III   C. IV   D. V   E. VII

15. Of the following, the one with the LOWEST freezing point is

    A. acetic acid   B. acetone   C. benzene
    D. mercury   E. water

16. Of the following groups of elements, the one whose oxides all form alkalies when dissolved in water is

    A. Al, C, Fe, and S   B. B, C, P, and S
    C. B, Ca, Mg, and P   D. Ba, Cl, Na, and S
    E. Ca, Mg, K, and Na

17. Of the following acids, the one whose dissociation constant is nearest to 10^{-5} is _____

    A. acetic   B. carbonic   C. hydrochloric
    D. nitric   E. sulfuric

18. Of the following salts, the one with the GREATEST solubility in water is _____

    A. cupric   B. cuprous   C. lead
    D. mercurous   E. silver

19. Of the following, the STRONGEST oxidizing agent is sodium

    A. dichromate and sulfuric acid
    B. iodide and sodium hydroxide
    C. nitrate and sodium hydroxide
    D. thiocyanate and ammonia
    E. thiosulfate and hydrochloric acid

20. The one of the following which is a sulfite is

    A. $NaHSO_4$ B. Na_2S C. Na_2SO_3 D. Na_2SO_4 E. $Na_2S_2O_4$

21. Of the following groups of elements, the one whose oxides all form acids when dissolved in water is

    A. Al, B, Fe, and S
    B. B, C, P, and S
    C. B, Be, P, and S
    D. C, Ca, N, and S
    E. Ca, K, Mg, and Na

22. The one of the following statements regarding the use of the analytical balance that is INCORRECT is

    A. analytical samples should be placed directly on the balance pan
    B. the beam and stirrups should be taken off their knife edges between weighings
    C. the empty balance need not be adjusted to *zero* before use
    D. the object to be weighed should be at the same temperature as the balance
    E. weights should be handled only with forceps

23. The one of the following sets of glassware that would be MOST useful for preparing a standard solution of potassium acid phthalate is weighing bottle,

    A. graduated cylinder, funnel, glass rod, and beaker
    B. graduated cylinder, funnel, glass rod, and transfer pipette
    C. volumetric flask, funnel, glass rod, and beaker
    D. volumetric flask, funnel, glass rod, and transfer pipette
    E. volumetric flask, glass rod, beaker, and transfer pipette

24. Reagent grade concentrated hydrochloric acid is APPROXIMATELY

    A. 6M B. 12M C. 18M D. 24M E. 36M

25. A common method for preparing a standardized 0.1N solution of NaOH is to

    A. dilute a clarified 50% (saturated) solution of sodium hydroxide with boiled water and standardize against crystalline potassium acid phthalate
    B. prepare a 0.1N solution of sodium bicarbonate and boil out the CO_2
    C. prepare a 0.1N solution of sodium carbonate and precipitate the carbonate with excess barium hydroxide
    D. weigh out exactly 2.30 g of sodium and dissolve it in one liter of water
    E. weigh out exactly 4.00 g of sodium hydroxide and dissolve it in a liter of water

26. When one drop of 0.1M potassium thiocyanate solution is added to 10 ml of 0.1M ferric chloride, the color of the mixture is

    A. blue   B. green   C. nearly colorless
    D. orange-yellow E. red

27. When a gas volume is measured over water, a correction should be made for the 27._____

   A. pressure and temperature of the aqueous phase
   B. solubility of the gas in the aqueous phase
   C. solubility of water in the gas phase
   D. vapor pressure of the water and solubility of the gas in water
   E. volume and temperature of the aqueous phase

28. The heat of combustion of C to form CO_2 is 97.1300 calories per mole of carbon, that of 28._____
   C to form CO is 29,400 calories per mole of carbon.
   Therefore, the heat of combustion of CO to CO_2 is

   A. 38,800 calories per mole
   B. 68,200 calories per mole
   C. 127,000 calories per mole
   D. 156,400 calories per mole
   E. impossible to determine from the information given

29. An intense blue solution is obtained when 29._____

   A. 0.1M sodium thiosulfate is added to 0.1M potassium permanganate
   B. 6M NH_3 is added to copper sulfide
   C. 6M NaOH is added to hydrated copper hydroxide
   D. 12M HCl is added to 1M nickel chloride solution
   E. a piece of copper is dropped into 1M $ZnSO_4$ solution

30. When 10 ml of 0.1M NaI is added to 1 ml of $Cu(NO_3)_2$, there is 30._____

   A. a blue precipitate formed
   B. a brownish solution formed
   C. a violet vapor formed
   D. a white precipitate formed
   E. no visible reaction

31. In the preparation of potassium permanganate solution, a period of storage is recom- 31._____
   mended before standardization to allow time for

   A. complete solution of the permanganate
   B. diffusion of the permanganate throughout the solution
   C. escape of air from the solution
   D. oxidation of accidentally included organic impurities, such as dust
   E. reduction of accidentally included organic impurities, such as dust

32. Comparing Solution #1 containing exactly 1 mole of NaCl and 1 mole of K_2SO_4 with 32._____
   Solution #2 containing 1 mole of KCl and 1 mole of Na_2SO_4, the solutions

   A. are identical   B. differ in acidity
   C. differ in Cl^- contents   D. differ in K+ contents
   E. differ in $SO_4^=$ contents

33. The fats and waxes are distinguished from each other by the

    A. iodine numbers of the substances
    B. presence of distinctly different groups of fatty acids in the substances
    C. presence of glycerol in the hydrolysis products of fats and of long chain alcohols in the hydrolysis products of waxes
    D. presence of long chain alcohols in the hydrolysis products of fats but not in the hydrolysis products of waxes
    E. relative softening points of the substances

34. When hydrogen sulfide is bubbled through aqueous solutions containing mild oxidizing agents, a hazy yellow solution sometimes results.
This is caused by

    A. an insufficiency of neutral salt in the solution
    B. bubbles of undissolved gas
    C. the formation of colloidal sulfur
    D. the formation of the unstable ion $S_2O_3^=$
    E. the reduction of the sulfide ion

35. A neutral solution will result when equal volumes of 0.1N solutions of the following two substances are mixed:

    A. acetic acid and sodium hydroxide
    B. hydrogen chloride and ammonium hydroxide
    C. hydrogen chloride and sodium hydroxide
    D. phosphoric acid and sodium hydroxide
    E. sodium chloride and ammonium chloride

36. Cupric salts react with iodides in slightly acid solutions to give

    A. copper tri-iodide
    B. cupric iodide
    C. hydrogen ions and cuprous salts
    D. iodine and cuprous iodide
    E. a complex copper iodide ion

37. The one of the following titrations in which phenolphthalein is useful as an indicator is

    A. acetic acid with sodium hydroxide
    B. ammonia with hydrochloric acid
    C. silver nitrate with hydrochloric acid
    D. sodium acetate with hydrochloric acid
    E. sodium carbonate with hydrochloric acid

38. Of the following reagents, the one which produces a characteristic red color in the presence of nickel is

    A. Benedict's solution   B. dimethylglyoxime
    C. 8-hydroxy quinoline   D. magnesium perchlorate
    E. Nessler's solution

39. Potassium permanganate may be used in analytical chemistry for the direct estimation of   39._____
    A. arsenious compounds, carbonate, and ferric chloride
    B. chloride, ferrocyanide, and sulfite
    C. chloride, oxalate, and sulfate
    D. ferricyanide, oxalate, and thiosulfate
    E. ferrocyanide, oxalate, and sulfite

40. The series in which each element will displace those following it from aqueous solutions   40._____
    of their salts is
    A. Ag, Cu, H, Ni, Co
    B. K, Ba, Fe, Cu, Na
    C. K, Fe, H, Hg, Pt
    D. K, Zn, Pb, Pt, H
    E. Na, H, Zn, Pb, Pt

KEY (CORRECT ANSWERS)

1. A	11. C	21. B	31. D
2. D	12. E	22. A	32. D
3. A	13. D	23. C	33. C
4. C	14. A	24. B	34. C
5. C	15. B	25. A	35. C
6. B	16. E	26. E	36. D
7. D	17. A	27. D	37. A
8. A	18. A	28. B	38. B
9. A	19. A	29. C	39. E
10. B	20. C	30. D	40. C

EXAMINATION SECTION
TEST 1

DIRECTIONS: Each question or incomplete statement is followed by several suggested answers or completions. Select the one that BEST answers the question or completes the statement. *PRINT THE LETTER OF THE CORRECT ANSWER IN THE SPACE AT THE RIGHT.*

1. A compound has the empirical formula NO_2. Its molecular formula could be

    A. NO_2 B. N_2O C. N_4O_2 D. N_4O_4

    1.____

2. Hydrogen bonds are STRONGEST between molecules of

    A. HBr(g)   B. HI(g)   C. HF(g)   D. HCl(g)

    2.____

3. Indicate which of the following molecule is a dipole.

    A. H_2 B. N_2 C. CH_4 D. HCl

    3.____

4. Which compound is ionic?

    A. HCl   B. $CaCl_2$ C. SO_2 D. N_2O

    4.____

5. In the reaction $Al^{3+} + 6H_2O \rightarrow Al(H_2O)_6^{3+}$, the Al^{3+} ion is undergoing the process called

    A. neutralization   B. addition
    C. hydrogenation   D. hydration

    5.____

6. Which element forms a diatomic moleicule containing a triple covalent bond?

    A. Hydrogen   B. Chlorine   C. Nitrogen   D. Oxygen

    6.____

7. As the elements in Group IIA are considered from beryllium to radium, the degree of metallic activity _____ and atomic radius _____.

    A. increases; increases   B. increases; decreases
    C. decreases; increases   D. decreases; decreases

    7.____

8. Which group of elements occur ONLY as compounds in nature because they are extremely reactive?

    A. IA   B. IB   C. VIA   D. 0

    8.____

9. Which element in Period 2 has the GREATEST tendency to gain electrons?

    A. Li   B. C   C. F   D. Ne

    9.____

10. If M represents an atom of an alkali metal, the CORRECT formula for a compound of this atom with chlorine is

    A. M_2Cl B. MCl_2 C. MCl_3 D. MCl

    10.____

11. At STP, 170. grains of NH_3 will occupy a total of _____ ℓ.

    A. 2.24   B. 22.4   C. 224   D. 2240

12. The total mass of iron in 1.0 mole of Fe_2O_3 is _____ grams.

    A. 160   B. 112   C. 72   D. 56

13. Given the reaction: $2CO + O_2 \rightarrow 2CO_2$.
    What is the MINIMUM number of moles of O_2 required to produce one mole of CO_2?

    A. 1.0   B. 2.0   C. 0.25   D. 0.50

14. A solution contains 70 grams of $NaNO_3$ in 100 grams of water at 10° C.
    How many additional grams of $NaNO_3$ are required to saturate this solution?

    A. 10   B. 20   C. 60   D. 70

15. How do the freezing and boiling points of a sample of water change when 1 mole of NaCl is dissolved in a sample of water.
    The freezing poing of the water _____, and the boiling point _____.

    A. decreases; increases
    B. increases; increases
    C. decreases; decreases
    D. increases; decreases

16. Given the reaction at equilibrium:

    $H_2(g) + 1/2\ O_2(g) \rightleftarrows H_2O(g)$ + heat.

    The value of the equilibrium constant for this reaction can be changed by

    A. changing the pressure
    B. changing the temperature
    C. adding more O_2
    D. adding a catalyst

17. Given the reaction at equilibrium:

    $1/2 N_2(g) + 1/2\ O_2(g) + 21.6\ kcal \rightleftarrows NO(g)$.

    The equilibrium will shift to the right if the

    A. temperature increases
    B. temperature decreases
    C. pressure increases
    D. pressure decreases

18. The heat of reaction (ΔH) is equal to the

    A. heat content of the products minus the heat content of the reactants
    B. heat content of the reactants minus the heat content of the products
    C. entropy of the products minus the entropy of the reactants
    D. entropy of the reactants minus the entropy of the products

19. Based on the table at the right, the formation of 1 mole of which of the following substances releases the GREATEST amount of energy?

    A. C_2H_2
    B. C_2H_4
    C. $CuSO_4$
    D. $BaSO_4$

Compound	Heat (Enthalpy) of Formation kcal/mole (ΔH_f°)	Free Energy of Formation kcal/mole (ΔG_f°)
Aluminum oxide Al_2O_3 (s)	—399.1	—376.8
Ammonia NH_3 (g)	—11.0	—4.0
Barium sulfate $BaSO_4$ (s)	—350.2	—323.4
Calcium hydroxide $Ca(OH)_2$ (s)	—235.8	—214.3
Carbon dioxide CO_2 (g)	—94.1	—94.3
Carbon monoxide CO (g)	—26.4	—32.8
Copper (II) sulfate $CuSO_4$ (s)	—184.0	—158.2
Ethane C_2H_6 (g)	—20.2	—7.9
Ethene C_2H_4 (g)	12.5	16.3
Ethyne (acetylene) C_2H_2 (g)	54.2	50.0
Hydrogen fluoride HF (g)	—64.2	—64.7
Hydrogen iodide HI (g)	6.2	0.3
Iodine chloride ICl (g)	4.2	—1.3
Lead (II) oxide PbO (s)	—52.4	—45.3
Magnesium oxide MgO (s)	—143.8	—136.1
Nitrogen (II) oxide NO (g)	21.6	20.7
Nitrogen (IV) oxide NO_2 (g)	8.1	12.4
Potassium chloride KCl (s)	—104.2	—97.6
Sodium chloride $NaCl$ (s)	—98.2	—91.8
Sulfur dioxide SO_2 (g)	—71.0	—71.8
Water H_2O (g)	—57.8	—54.6
Water H_2O (ℓ)	—68.3	—56.7

Sample equation

$2Al\ (s) + \tfrac{3}{2}O_2\ (g) \rightarrow Al_2O_3\ (s)$

20. The reaction $CH_3COOH(aq) \rightleftharpoons CH_3COO^-(aq) + H^+(aq)$ has a K_a equal to 1.8×10^{-5} at 25° C.

    In a solution of this acid at 25° C, the concentration of CH_3COOH is _____ the concentration of _____ ions.

    A. less than; H^+
    B. equal to; H+
    C. greater than; CH_3COO^-
    D. equal to; CH_3COO^-

21. The conjugate base of NH_3 is

    A. NH_2^-
    B. NH_3
    C. NO_3^-
    D. NO_2^-

22. Which salt will hydrolyze in water to produce a basic solution?

    A. BaI_2
    B. $NaNO_2$
    C. $CaCl_2$
    D. $MgSO_4$

23. How many moles of KOH are needed to exactly neutralize 500. ml of a 1.0 M HCl solution?

    A. 1.0
    B. 2.0
    C. 0.25
    D. 0.50

24. In a 0.01 M solution of HCl, litmus will be _____ and phenolphthalein will be _____

    A. blue; colorless
    B. blue; pink
    C. red; colorless
    D. red; pink

25. Pure water is similar to 0.1 M HCl in that they both

    A. contain H_3O^+ ions
    B. are neutral to litmus
    C. are good conductors of electricity
    D. have a pH greater than 7

26. Which half-reaction CORRECTLY represents reduction?

    A. $Sn^{2+} + 2e^- \rightarrow Sn^{4+}$
    B. $Sn^{2+} \rightarrow Sn^{4+} + 2e^-$
    C. $Sn^{2+} + 2e^- \rightarrow Sn^0$
    D. $Sn^{2+} \rightarrow Sn^0 + 2e^-$

27. Which ion is MOST easily oxidized?

    A. Br^- B. Cl^- C. F^- D. I^-

28. In the reaction $MnO_2 + 4HCl \rightarrow MnCl_2 + 2H_2O + Cl_2$, which species is reduced?

    A. Mn^{4+} B. O^{2-} C. H^+ D. Cl^-

29. During the electrolysis of fused NaCl, which half-reaction occurs at the negative electrode?

    A. $Na^+ + 1e^- \rightarrow Na^0$
    B. $Na^0 \rightarrow Na^+ + 1e^-$
    C. $2Cl^- \rightarrow Cl_2^0 + 2e^-$
    D. $Cl_2^0 + 2e^- \rightarrow 2Cl^-$

30. Given the reaction:
    $\_Cr^{3+} + 10\ OH^- + \_ClO_3 \rightarrow \_CrO_4^{2-} + \_Cl^- + 5H_2O$.
    When the reaction is completely balanced using the smallest whole numbers, the coefficient of Cr^{3+} will be

    A. 1   B. 2   C. 3   D. 4

31. An organic acid is represented by the formula

    A. CH_3COOH B. CH_3OH C. CH_3OCH_3 D. CH_3COOCH_3

32. Which equation represents an esterification reaction?

    A. $C_6H_{12}O_6 \rightarrow 2C_2H_5OH + 2CO_2$
    B. $C_5H_{10} + H_2 \rightarrow C_5H_{12}$
    C. $C_3H_8 + Cl_2 \rightarrow C_3H_7Cl + HCl$
    D. $HCOOH + CH_3OH \rightarrow HCOOCH_3 + HOH$

33. The compound $CH_3CH_2CH_2CH_3$ belongs to the series that has the general formula

    A. C_nH_{2n-2} B. C_nH_{2n+2} C. C_nH_{n-6} D. C_nH_{n+6}

34. Which molecule contains a triple covalent bond between adjacent carbon atoms?   34.____

    A. C_2H_4 B. C_2H_2 C. C_3H_6 D. C_3H_8

35. The total number of OH groups in a molecule of glycerol is   35.____

    A. 1   B. 2   C. 3   D. 4

KEY (CORRECT ANSWERS)

1.	A	16.	B
2.	C	17.	A
3.	D	18.	A
4.	B	19.	D
5.	D	20.	C
6.	C	21.	A
7.	A	22.	B
8.	A	23.	D
9.	C	24.	C
10.	D	25.	A
11.	C	26.	C
12.	B	27.	D
13.	D	28.	A
14.	A	29.	A
15.	A	30.	B

31. A
32. D
33. B
34. B
35. C

TEST 2

DIRECTIONS: Each question or incomplete statement is followed by several suggested answers or completions. Select the one that BEST answers the question or completes the statement. *PRINT THE LETTER OF THE CORRECT ANSWER IN THE SPACE AT THE RIGHT.*

1. According to the chart at the right, a compound which forms spontaneously from its elements is
   A. NO
   B. NO_2
   C. C_2H_4
   D. C_2H_6

1._____

Standard Energies of Formation of Compounds at 1 atm and 298 K		
Compound	Heat (Enthalpy) of Formation kcal/mole (ΔH_f)	Free Energy of Formation kcal/mole (ΔG_f)
Aluminum oxide Al_2O_3 (s)	—399.1	—376.8
Ammonia NH_3 (g)	—11.0	—4.0
Barium sulfate $BaSO_4$ (s)	—350.2	—323.4
Calcium hydroxide $Ca(OH)_2$ (s)	—235.8	—214.3
Carbon dioxide CO_2 (g)	—94.1	—94.3
Carbon monoxide CO (g)	—26.4	—32.8
Copper (II) sulfate $CuSO_4$ (s)	—184.0	—158.2
Ethane C_2H_6 (g)	—20.2	—7.9
Ethene C_2H_4 (g)	12.5	16.3
Ethyne (acetylene) C_2H_2 (g)	54.2	50.0
Hydrogen fluoride HF (g)	—64.2	—64.7
Hydrogen iodide HI (g)	6.2	0.3
Iodine chloride ICl (g)	4.2	—1.3
Lead (II) oxide PbO (s)	—52.4	—45.3
Magnesium oxide MgO (s)	—143.8	—136.1
Nitrogen (II) oxide NO (g)	21.6	20.7
Nitrogen (IV) oxide NO_2 (g)	8.1	12.4
Potassium chloride KCl (s)	—104.2	—97.6
Sodium chloride NaCl (s)	—98.2	—91.8
Sulfur dioxide SO_2 (g)	—71.0	—71.8
Water H_2O (g)	—57.8	—54.6
Water H_2O (ℓ)	—68.3	—56.7
Sample equation		
$2Al (s) + \tfrac{3}{2}O_2 (g) \rightarrow Al_2O_3 (s)$		

2. A neutralization reaction is demonstrated by the equation

   A. $NaOH + HCl \rightarrow NaCl + H_2O$
   B. $2Na + 2H_2O \rightarrow 2NaOH + H_2$
   C. $Zn + CuSO_4 \rightarrow ZnSO_4 + Cu$
   D. $AgNO_3 + NaCl \rightarrow AgCl + NaNO_3$

2._____

3. The concentration of H_3O^+ ions, in moles per liter, of a 0.0001 M HCl solution is 1 x

   A. 10^{-1} B. 10^{-2} C. 10^{-3} D. 10^{-4}

3._____

4. As HF dissolves in water, the following ionization reaction occurs: $HF + H_2O + H_3O^+ + F^-$. In this reaction, a proton is donated to

   A. H_3O^+ by H_2O B. H_2O by HF
   C. H_3O^+ by F^- D. HF by F^-

4._____

5. How many milliliters of 1.0 M H_2SO_4 are needed to EXACTLY neutralize 15 milliliters of 2.0 M $Ba(OH)_2$? _____ ml.

   A. 7.5   B. 10.   C. 15   D. 30.

5._____

6. A 0.1 M solution of which acid is the BEST conductor of electricity at 25° C? 6._____

A. $H_3PO_4(K_a = 7.1 \times 10^{-3})$

B. $HNO_2(K_a = 5.1 \times 10^{-4})$

C. $CH_3COOH(K_a = 1.8 \times 10^{-5})$

D. $H_2S(K_a = 1.0 \times 10^{-7})$

7. What is the pH of a solution if the hydroxide ion concentration is 1×10^{-7} mole per liter? 7._____

A. 1 B. 7 C. 10 D. 14

8. Which is a redox reaction? 8._____

A. $Mg + 2HCl \rightarrow MgCl_2 + H_2$

B. $Mg(OH)_2 + 2HCl \rightarrow MgCl_2 + 2H_2O$

C. $Mg^2 +$ (aq) + $2OH^-$(aq) $\rightarrow Mg(OH)_2$

D. $MgCl_2 + 6H_2O \rightarrow MgCl_2.6H_2O$

9. In the reaction $Zn + Cu^{2+} \rightarrow Zn^{2+} + Cu$, the oxidizing agent 9._____

A. gains protons
B. loses electrons
C. is reduced
D. is oxidized

10. A chemical cell has a net reaction of $Cu + 2Ag^+ = Cu^{2+} + 2Ag$. 10._____
At equilibrium, the cell potential, in volts, is

A. -0.46 B. 0.00 C. +0.34 D. +0.80

Questions 11-12.

DIRECTIONS: Questions 11 and 12 are to be answered on the basis of the following chart.

STANDARD ELECTRODE POTENTIALS

Ionic Concentrations 1 M Water at 298 K, 1 atm

Half-Reaction	$E°$ *(volts)*
$F_2(g) + 2e^- \longrightarrow 2F^-$	+2.87
$MnO_4^- + 8H^+ + 5e^- \longrightarrow Mn^{2+} + 4H_2O$	+1.52
$Au^{3+} + 3e^- \longrightarrow Au(s)$	+1.50
$Cl_2(g) + 2e^- \longrightarrow 2Cl^-$	+1.36
$Cr_2O_7^{2-} + 14H^+ + 6e^- \longrightarrow 2Cr^{3+} + 7H_2O$	+1.33
$MnO_2(s) + 4H^+ + 2e^- \longrightarrow Mn^{2+} + 2H_2O$	+1.28
$\frac{1}{2}O_2(g) + 2H^+ + 2e^- \longrightarrow H_2O$	+1.23
$Br_2(\ell) + 2e^- \longrightarrow 2Br^-$	+1.06
$NO_3^- + 4H^+ + 3e^- \longrightarrow NO(g) + 2H_2O$	+0.96
$\frac{1}{2}O_2(g) + 2H^+(10^{-7}M) + 2e^- \longrightarrow H_2O$	+0.82
$Ag^+ + e^- \longrightarrow Ag(s)$	+0.80
$\frac{1}{2}Hg_2^{2+} + e^- \longrightarrow Hg(\ell)$	+0.79
$Hg^{2+} + 2e^- \longrightarrow Hg(\ell)$	+0.78
$NO_3^- + 2H^+ + e^- \longrightarrow NO_2(g) + H_2O$	+0.78
$Fe^{3+} + e^- \longrightarrow Fe^{2+}$	+0.77
$I_2(s) + 2e^- \longrightarrow 2I^-$	+0.53
$Cu^+ + e^- \longrightarrow Cu(s)$	+0.52
$Cu^{2+} + 2e^- \longrightarrow Cu(s)$	+0.34
$SO_4^{2-} + 4H^+ + 2e^- \longrightarrow SO_2(g) + 2H_2O$	+0.17
$Sn^{4+} + 2e^- \longrightarrow Sn^{2+}$	+0.15
$2H^+ + 2e^- \longrightarrow H_2(g)$	0.00
$Pb^{2+} + 2e^- \longrightarrow Pb(s)$	−0.13
$Sn^{2+} + 2e^- \longrightarrow Sn(s)$	−0.14
$Ni^{2+} + 2e^- \longrightarrow Ni(s)$	−0.25
$Co^{2+} + 2e^- \longrightarrow Co(s)$	−0.28
$2H^+(10^{-7}M) + 2e^- \longrightarrow H_2(g)$	−0.41
$Fe^{2+} + 2e^- \longrightarrow Fe(s)$	−0.44
$Cr^{3+} + 3e^- \longrightarrow Cr(s)$	−0.74
$Zn^{2+} + 2e^- \longrightarrow Zn(s)$	−0.76
$2H_2O + 2e^- \longrightarrow 2OH^- + H_2(g)$	−0.83
$Mn^{2+} + 2e^- \longrightarrow Mn(s)$	−1.18
$Al^{3+} + 3e^- \longrightarrow Al(s)$	−1.66
$Mg^{2+} + 2e^- \longrightarrow Mg(s)$	−2.37
$Na^+ + e^- \longrightarrow Na(s)$	−2.71
$Ca^{2+} + 2e^- \longrightarrow Ca(s)$	−2.87
$Sr^{2+} + 2e^- \longrightarrow Sr(s)$	−2.89
$Ba^{2+} + 2e^- \longrightarrow Ba(s)$	−2.90
$Cs^+ + e^- \longrightarrow Cs(s)$	−2.92
$K^+ + e^- \longrightarrow K(s)$	−2.92
$Rb^+ + e^- \longrightarrow Rb(s)$	−2.93
$Li^+ + e^- \longrightarrow Li(s)$	−3.00

11. Which half-reaction has a reduction potential (E°) of +1.50 volts?

   A. $Au^{3+} + 3e^- \rightarrow Au(s)$
   B. $Cr^{3+} + 3e^- \rightarrow Cr(s)$
   C. $Sn^{2+} + 2e^- \rightarrow Sn(s)$
   D. $Ba^{2+} + 2e^- \rightarrow Ba(s)$

12. Which metal will react spontaneously with H^+?

   A. Au   B. Ag   C. Cr   D. Cu

13. Given the reaction: $3Mg(s) + 2Cr^{3+}(aq) \rightarrow 3Mg^{2+}(aq) + 2Cr(s)$ What is the potential (E°) for the overall reaction? _____ volts.

   A. +3.11   B. -3.11   C. +1.63   D. -1.63

14. In the reaction $4NH_3 + 5O_2 \rightarrow 4NO + 6H_2O$, the oxidation number of nitrogen changes from

   A. -2 to -3   B. -2 to +3   C. -3 to -2   D. -3 to +2

15. An unsaturated hydrocarbon is represented by the formula

   A. C_3H_8 B. C_3H_7Cl C. C_3H_6 D. CCl_4

16. The isomers 1-chloropropane and 2-chloropropane differ ONLY in

   A. molecular composition
   B. molecular structure
   C. the number of chloro groups per molecule
   D. the number of carbon atoms per molecule

17. Which structural formula represents ethene?

   A.
   ```
      H H
      | |
   H-C-C-H
      | |
      H H
   ```
   B.
   ```
      H H
      | |
   H-C=C-H
   ```
   C.
   ```
      H H H
      | | |
   H-C-C-C-H
      | | |
      H H H
   ```
   D.
   ```
      H H H
      | | |
   H-C=C-C-H
         ||
         H
   ```

18. Which diagram may be used to represent a benzene ring?

   A.    B.    C.    D.

19. A compound with the structural formula is

$$\begin{array}{c} H\ H\ H \\ |\ \ |\ \ | \\ H-C-C-C-H \\ |\ \ \ |\ \ \ | \\ H\ OH\ H \end{array}$$

classified as an

   A. alcohol
   B. acid
   C. alkane
   D. alkene

20. As the temperature of a liquid *increases,* its vapor pressure

   A. decreases
   B. increases
   C. remains the same
   D. increases, then decreases

21. As a sulfur atom gains electrons, its radius

   A. decreases
   B. increases
   C. remains the same
   D. increases, then decreases

22. As the H_3O^+ ion concentration of a solution increases and the OH^- concentration decreases, the pH of the solution

   A. decreases
   B. increases
   C. remains the same
   D. cannot be determined from the information given

23. Given the system $CO_2(s) \rightleftarrows CO_2(g)$ at equilibrium.
    As the pressure increases at constant temperature, the amount of $CO_2(g)$ will

   A. decrease
   B. increase
   C. remain the same
   D. decrease, then increase

24. When a catalyst lowers the activation energy of a reaction, the rate of the reaction

   A. decreases
   B. increases
   C. remains the same
   D. decreases, then increases

25. A sample of a gas is at STP.
    As the pressure decreases and the temperature increases, the volume of the gas

   A. decreases
   B. increases
   C. remains the same
   D. decreases, then increases

Questions 26-30.

DIRECTIONS: Questions 26 through 30 are to be answered on the basis of the graphs below.

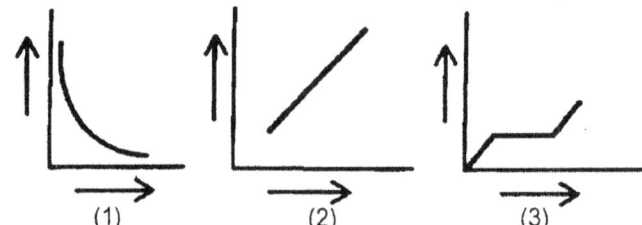

26. Which graph BEST represents how the volume of a given mass of a gas varies with the Kelvin (absolute) temperature at constant pressure?

   A. 1
   B. 2
   C. 3
   D. None of the above

27. Which graph BEST represents how the volume of a given mass of a gas varies with the pressure exerted on it at constant temperature?

   A. 1
   B. 2
   C. 3
   D. None of the above

28. Which represents a homogeneous mixture?

   A. $CuSO_4(s)$
   B. $Br_2(l)$
   C. $NaCl(aq)$
   D. $CO_2(g)$

29. A 16.0 gram sample of $CH_4(g)$ is at 0° C and 1 atmosphere. The volume of the gas sample in liters at 27° C and 1 atmosphere is equal to

   A. 16.0 x 1/27
   B. 16.0 x 27/1
   C. 22.4 x 273/300
   D. 22.4 x 300/273

30. At STP, 32 grams of O_2 would occupy the same volume as

   A. 64 g of H_2
   B. 32 g of SO_2
   C. 8.0 g of CH_4
   D. 4.0 g of He

31. The mass number of a ^3_1H atom is

   A. 1
   B. 2
   C. 3
   D. 4

32. Which orbital notation CORRECTLY represents the outermost principal energy level of a sulfur atom in the ground state?

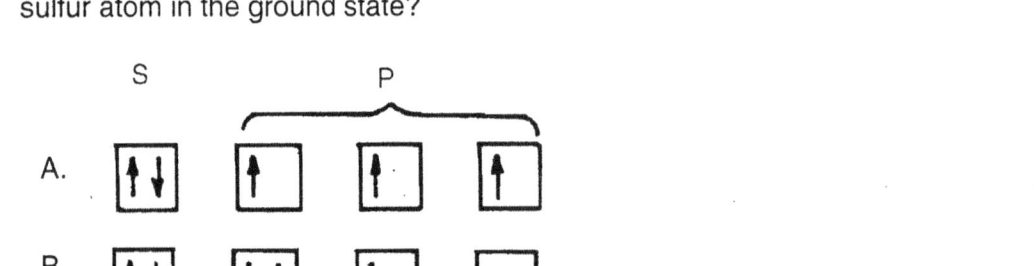

C. [↑↓] [↑↓] [↑↓] [ ]

D. [↑↓] [↑↓] [↑] [↑]

33. A radioactive source emits radiation which is deflected as shown in the diagram at the right. This radiation could be

   A. $^{0}_{-1}e$
   B. $^{4}_{2}He$
   C. $^{1}_{1}H$
   D. $^{1}_{0}n$

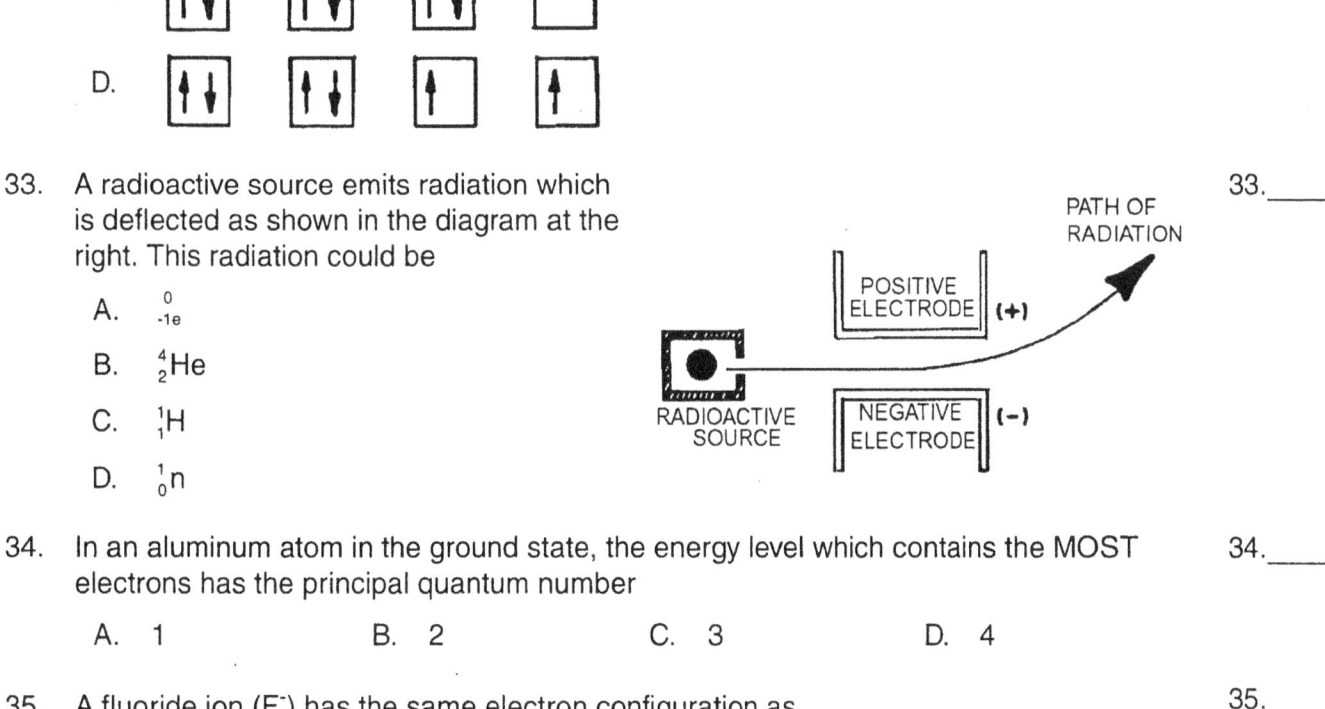

34. In an aluminum atom in the ground state, the energy level which contains the MOST electrons has the principal quantum number

   A. 1   B. 2   C. 3   D. 4

35. A fluoride ion (F⁻) has the same electron configuration as

   A. Na   B. Na⁺   C. Cl   D. Cl⁻

KEY (CORRECT ANSWERS)

1.	D	16.	B
2.	A	17.	B
3.	D	18.	C
4.	B	19.	A
5.	D	20.	B
6.	A	21.	B
7.	B	22.	A
8.	A	23.	A
9.	C	24.	B
10.	B	25.	B
11.	A	26.	B
12.	C	27.	A
13.	C	28.	C
14.	D	29.	D
15.	C	30.	D

31. C
32. D
33. A
34. B
35. B

TEST 3

DIRECTIONS: Each question or incomplete statement is followed by several suggested answers or completions. Select the one that BEST answers the question or completes the statement. *PRINT THE LETTER OF THE CORRECT ANSWER IN THE SPACE AT THE RIGHT.*

1. The molecules of _____ have the HIGHEST average kinetic energy.

    A. He(g) at 0° C
    B. CO_2(g) at 20° C
    C. HCl(g) at 40° C
    D. N_2(g) at 60° C

2. The temperature of 50 grams of water was raised to 50° C by the addition of 1,000 calories of heat energy.
    The initial temperature of the water was _____ ° C.

    A. 10   B. 20   C. 30   D. 60

3. Which gas will MOST closely resemble an ideal gas at STP?

    A. SO_2 B. NH_3 C. Cl_2 D. H_2

4. When water freezes, each gram loses an amount of heat equal to its heat of

    A. fusion
    B. vaporization
    C. sublimation
    D. reaction

5. Equal volumes of all gases at the same temperature and pressure contain an equal number of

    A. molecules   B. atoms   C. electrons   D. protons

6. Which is the electron configuration of an atom in the ground state?

    A. $1s^2 2s^1 2p^2$
    B. $1s^2 2s^2 2p^5 3s^2$
    C. $1s^2 2s^2 3s^1$
    D. $1s^2 2s^2 2p^6 3s^1$

7. An electron in an atom will emit energy when it moves from energy level

    A. 2s to 3p   B. 2s to 2p   C. 2p to 3s   D. 2p to 1s

8. Which atom has a COMPLETELY filled 3rd principal energy level?

    A. Ar   B. Zn   C. Ca   D. K

9. The electron dot symbol $:\ddot{X}:^-$ represents an ion of atom X. Atom X could be an atom of

    A. K   B. H   C. I   D. S

10. Which of the following elements has the HIGHEST first ionization energy?

    A. Li   B. Na   C. K   D. Rb

11. There are no known stable isotopes of the element with an atomic number of
    A. 20   B. 38   C. 56   D. 88

12. The TOTAL number of protons found in an OH⁻ ion is
    A. 1   B. 8   C. 9   D. 17

13. Two atoms of element A unite to form a molecule with the formula A_2. The bond between the atoms in the molecule is
    A. electrovalent
    B. ionic
    C. nonpolar covalent
    D. polar covalent

14. Which bond has the GREATEST degree of ionic character?
    A. H-Cl   B. I-Cl   C. Cl-Cl   D. K-Cl

15. Which substance will conduct electricity in both the solid phase and the liquid phase?
    A. AgCl   B. Ag   C. H_2 D. HCl

16. Indicate which of the following statements BEST explains why a CH_4 molecule is nonpolar.
    A. C and H are nonmetals.
    B. C and H have the same electronegativity.
    C. CH_4 has a symmetrical charge distribution.
    D. CH_4 is a gas at room temperature.

17. Mercury (I) chloride is CORRECTLY represented by the formula
    A. HG_2Cl B. $HgCl_2$ C. Hg_2Cl_2 D. Hg_2Cl_4

18. An example of an empirical formula is
    A. C_2H_2 B. H_2O_2 C. C_2Cl_2 D. $CaCl_2$

19. When the equation $H_2 + N_2 \rightarrow NH_3$ is completely balanced using smallest whole numbers, the sum of all the coefficients will be
    A. 6   B. 7   C. 3   D. 12

20. Which particle has the LARGEST radius?
    A. Cu   B. Cu^{2+} C. Se   D. Se^2

21. Which atom may form a negative ion with the electron configuration $1s^2$?
    A. H   B. He   C. Li   D. Be

22. Group _____ is known as the halogens.
    A. IA   B. IIA   C. VIIA   D. 0

23. Which element exhibits BOTH metallic and nonmetallic properties?
    A. B   B. Ba   C. K   D. Kr

24. In which group are all of the elements solids at STP?

    A. VIIA   B. VIA   C. VA   D. IVA

25. A white anhydrous powder that dissolves in water to form a blue aqueous solution could be

    A. $MgSO_4$ B. $BaSO_4$ C. $CuSO_4$ D. $CaSO_4$

26. There are _____ x 10^{23} molecules in 0.25 mole of O_2.

    A. 12   B. 6.0   C. 3.0   D. 1.5

27. A 10.0 gram sample of a hydrate was heated until all the water of hydration was driven off. The mass of anhydrous product remaining was 8.00 grams. The percent of water in the hydrate is _____ percent.

    A. 12.5   B. 20.0   C. 25.0   D. 80.0

28. A compound contains 50% sulfur and 50% oxygen by mass. What is the empirical formula of the compound?

    A. SO   B. SO_2 C. SO_3 D. SO_4

29. The density, in grams per liter, of N_2 gas at STP is

    A. 28.0   B. 14.0   C. 1.25   D. 0.800

30. Given the balanced equation: $3Fe + 4H_2O \rightarrow Fe_3O_4 + 4H_2$. When 36.0 grams of H_2O is consumed, the TOTAL number of liters of H_2 produced at STP is

    A. 22.4   B. 33.6   C. 44.8   D. 89.6

31. What is the TOTAL number of grams of KC1 (formula mass = 74.6) in 1.00 liter of 0.200 molar solution? _____ grams.

    A. 7.46   B. 14.9   C. 22.4   D. 29.8

32. According to the table at the right, in which reaction do the products have a HIGHER energy content than the reactants?

    A. $CH_4(g) + 2O_2(g) \rightarrow CO_2(g) + 2H_2O(\ell)$

    B. $CH_3OH(\ell) + \frac{3}{2}O_2(g) \rightarrow CO_2(g) + 2H_2O(\ell)$ H_2O

    C. $NH_4Cl(s) \rightarrow NH_4^+(aq) + Cl^-(aq)$ H_2O

    D. $NaOH(s) \rightarrow Na^+(aq) + OH^-(aq)$

    Heats of Reaction at 1 atm and 298K

Reaction	ΔH (kcal)
$CH_4(g) + 2O_2(g) \rightarrow CO_2(g) + 2H_2O(\ell)$	—212.8
$C_2H_6(g) + 5O_2(g) \rightarrow 3CO_2(g) + 4H_2O(\ell)$	—530.6
$CH_3OH(\ell) + \frac{3}{2}O_2(g) \rightarrow CO_2(g) + 2H_2O(\ell)$	—173.6
$C_6H_{12}O_6(s) + 6O_2(g) \rightarrow 6CO_2(g) + 6H_2O(\ell)$	—669.9
$CO(g) + \frac{1}{2}O_2(g) \rightarrow CO_2(g)$	—67.7
$NaOH(s) \xrightarrow{H_2O} Na^+(aq) + OH^-(aq)$	—10.6
$NH_4Cl(s) \xrightarrow{H_2O} NH_4^+(aq) + Cl^-(aq)$	+3.5
$H^+(aq) + OH^-(aq) \rightarrow H_2O(\ell)$	—13.8

33. According to the table at the right, which compound is MOST soluble in water?
    A. BaCO$_3$
    B. BaSO$_4$
    C. ZnCO$_3$
    D. ZnSO$_4$

34. Given the reaction H$_2$(g) + I$_2$(g) ⇌ 2HI(g).
    What is the CORRECT equilibrium expression for this reaction?
    k$_{eq}$=

    A. $\dfrac{[HI]^2}{[H_2][I_2]}$
    B. $\dfrac{[HI]^2}{[2H][2I]}$
    C. $\dfrac{[H_2][I_2]}{[HI]}$
    D. $\dfrac{[HI]^2}{[H]^2[I]^2}$

35. Given the reaction at equilibrium: A(g) + B(g) ⇌ AB(g).
    Indicate which equilibrium constant, K$_{eq}$, MOST favors the formation of AB(g)?

    A. 1×10^{-3}
    B. 2×10^{-6}
    C. 3×10^{-9}
    D. 4×10^{-12}

KEY (CORRECT ANSWERS)

1.	D	16.	C
2.	C	17.	C
3.	D	18.	D
4.	A	19.	A
5.	A	20.	D
6.	D	21.	A
7.	D	22.	C
8.	B	23.	A
9.	C	24.	D
10.	A	25.	C
11.	D	26.	D
12.	C	27.	B
13.	C	28.	B
14.	D	29.	C
15.	B	30.	C

31.	B
32.	C
33.	D
34.	A
35.	A

EXAMINATION SECTION
TEST 1

DIRECTIONS: Each question or incomplete statement is followed by several suggested answers or completions. Select the one that BEST answers the question or completes the statement. *PRINT THE LETTER OF THE CORRECT ANSWER IN THE SPACE AT THE RIGHT.*

1. The reactivity of the metals in Groups IA and IIA generally INCREASES with

    A. *increased* ionization energy
    B. *increased* atomic radius
    C. *decreased* nuclear charge
    D. *decreased* mass

2. The heat of vaporization for water is 540 calories per gram. What is the MINIMUM number of calories needed to change 40.0 grams of water at 100° C to steam at the same temperature and pressure?

    A. 43,200   B. 21,600   C. 540.   D. 40.0

3. A compound contains 40% calcium, 12% carbon, and 48% oxygen by mass. What is the empirical formula of this compound?

    A. $CaCO_3$ B. CaC_2O_4 C. CaC_3O_6 D. $CaCO_2$

4. If the density of a gas at STP is 2.50 grams per liter, what is the gram molecular mass of the gas?

    A. 2.50   B. 22.4   C. 56.0   D. 89.6

5. Which solution will freeze at the LOWEST temperature?
   _____ of sugar in _____ grams of water.

    A. 1 mole; 500
    B. 1 mole; 1,000
    C. 2 moles; 500
    D. 2 moles; 1,000

6. What is the total number of carbon atoms contained in 22.4 liters of CO gas at STP?

    A. 1.00
    B. 0.500
    C. 3.01×10^{23}
    D. 6.02×10^{23}

7. Which statement is TRUE if the free energy (ΔG) of a reaction is zero? The

    A. rate of the forward reaction is zero
    B. rate of the reverse reaction is zero
    C. reaction is approaching equilibrium
    D. reaction is at equilibrium

8. According to the chart at the right, which compound is MORE soluble than $BaSO_4$ at 1 atmosphere and 298 K? 8.____

A. AgBr
B. $PbCl_2$
C. AgI
D. ZnS

Constants for Various Equilibria at 1 atm and 298 K

$H_2O = H^+(aq) + OH^-(aq)$	$K_w = 1.0 \times 10^{-14}$
$CH_3COO^-(aq) + H_2O = CH_3COOH(aq) + OH^-(aq)$	$K_b = 5.6 \times 10^{-10}$
$NH_3(aq) + H_2O = NH_4^+(aq) + OH^-(aq)$	$K_b = 1.8 \times 10^{-5}$
$CO_3^{2-}(aq) + H_2O = HCO_3^-(aq) + OH^-(aq)$	$K_b = 2.1 \times 10^{-4}$
$Ag(NH_3)_2^+(aq) = Ag^+(aq) + 2NH_3(aq)$	$K_{eq} = 6.3 \times 10^{-8}$
$N_2(g) + 3H_2(g) = 2NH_3(g)$	$K_{eq} = 6.7 \times 10^{5}$
$H_2(g) + I_2(g) = 2HI(g)$	$K_{eq} = 3.5 \times 10^{-1}$

Compound	K_{sp}	*Compound*	K_{sp}
AgCl	1.6×10^{-10}	$PbCl_2$	1.6×10^{-5}
AgBr	7.7×10^{-13}	$PbCrO_4$	1.8×10^{-14}
AgI	1.5×10^{-16}	PbI_2	1.4×10^{-8}
$BaSO_4$	1.1×10^{-10}	ZnS	1.6×10^{-23}

9. A chemical reaction will ALWAYS occur spontaneously if the reaction has a 9.____

A. negative ΔG
B. positive ΔG
C. negative ΔH
D. positive ΔH

10. The free energy change, ΔG, must be negative when ΔH is ______ and ΔS is ______. 10.____

A. positive; positive
B. positive; negative
C. negative; positive
D. negative; negative

11. Given the reaction at equilibrium: 11.____
$NaCl(s) = Na^+(aq) + Cl^-(aq)$.
The addition of KC1 to this system will cause a shift in the equilibrium to the ______ and the concentration of $Na^+(aq)$ ions will ______.

A. left; increase
B. right; increase
C. left; decrease
D. right; decrease

12. What is the pH of an aqueous solution of $C_6H_{12}O_6$? 12.____

A. 1
B. 7
C. 11
D. 14

13. A sample of pure water contains 13.____

A. neither OH^- ions nor H_3O^+ ions
B. equal concentrations of OH^- and H_3O^+ ions
C. a larger concentration of H_3O^+ ions than OH^- ions
D. a smaller concentration of H_3O^+ ions than OH^- ions

14. Which of the following acids ionizes to the LEAST extent at 298 K? 14.____

A. HF
B. HNO_2
C. H_2S
D. H_2O

15. According to the chart at the right, which substance is amphiprotic?

    A. H_2SO_4
    B. HNO_3
    C. NH_3
    D. HBr

16. As 0.1 M HCl is added to 0.1 M KOH, the pH of the basic solution _____ and basicity _____.

    A. decreases; decreases
    B. increases; decreases
    C. decreases; increases
    D. increases; increases

17. In order for a redox reaction to be spontaneous, the potential (E^o) for the overall reaction must be

    A. greater than zero
    B. zero
    C. between zero and -1
    D. less than -1

18. Given the reaction:
    $2Au^{3+}(aq) + 3Ni^0 \rightarrow 2Au^0 + 3Ni^{2+}(aq)$.
    The cell potential (E^o) for the overall reaction is _____ volts.

    A. 3.75   B. 2.25   C. 1.75   D. 1.25

19. Which half-reaction occurs at the cathode in an electrolytic cell in which an object is being plated with copper?

    A. $Cu(s) \rightarrow Cu^{2+} + 2e^-$
    B. $Cu(s) + 2e^- \rightarrow Cu^{2+}$
    C. $Cu^{2+} \rightarrow Cu(s) + 2e^-$
    D. $Cu^{2+} + 2e^- \rightarrow Cu(s)$

20. Which will oxidize $Zn(s)$ to Zn^{2+} but will NOT oxidize $Pb(s)$ to Pb^{2+}?

    A. Al^{3+} B. Au^{3+} C. Co^{2+} D. Mg^{2+}

21. According to the table at the right, which halogen will react spontaneously with Au(s) to produce Au³⁺?

    A. Br₂
    B. F₂
    C. I₂
    D. Cl₂

21._____

22. Which is the structure for 1,2-dibromoethane?

    A. Br—C(H)(H)—Br (with one carbon)
    B. H—C(H)(Br)—C(H)(Br)—H
    C. H—C(H)(H)—C(H)(Br)—Br
    D. H—C(H)(H)—C(Br)(Br)—C(H)(H)—H

22._____

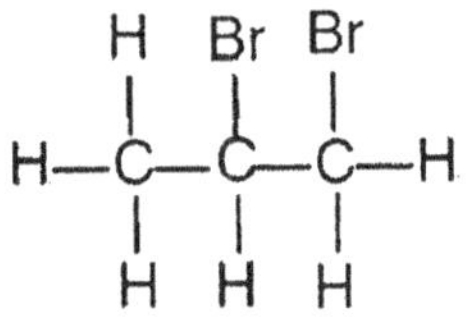

23. Which organic reaction involves the bonding of monomers by a dehydration process?

    A. Substitution
    B. Oxidation
    C. Addition polymerization
    D. Condensation polymerization

23._____

24. Which is the CORRECT structural formula for glycerol?

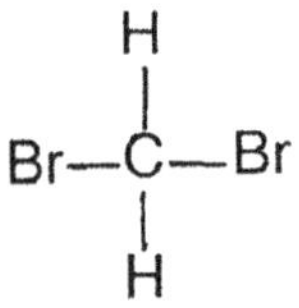

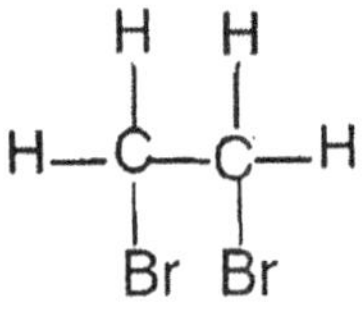

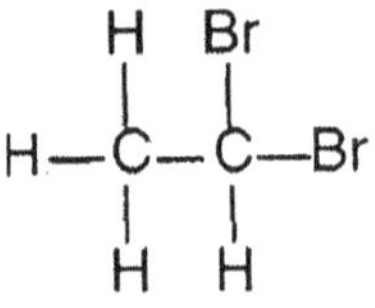

    A. Two-carbon chain with H, OH on each C
    B. One carbon with H, OH, H
    C. One carbon with OH, OH, OH, H
    D. Three-carbon chain with OH on each C

24._____

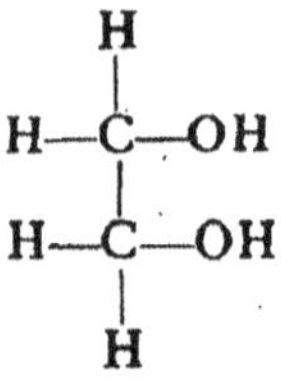

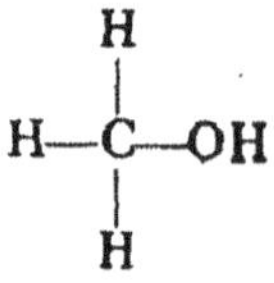

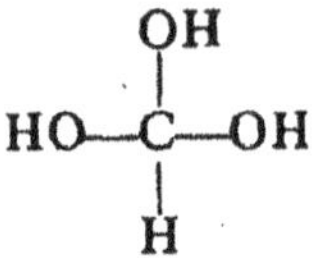

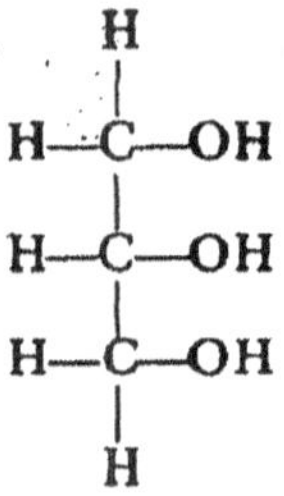

25. Which is represented by the structural formula shown at the right?   25._____ 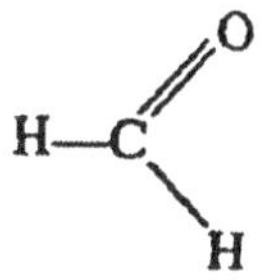
    An
    A. aldehyde
    B. alcohol
    C. alkane
    D. acid

26. Which is the general formula for an ether?   26._____

    A. R—OH
    B. R_1—O—R_2
    C. 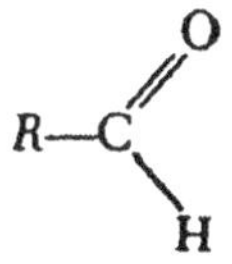 R—C(=O)H (with H below)
    D. 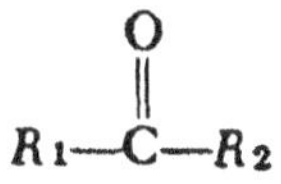 R_1—C(=O)—R_2

27. In crude petroleum, fractions can be separated according to their differing boiling points by   27._____

    A. the contact process
    B. the Haber process
    C. fractional distillation
    D. cracking

28. Which type of chemical reaction is the corrosion of iron?   28._____

    A. Reduction-oxidation
    B. Substitution
    C. Polymerization
    D. Decomposition

29. Which equation represents a simple example of cracking?   29._____

    A. $N_2 + 3H_2 \xrightarrow{600°C} 2NH_3$
    B. $S + O_2 \rightarrow SO_2$
    C. $C_3H_8 + 5O_2 \rightarrow 3CO_2 + 4H_2O$
    D. $C_{14}H_{30} \xrightarrow{600°C} C_7H_{16} + C_7H_{14}$

30. The Haber process is used to produce   30._____

    A. sulfur dioxide
    B. ammonia
    C. sulfuric acid
    D. sodium chloride

31. Which of the following metals forms a self-protective coating when exposed to air and moisture?   31._____

    A. Zinc   B. Calcium   C. Iron   D. Sodium

32. When a uranium nucleus breaks up into fragments, which type of nuclear reaction occurs?   32._____

    A. Fusion
    B. Fission
    C. Replacement
    D. Redox

33. The MAIN purpose of the moderator in a fission reactor is to   33._____

    A. remove heat
    B. produce heat
    C. slow down neutrons
    D. speed up neutrons

34. In the reaction $X + {}^1_1H \rightarrow {}^6_3Li + {}^4_2He$, the nucleus represented by X is

   A. ${}^9_3Li$ B. ${}^{10}_5B$ C. ${}^9_4Be$ D. ${}^{10}_6C$

34.____

35. Which particle can NOT be accelerated by the electric or magnetic fields in a particle accelerator?

   A. Neutron
   B. Proton
   C. Alpha particle
   D. Beta particle

35.____

36. Which equation represents artificial transmutation?

   A. $H_2O \rightarrow H^+ + OH^-$
   B. $UF_6 + 6Na \rightarrow 6NaF + U$
   C. ${}^{238}_{92}U \rightarrow {}^{234}_{90}TH + {}^4_2He$
   D. ${}^{27}_{13}Al + {}^4_2HE \rightarrow {}^{30}_{15}P + {}^1_0n$

36.____

37. The diagram at the right shows a eudiometer tube in a water bath. The water levels inside and outside the tube are equal. If the atmospheric pressure is 750 torr, the pressure inside the tube is _____ torr.

   A. 740
   B. 750
   C. 760
   D. 800

37.____

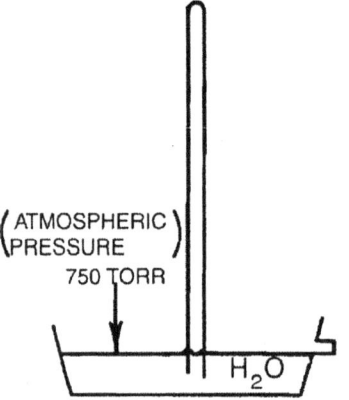

38. The volume of an acid required to neutralize exactly 15.00 milliliters (ml) of a base could be measured MOST precisely if it were added to the base solution from a

   A. 100 ml graduate
   B. 125 ml Erlenmeyer flask
   C. 50 ml buret
   D. 50 ml beaker

38.____

Questions 39-40.

DIRECTIONS: Questions 39 and 40 are to be answered on the basis of the table below which shows the data collected during the heating of a 5.0 gram sample of a hydrated salt.

Mass of Salt (g)	Heating Time (min)
5.0	0.0
4.1	5.0
3.1	10.
3.0	15.
3.0	30.
3.0	60.

39. After 60 minutes, how many grams of water appear to remain in the salt?

   A. 0.00 B. 2.0 C. 1.9 D. 0.90

39.____

40. The original sample contains _____ percent water.   40._____
    A. 82.   B. 60.   C. 30.   D. 40.

KEY (CORRECT ANSWERS)

1. B	11. C	21. B	31. A
2. B	12. B	22. B	32. B
3. A	13. B	23. D	33. C
4. C	14. D	24. D	34. C
5. C	15. C	25. A	35. A
6. D	16. A	26. C	36. D
7. D	17. A	27. C	37. B
8. B	18. C	28. A	38. C
9. A	19. D	29. D	39. A
10. C	20. C	30. B	40. D

TEST 2

DIRECTIONS: Each question or incomplete statement is followed by several suggested answers or completions. Select the one that BEST answers the question or completes the statement. *PRINT THE LETTER OF THE CORRECT ANSWER IN THE SPACE AT THE RIGHT.*

1. Given the system at chemical equilibrium:
   $2O_3(g) \rightleftarrows 3O_2(g)$ ($K_{eq} = 2.5 \times 10^{12}$).
   The concentration of O_3 and O_2 must be

   A. constant
   B. equal
   C. increasing
   D. decreasing

2. If HCl and H_2O react together in an acid-base reaction to form their Brönsted-Lowry conjugates, the products would be

   A. HCl and H_3O^+
   B. Cl^- and OH^-
   C. Cl_2 and H_2
   D. Cl^- and H_3O^+

3. What is the hydronium ion concentration of a solution at 298 K whose hydroxide ion concentration is 1×10^{-8}?
   $1 \times$

   A. 10^{-6}
   B. 10^{-7}
   C. 10^{-8}
   D. 10^{-14}

4. A 0.1 M acid solution at 298 K would conduct electricity BEST if the acid had a K_a value of

   A. 1.0×10^{-7}
   B. 1.8×10^{-5}
   C. 6.7×10^{-4}
   D. 1.7×10^{-2}

5. If 50 milliliters (ml) of a 0.01 M HCl solution is required to neutralize exactly 25 milliliters (ml) of NaOH, what is the concentration of the base?
   _____ M.

   A. 0.01
   B. 0.02
   C. 0.0005
   D. 0.04

6. When tested, a solution turns red litmus to blue. This indicates that the solution contains more

   A. H^+ ions than OH^- ions
   B. H_3O^+ ions than OH^- ions
   C. OH^- ions than H_3O^+ ions
   D. H^+ and OH^- ions than H_2O molecules

7. Oxygen has a positive oxidation number in the compound

   A. H_2O
   B. H_2O_2
   C. OF_2
   D. IO_2

8. In a chemical cell composed of two half-cells, ions are allowed to flow from one half-cell to another by means of

   A. electrodes
   B. an external conductor
   C. a voltmeter
   D. a salt bridge

9. Which occurs in the half-reaction Na(s) → Na⁺ + e⁻?

   A. Na(s) is reduced.
   B. Na(s) is oxidized.
   C. Na(s) gains electrons.
   D. Na⁺ is oxidized.

10. What is the oxidizing agent in the reaction $Zn^0 + 2Ag^+ \rightarrow Zn^{2+} + 2Ag^0$?

    A. Zn^0 B. Ag^0 C. Zn^{2+} D. Ag^+

11. Which is a redox reaction?

    A. $CaCO_3 \rightarrow CaO + CO_2$
    B. $NaOH + HCl \rightarrow NaCl + H_2O$
    C. $2NH_4Cl + Ca(OH)_2 \rightarrow 2NH_3 + 2H_2O + CaCl_2$
    D. $2H_2O \rightarrow 2H_2 + O_2$

12. Given the unbalanced equation: $Ca^0 + Al^{3+} \rightarrow Ca^{2+} + Al^0$. When the equation is completely balanced with the SMALLEST whole-number coefficients, what is the coefficient of Ca?

    A. 1   B. 2   C. 3   D. 4

13. Organic compounds that are essentially non-polar and exhibit weak intermolecular forces have

    A. low melting points
    B. low vapor pressure
    C. high conductivity in solution
    D. high boiling points

14. What is the formula for pentanol?

    A. C_5H_{12} B. $C_5H_{11}OH$ C. C_4H_{10} D. C_4H_9OH

15. The functional group

    $-\overset{O}{\underset{OH}{C}}$

    is ALWAYS found in an organic

    A. acid
    B. ester
    C. ether
    D. aldehyde

16. Which compound is a member of the alkene series of hydrocarbons?

    A. Benzene   B. Propene   C. Toluene   D. Butadiene

17. Which compound contains a triple bond?

    A. CH_4 B. C_2H_2 C. C_3H_6 D. C_4H_{10}

18. As additional KCl is added to a saturated solution of KCl, the conductivity of the solution   18.____

    A. decreases
    B. increases
    C. remains the same
    D. cannot be determined from the information given

19. As the pressure on a sample of gas increases at constant temperature, the volume of the gas   19.____

    A. decreases
    B. increases
    C. remains the same
    D. cannot be determined from the information given

20. As 1 gram of H_2O (ℓ) changes to 1 gram of $H_2O(s)$, the entropy of the system   20.____

    A. decreases
    B. increases
    C. remains the same
    D. cannot be determined from the information given

21. Given the reaction at equilibrium: 21.____
    $A(g) + B(g) + \text{heat} = AB(g)$.
    As the pressure increases at constant temperature, the value of the equilibrium constant

    A. decreases
    B. increases
    C. remains the same
    D. cannot be determined from the information given

22. The graph at the right represents changes of state for an unknown substance. What is the boiling temperature of the substance?   22.____

    ____ °C.
    A. 0
    B. 20
    C. 70
    D. 40

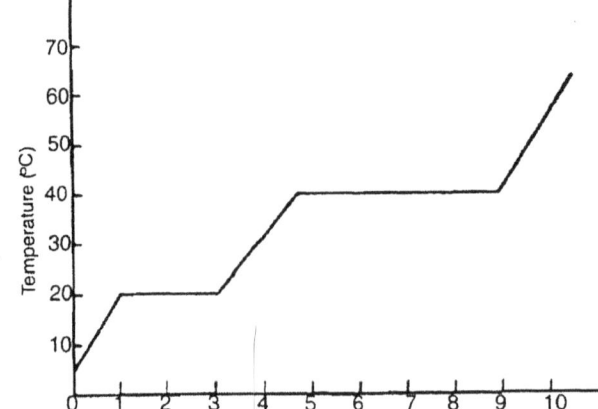

23. Which is the formula of a binary compound?   23.____

    A. KOH   B. $NaClO_3$ C. Al_2S_3 D. $Bi(NO_3)_3$

24. At constant pressure, 50. milliliters (ml) of a gas at 20.°C is heated to 30.°C. The new volume of the gas in milliliters (ml) is equal to 50. x

    A. 20./30.　　B. 30./20.　　C. 293/303　　D. 303/293

25. Which of the following substances is made up of particles with the HIGHEST average kinetic energy? _____ °C.

    A. Fe(s) at 35
    B. Br_2 (ℓ) at 20
    C. H_2O (ℓ) at 30
    D. CO_2(g) at 25

26. Solid substances are MOST likely to sublime if they have _____ vapor pressure and _____ intermolecular attractions.

    A. high; strong
    B. high; weak
    C. low; strong
    D. low; weak

27. Which of the following atoms has the GREATEST nuclear charge?

    A. $^{14}_{7}N$　　B. $^{12}_{6}C$　　C. $^{2}_{1}H$　　D. $^{4}_{2}He$

28. Potassium-42 requires _____ hours to undergo three half-life periods.

    A. 6.2　　B. 12.4　　C. 24.8　　D. 37.2

29. Usually, the term *kernel* includes all parts of the atom EXCEPT the

    A. neutrons
    B. protons
    C. valence electrons
    D. orbital electrons

30. Which nuclear emission moving through an electric field would be deflected toward the positive electrode?

    A. Alpha particle
    B. Beta particle
    C. Gamma radiation
    D. Proton

31. What is the electron configuration for Be^{2+} ions?

    A. $1s^1$　　B. $1s^2$　　C. $1s^22s^1$　　D. $1s^22s^2$

32. What type of bonding is found in the molecule HBr?

    A. Ionic
    B. Metallic
    C. Nonpolar covalent
    D. Polar covalent

33. What is the name of the calcium salt of sulfuric acid? Calcium

    A. thiosulfate
    B. sulfate
    C. sulfide
    D. sulfite

34. What is the formula of nitrogen (I) oxide?

    A. NO　　B. N_2O　　C. NO_2　　D. N_2O_4

35. When a reaction occurs between atoms with ground state electron configurations $1s^22s^1$ and $1s^22s^22p^5$, the predominant type of bond formed is

    A. polar covalent
    B. nonpolar covalent
    C. ionic
    D. metallic

36. Which represents both an empirical and a molecular formula?

    A. P_2O_5
    B. N_2O_4
    C. C_3H_6
    D. $C_6H_{12}O_6$

37. In Period 2, as the elements are considered from left to right, there is a DECREASE in

    A. ionization energy
    B. atomic mass
    C. metallic character
    D. nonmetallic character

38. Which molecule is relatively inactive and contains a triple bond?

    A. N_2
    B. O_2
    C. Cl_2
    D. H_2

39. Atoms of metallic elements tend to _____ electrons and form _____ ions.

    A. gain; negative
    B. gain; positive
    C. lose; negative
    D. lose; positive

40. Alkali metals, alkaline earth metals, and halogens are elements found respectively in Groups

    A. IA, IIA, and O
    B. HA, IIIA, and VIIA
    C. IA, IIA, and IVA
    D. IA, IIA, and VIIA

KEY (CORRECT ANSWERS)

1. A	11. D	21. C	31. B
2. D	12. C	22. D	32. D
3. A	13. A	23. C	33. B
4. D	14. B	24. D	34. B
5. B	15. A	25. A	35. C
6. C	16. B	26. B	36. A
7. C	17. B	27. A	37. C
8. D	18. C	28. D	38. A
9. B	19. A	29. C	39. D
10. D	20. A	30. B	40. D

TEST 3

DIRECTIONS: Each question or incomplete statement is followed by several suggested answers or completions. Select the one that BEST answers the question or completes the statement. *PRINT THE LETTER OF THE CORRECT ANSWER IN THE SPACE AT THE RIGHT.*

1. A 1-liter flask contains two gases at a total pressure of 3.0 atmospheres. If the partial pressure of one of the gases is 0.5 atmosphere, then the partial pressure of the other gas MUST be _____ atm.

    A. 1.0 B. 2.5 C. 1.5 D. 0.50

2. Which of the following BEST describes exothermic chemical reactions? They

    A. *never* release heat
    B. *always* release heat
    C. *never* occur spontaneously
    D. *always* occur spontaneously

3. What is the TOTAL number of molecules in 1.0 mole of $Cl_2(aq)$?

    A. 35
    B. 70
    C. 6.0×10^{23}
    D. 12×10^{24}

4. The number of calories needed to raise the temperature of 10 grams of water from 20°C to 30°C is

    A. 10 B. 20 C. 100 D. 40

5. The heat of fusion for ice is 80 calories per gram. Adding 80 calories of heat to one gram of ice at STP will cause the ice to _____ temperature.

    A. increase in
    B. decrease in
    C. change to water at a higher
    D. change to water at the same

6. Which 1-mole sample of atoms requires the LEAST energy to form a mole of positive ions?

    A. Ge B. Ca C. Ga D. K

7. The atomic number of an atom is ALWAYS equal to the total number of

    A. neutrons in the nucleus
    B. protons in the nucleus
    C. neutrons plus protons in the atom
    D. protons plus electrons in the atom

8. Which electron configuration represents an atom in an excited state?

    A. $1s^2 2s^2 2p^6 3p^1$
    B. $1s^2 2s^2 2p^6 3s^2 3p^1$
    C. $1s^2 2s^2 2p^6 3s^2 3p^2$
    D. $1s^2 2s^2 2p^6 3s^2$

9. Which principal energy level can hold a MAXIMUM of 18 electrons?

    A. 5   B. 2   C. 3   D. 4

10. Which is the CORRECT electron dot representation of an atom of sulfur in the ground state?

    A. S: B. ·S: C. :̇S: D. :S̈:

11. The TOTAL number of d orbitals in the third principal energy level is

    A. one   B. five   C. three   D. seven

12. Which of the following nuclei is an isotope of (10p, 11n)?

    A. (10p, 9n)   B. (11p, 10n)   C. (9p, 11n)   D. (11p, 12n)

13. When the equation $NH_3 + O_2 \rightarrow HNO_3 + H_2O$ is completely balanced using SMALLEST whole numbers, the coefficient of O_2 would be

    A. 1   B. 2   C. 3   D. 4

14. The bonding in NH_3 is MOST similar to the bonding in

    A. H_2O B. NaCl   C. MgO   D. KF

15. Which is the formula of an ionic compound?

    A. SO_2 B. CO_2 C. CH_3OH D. NaOH

16. Which electron dot formula represents a molecule that contains a nonpolar covalent bond?

    A. ˣˣBr ˣ Brˣˣ ··

    B. Na⁺ [:F:]⁻

    C. H ˣ Br:

    D. H ˣ F ˣ

17. Molecule-ion attractions are found in

    A. Cu(s)   B. CO(g)   C. KBr( )   D. NaCl(aq)

18. Hydrogen bonds are STRONGEST between the molecules of

    A. HF (ℓ)   B. HCl (ℓ)   C. HBr (ℓ)   D. HI (ℓ)

19. The bonds present in silicon carbide (SiC) are

    A. covalent   B. ionic
    C. metallic   D. van der Waals

20. As the elements are considered from the top to the bottom of Group VA, which sequence in properties occurs?

    A. Metal → metalloid → nonmetal
    B. Metal → nonmetal → metalloid
    C. Metalloid → metal → nonmetal
    D. Nonmetal → metalloid → metal

21. The element found in Group IIIA and in Period 2 is

    A. Be   B. Mg   C. B   D. Al

22. Which element is considered malleable?

    A. Gold   B. Hydrogen C. Sulfur   D. Radon

23. The MOST active nonmetal in the Periodic Table of the Elements is

    A. Na   B. F   C. I   D. Cl

24. Element M has an electronegativity of less than 1.2 and reacts with bromine to form the compound MBr_2.
    Element M could be

    A. Al   B. Na   C. Ca   D. K

25. A chloride dissolves in water to form a colored solution.
    The chloride could be

    A. HCl   B. KCl   C. $CaCl_2$ D. $CuCl_2$

26. Which of the following particles has the SMALLEST radius?

    A. Na^0 B. K^0 C. Na^+ D. K^+

27. The gram molecular mass of CO_2 is the same as the gram molecular mass of

    A. CO   B. SO_2 C. C_2H_6 D. C_3H_8

28. The empirical formula of a compound is CH_2 and its molecular mass is 70.
    What is the molecular formula of the compound?

    A. C_2H_2 B. C_2H_4 C. C_4H_{10} D. C_5H_{10}

29. Consider the following reaction:
    $2Na + 2H_2O \rightarrow 2NaOH + H_2$.
    What is the TOTAL number of moles of hydrogen produced when 4 moles of sodium react completely?

    A. One   B. Two   C. Three   D. Four

30. The percent by mass of nitrogen in $Mg(CN)_2$ is equal to _____ x 100.

    A. 14/76   B. 14/50   C. 28/76   D. 28/50

31. What is the molarity of a solution of KNO_3 (molecular mass = 101) that contains 404 grams of KNO_3 in 2.00 liters of solution?

   A. 1.00   B. 2.00   C. 0.500   D. 4.00

32. The graph at the right represents the potential energy changes that occur in a chemical reaction. Which letter represents the activated complex?

   A. A
   B. B
   C. C
   D. D

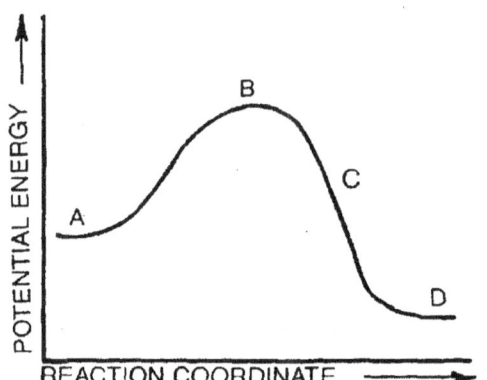

33. According to the chart at the right, which of the following substances is MOST soluble at 60°C?
   A. NH_4Cl
   B. KCl
   C. NaCl
   D. NH_3

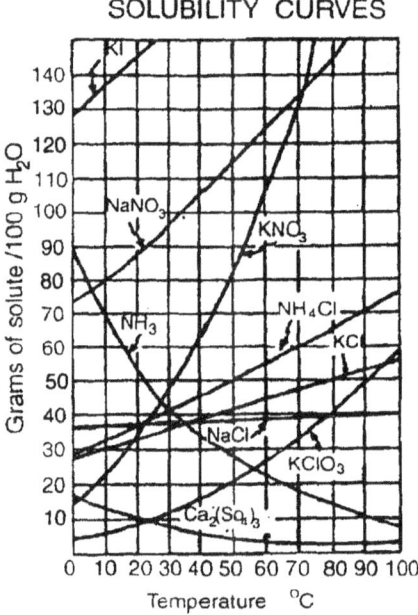

34. In a chemical reaction, the difference in potential energy between the products and the reactants is equal to

   A. ΔS B. ΔG C. ΔH D. ΔT

35. Given the reaction at equilibrium:
   $2CO(g) + O_2(g) = 2CO_2(g)$.
   The CORRECT equilibrium expression for this reaction is K_{eq} =

   A. $\dfrac{[2CO][O_2]}{[2CO_2]}$

   B. $\dfrac{[CO]^2[O_2]}{[CO_2]^2}$

   C. $\dfrac{[2CO_2]}{[2CO][O_2]}$

   D. $\dfrac{[CO_2]^2}{[CO]^2[O_2]}$

KEY (CORRECT ANSWERS)

1.	B	16.	A
2.	B	17.	D
3.	C	18.	A
4.	C	19.	A
5.	D	20.	D
6.	D	21.	C
7.	B	22.	A
8.	A	23.	B
9.	C	24.	C
10.	C	25.	D
11.	B	26.	C
12.	A	27.	D
13.	B	28.	D
14.	A	29.	B
15.	D	30.	C

31. B
32. B
33. A
34. C
35. D

EXAMINATION SECTION
TEST 1

DIRECTIONS: Each question or incomplete statement is followed by several suggested answers or completions. Select the one that BEST answers the question or completes the statement. *PRINT THE LETTER OF THE CORRECT ANSWER IN THE SPACE AT THE RIGHT.*

1. Which substance is an ionic solid?
   A. LiCl   B. HCl   C. Ne   D. Fe

2. The element in Group VIA whose isotopes are all radioactive is
   A. O   B. S   C. Te   D. Po

3. Which particle has the LARGEST radius?
   A. F^- B. Ne   C. Cl^- D. Ar

4. Which element occurs in nature ONLY in compounds?
   A. Au   B. Ag   C. Ne   D. Na

5. In the Periodic Table, the transition elements are found in the
   A. A groups *only*
   B. B groups *only*
   C. A groups and Group O
   D. B groups and Group VIII

6. In the ground state, how many electrons are in the outermost s sublevel of each element in Group VIIA?
   A. Five   B. Two   C. Seven   D. Eight

7. The gram-molecular mass of a gas is 44.0 grams. Its density at STP is _____ g/ℓ.
   A. 0.509   B. 1.43   C. 1.96   D. 2.84

8. At standard pressure, a 1 molal solution of sugar has a boiling point _____ than 100° C and a freezing point than 0° C.
   A. greater; greater
   B. greater; less
   C. less; greater
   D. less; less

9. In the reaction $N_2 + 3H_2 \rightarrow 2NH_3$, _____ gram(s) of H_2 are needed to produce EXACTLY 1 mole of ammonia.
   A. one   B. two   C. three   D. four

10. The volume of 16.0 grams of $SO_2(g)$ at STP is CLOSEST to _____ ℓ.
    A. 5.60   B. 11.2   C. 22.4   D. 44.8

11. A compound is 92.3% carbon and 7.7% hydrogen. The empirical formula of this compound is

    A. CH B. CH_2 C. CH_3 D. CH_4

12. The ΔG of a chemical reaction refers to the change in

    A. entropy
    B. state
    C. activation energy
    D. free energy

13. Based on the chart at the right, a compound which forms spontaneously from its elements is
    A. ethene
    B. ethane
    C. nitrogen (II) oxide
    D. nitrogen (IV) oxide

Standard Energies of Formation of Compounds at 1 atm and 298 K

Compound	Heat (Enthalpy) of Formation kcal/mole (ΔH_f)	Free Energy of Formation kcal/mole (ΔG_f)
Aluminum oxide Al_2O_3 (s)	−399.1	−376.8
Ammonia NH_3 (g)	−11.0	−4.0
Barium sulfate $BaSO_4$ (s)	−350.2	−323.4
Calcium hydroxide $Ca(OH)_2$ (s)	−235.8	−214.3
Carbon dioxide CO_2 (g)	−94.1	−94.3
Carbon monoxide CO (g)	−26.4	−32.8
Copper (II) sulfate $CuSO_4$ (s)	−184.0	−158.2
Ethane C_2H_6 (g)	−20.2	−7.9
Ethene C_2H_4 (g)	12.5	16.3
Ethyne (acetylene) C_2H_2 (g)	54.2	50.0
Hydrogen fluoride HF (g)	−64.2	−64.7
Hydrogen iodide HI (g)	6.2	0.3
Iodine chloride ICl (g)	4.2	−1.3
Lead (II) oxide PbO (s)	−52.4	−45.3
Magnesium oxide MgO (s)	−143.8	−136.1
Nitrogen (II) oxide NO (g)	21.6	20.7
Nitrogen (IV) oxide NO_2 (g)	8.1	12.4
Potassium chloride KCl (s)	−104.2	−97.6
Sodium chloride NaCl (s)	−98.2	−91.8
Sulfur dioxide SO_2 (g)	−71.0	−71.8
Water H_2O (g)	−57.8	−54.6
Water H_2O (ℓ)	−68.3	−56.7

Sample equation
$2Al(s) + \frac{3}{2}O_2(g) \rightarrow Al_2O_3(s)$

14. Given the reaction at equilibrium:

    $AgI(s) \rightleftarrows Ag^+(aq) + I^-(aq)$.

    Which is the CORRECT solubility product constant expression for the reaction?
    $K_{sp} =$

    A. $[Ag+][I^-]$
    B. $\dfrac{1}{[Ag^+][I^-]}$
    C. $[Ag+] + [I^-]$
    D. $\dfrac{1}{[Ag^+]+[I^-]}$

15. Given the reaction at equilibrium:

    $CH_3COOH(aq) + H_2O(\ell) \rightleftarrows H_3O^+(aq) + CH_3COO^-(aq)$.

    The addition of which ion will cause an INCREASE in the concentration of CH_3COO^-(aq)?

    A. H_3O^+ B. Cl^- C. Na^+ D. OH^-

16. Given the reaction at equilibrium:

    $H_2(g) + Cl_2(g) \rightleftharpoons 2HCl(g) + heat$.

    The equilibrium will shift to the right when there is an INCREASE in

    A. temperature
    B. pressure
    C. concentration of $H_2(g)$
    D. concentration of $HCl(g)$

    16.____

17. How many milliliters of 5.0 M NaOH are needed to EXACTLY neutralize 40. milliliters of 2.0 M HCl?

    A. 8.0 B. 10. C. 16 D. 40.

    17.____

18. A 0.1 M HCl solution DIFFERS from a 0.1 M NaOH solution in that the HCl solution

    A. has a lower pH
    B. turns litmus blue
    C. contains H_3O^+ ions
    D. does not contain OH^-

    18.____

19. Which compound is a strong electrolyte?

    A. CH_3COOH B. H_2S C. $C_{12}H_{22}O_{11}$ D. HNO_3

    19.____

20. What is the $[H_3O^+]$ of a 0.001 M NaOH solution?
    1 X

    A. 10^{-1} B. 10^{-7} C. 10^{-11} D. 10^{-14}

    20.____

21. What are the two Bronsted acids in the reaction below?

    $HPO_4^{2-} + H_2O = PO_4^{3-} + H_3O^+$

    A. HPO_4^{2-} and PO_4^{3-}
    B. HPO_4^{2-} and $H3O^+$
    C. H_2O and H_3O^+
    D. H_2O and PO_4^{3-}

    21.____

22. In an electrolytic cell, a Cl^- ion would be attracted to the_____ electrode and_____ .

    A. positive; oxidized
    B. positive; reduced
    C. negative; oxidized
    D. negative; reduced

    22.____

STANDARD ELECTRODE POTENTIALS	
Ionic Concentrations 1 M Water at 298 K, 1 atm	
Half-Reaction	$E°$ (volts)
$F_2(g) + 2e^- \longrightarrow 2F^-$	+2.87
$MnO_4^- + 8H^+ + 5e^- \longrightarrow Mn^{2+} + 4H_2O$	+1.52
$Au^{3+} + 3e^- \longrightarrow Au(s)$	+1.50
$Cl_2(g) + 2e^- \longrightarrow 2Cl^-$	+1.36
$Cr_2O_7^{2-} + 14H^+ + 6e^- \longrightarrow 2Cr^{3+} + 7H_2O$	+1.33
$MnO_2(s) + 4H^+ + 2e^- \longrightarrow Mn^{2+} + 2H_2O$	+1.28
$\frac{1}{2}O_2(g) + 2H^+ + 2e^- \longrightarrow H_2O$	+1.23
$Br_2(\ell) + 2e^- \longrightarrow 2Br^-$	+1.06
$NO_3^- + 4H^+ + 3e^- \longrightarrow NO(g) + 2H_2O$	+0.96
$\frac{1}{2}O_2(g) + 2H^+(10^{-7}M) + 2e^- \longrightarrow H_2O$	+0.82
$Ag^+ + e^- \longrightarrow Ag(s)$	+0.80
$\frac{1}{2}Hg_2^{2+} + e^- \longrightarrow Hg(\ell)$	+0.79
$Hg^{2+} + 2e^- \longrightarrow Hg(\ell)$	+0.78
$NO_3^- + 2H^+ + e^- \longrightarrow NO_2(g) + H_2O$	+0.78
$Fe^{3+} + e^- \longrightarrow Fe^{2+}$	+0.77
$I_2(s) + 2e^- \longrightarrow 2I^-$	+0.53
$Cu^+ + e^- \longrightarrow Cu(s)$	+0.52
$Cu^{2+} + 2e^- \longrightarrow Cu(s)$	+0.34
$SO_4^{2-} + 4H^+ + 2e^- \longrightarrow SO_2(g) + 2H_2O$	+0.17
$Sn^{4+} + 2e^- \longrightarrow Sn^{2+}$	+0.15
$2H^+ + 2e^- \longrightarrow H_2(g)$	0.00
$Pb^{2+} + 2e^- \longrightarrow Pb(s)$	−0.13
$Sn^{2+} + 2e^- \longrightarrow Sn(s)$	−0.14
$Ni^{2+} + 2e^- \longrightarrow Ni(s)$	−0.25
$Co^{2+} + 2e^- \longrightarrow Co(s)$	−0.28
$2H^+(10^{-7}M) + 2e^- \longrightarrow H_2(g)$	−0.41
$Fe^{2+} + 2e^- \longrightarrow Fe(s)$	−0.44
$Cr^{3+} + 3e^- \longrightarrow Cr(s)$	−0.74
$Zn^{2+} + 2e^- \longrightarrow Zn(s)$	−0.76
$2H_2O + 2e^- \longrightarrow 2OH^- + H_2(g)$	−0.83
$Mn^{2+} + 2e^- \longrightarrow Mn(s)$	−1.18
$Al^{3+} + 3e^- \longrightarrow Al(s)$	−1.66
$Mg^{2+} + 2e^- \longrightarrow Mg(s)$	−2.37
$Na^+ + e^- \longrightarrow Na(s)$	−2.71
$Ca^{2+} + 2e^- \longrightarrow Ca(s)$	−2.87
$Sr^{2+} + 2e^- \longrightarrow Sr(s)$	−2.89
$Ba^{2+} + 2e^- \longrightarrow Ba(s)$	−2.90
$Cs^+ + e^- \longrightarrow Cs(s)$	−2.92
$K^+ + e^- \longrightarrow K(s)$	−2.92
$Rb^+ + e^- \longrightarrow Rb(s)$	−2.93
$Li^+ + e^- \longrightarrow Li(s)$	−3.00

23. Based on the chart at the right, which pair will react spontaneously? 23._____

A. I_2 and F^-

B. I_2 and Cl^-

C. I_2 and Ag

D. I_2 and Zn

24. In the reaction $Cl_2 + 2Br^-(aq) \rightarrow 2Cl^-(aq) + Br_2$, which half-reaction CORRECTLY represents oxidation? 24._____

A. $2Br^- \rightarrow Br_2 + 2e^-$

B. $Cl_2 \rightarrow 2Cl^- + 2e^-$

C. $2Br^- + 2e^- \rightarrow Br_2$

D. $Cl_2 + 2e^- \rightarrow 2Cl^-$

25. Given the reaction: 25._____

$_K_2Cr_2O_7 + _HCl \rightarrow _KCl + _CrCl_3 + _Cl_2 + _H_2O$. When the reaction is completely balanced using SMALLEST whole numbers, the coefficient of Cl_2 will be

A. 1 B. 2 C. 3 D. 4

26. Given the reaction: 26._____

$2Cr(s) + 3Cu^{+2}(aq) \rightarrow 2Cr^{+3}(aq) + 3Cu(s)$.

The potential difference (E) of this cell is _______ V.

A. 0.40 B. 1.08 C. 1.25 D. 2.50

27. What is the CORRECT I.U.P.A.C. name for a compound with the structural formula shown at the right? 27._____

A. 1, 3-dichloropentane

B. 2, 4-dichloropentane

C. 1, 3-dichlorobutane

D. 2, 4-dichlorobutane

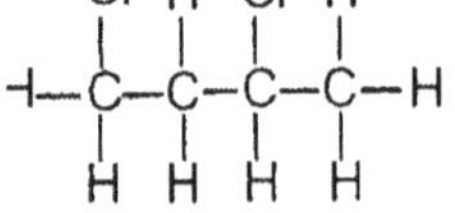

28. The reaction represented by the equation $nC_2H_4 \rightarrow (-C_2H_4-)_n$ is called 28._____

A. saponification

B. fermentation

C. esterification

D. polymerization

29. Which compound is a trihydroxy alcohol?

    A. Glycerol B. Butanol C. Ethanol D. Methanol

30. Which formula represents an acid?

    A.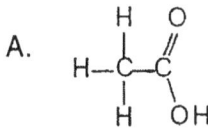

    B. H-C(H)(H)-C(H)(H)-OH

    C. H-C(H)(H)-C(H)(=O)-H

    D. H-C(H)(OH)-C(H)(OH)-H

31. Organic compounds DIFFER from inorganic compounds in that organic compounds generally have _____ melting points and are _____ .

    A. high; electrolytes   B. high; nonelectrolytes
    C. low; electrolytes   D. low; nonelectrolytes

32. Group IA metals are obtained commercially from their fused salts by

    A. transmutation   B. fractional distillation
    C. electrolysis   D. polymerization

33. When large hydrocarbon molecules are broken down into smaller hydrocarbon molecules, the reaction is known as

    A. cracking   B. distilling
    C. reduction   D. oxidation

34. Which equation represents the reaction that occurs during the Haber process?

    A. $ZnO + C \rightarrow Zn + CO$
    B. $2Al + Cr_2O_3 \rightarrow Al_2O_3 + 2Cr$
    C. $S + O_2 \rightarrow SO_2$
    D. $N_2 + 3H_2 \rightarrow 2NH_3$

35. Given the probable reaction for the nickel-cadmium battery: $2Ni(OH)_3 + Cd \rightleftarrows 2Ni(OH)_2 + Cd(OH)_2$.
    Which species is oxidized during the discharge of the battery?

    A. Ni^{3+} B. Ni^{2+} C. Cd^0 D. Cd^{2+}

36. Which metal may be connected to an iron pipe to prevent the corrosion of the iron?

    A. Co   B. Sn   C. Pb   D. Mg

37. The mass number of a deuterium atom is

    A. one   B. two   C. three   D. four

38. In a nuclear reactor, boron and cadmium are COMMONLY used in

    A. fuels
    B. coolants
    C. moderators
    D. control rods

39. Which atom can undergo nuclear fission when its nucleus captures a neutron?

    A. $_{1}^{1}H$
    B. $_{1}^{2}H$
    C. $_{92}^{235}U$
    D. $_{92}^{238}U$

40. Consider the reaction $_{13}^{27}Al + _{2}^{4}He \rightarrow _{15}^{30}P + _{0}^{1}n$. This reaction is BEST described as

    A. beta decay
    B. artificial transmutation
    C. fission
    D. fusion

KEY (CORRECT ANSWERS)

1. A	11. A	21. B	31. D
2. D	12. D	22. A	32. C
3. C	13. B	23. D	33. A
4. D	14. A	24. A	34. D
5. D	15. D	25. C	35. C
6. B	16. C	26. B	36. D
7. C	17. C	27. C	37. B
8. B	18. A	28. D	38. D
9. C	19. D	29. A	39. C
10. A	20. C	30. A	40. B

TEST 2

DIRECTIONS: Each question or incomplete statement is followed by several suggested answers or completions. Select the one that BEST answers the question or completes the statement. *PRINT THE LETTER OF THE CORRECT ANSWER IN THE SPACE AT THE RIGHT.*

1. Given the reaction: A + B $\rightleftharpoons$ AB

    The GREATEST amount of AB would be produced if the equilibrium constant of the reaction is equal to 1.0 x

    A. 10^{-5} B. 10^{-1} C. 10^1 D. 10^5

    1.____

2. Based on the chart at the right, the MOST energy would be released when oxygen reacts completely with 1.0 mole of

    A. CH_4
    B. CO
    C. $C_6H_{12}O_6$
    D. CH_3OH

Heats of Reaction at 1 atm and 298K	
Reaction	ΔH (kcal)
CH_4 (g) + $2O_2$ (g) → CO_2 (g) + $2H_2O$ (ℓ)	—212.8
C_3H_8 (g) + $5O_2$ (g) → $3CO_2$ (g) + $4H_2O$ (ℓ)	—530.6
CH_3OH (ℓ) + $\frac{3}{2}O_2$ (g) → CO_2 (g) + $2H_2O$ (ℓ)	—173.6
$C_6H_{12}O_6$ (s) + $6O_2$ (g) → $6CO_2$ (g) + $6H_2O$ (ℓ)	—669.9
CO (g) + $\frac{1}{2}O_2$ (g) → CO_2 (g)	—67.7
NaOH (s) $\xrightarrow{H_2O}$ Na^+ (aq) + OH^- (aq)	—10.6
NH_4Cl (s) $\xrightarrow{H_2O}$ NH_4^+ (aq) + Cl^- (aq)	+3.5
H^+ (aq) + OH^- (aq) → H_2O (ℓ)	—13.8

    2.____

3. At which pressure would carbon dioxide gas be MOST soluble in 100 grams of water at a temperature of 25° C? _____ atm.

    A. 1   B. 2   C. 3   D. 4

    3.____

4. According to the table at the right, which species can act as both a Bronsted acid and a Bronsted base?

    A. NO_2^-
    B. NO_3^-
    C. HF
    D. NH_3

    4.____

5. The ionization constant, K_a, for acetic acid at 1 atmosphere and 298 K is

    A. 2.5×10^{-11} B. 2.1×10^{-8}
    C. 1.8×10^{-5} D. 1.3×10^{-2}

    5.____

6. The H_3O^+ ion concentration of a solution is 1×10^{-5} mole per liter. This solution is ______ and has a pH of ______ 6.____

A. acidic; 5
B. acidic; 9
C. basic; 5
D. basic; 9

7. According to the Arrhenius theory, a substance that yields hydrogen ions as the only positive ion in an aqueous solution is a(n) 7.____

A. salt
B. base
C. acid
D. nonelectrolyte

8. How many moles of HCl can be neutralized by 0.1 liter of 0.5 M NaOH? 8.____

A. 0.1
B. 0.05
C. 0.5
D. 0.4

9. A 0.1 M solution of HCl contains 9.____

A. fewer H_3O^+ ions than OH^- ions
B. more H_3O^+ ions than OH^- ions
C. an equal number of H_3O^+ and OH^- ions
D. neither H_3O^+ ions nor OH^- ions

10. In the reaction $Cl_2 + H_2O \rightarrow HClO + HCl$, the oxidation number of chlorine 10.____

A. decreases *only*
B. increases *only*
C. neither decreases nor increases
D. both decreases and increases

11. According to the chart at the right, which can act as both a reducing agent and an oxidizing agent? 11.____

A. Au^{3+}
B. Al^{3+}
C. Fe^{2+}
D. Zn^{2+}

STANDARD ELECTRODE POTENTIALS

Ionic Concentrations 1 M Water at 298 K, 1 atm

Half-Reaction	$E°$ *(volts)*
$F_2(g) + 2e^- \longrightarrow 2F^-$	+2.87
$MnO_4^- + 8H^+ + 5e^- \longrightarrow Mn^{2+} + 4H_2O$	+1.52
$Au^{3+} + 3e^- \longrightarrow Au(s)$	+1.50
$Cl_2(g) + 2e^- \longrightarrow 2Cl^-$	+1.36
$Cr_2O_7^{2-} + 14H^+ + 6e^- \longrightarrow 2Cr^{3+} + 7H_2O$	+1.33
$MnO_2(s) + 4H^+ + 2e^- \longrightarrow Mn^{2+} + 2H_2O$	+1.28
$\frac{1}{2}O_2(g) + 2H^+ + 2e^- \longrightarrow H_2O$	+1.23
$Br_2(\ell) + 2e^- \longrightarrow 2Br^-$	+1.06
$NO_3^- + 4H^+ + 3e^- \longrightarrow NO(g) + 2H_2O$	+0.96
$\frac{1}{2}O_2(g) + 2H^+(10^{-7}M) + 2e^- \longrightarrow H_2O$	+0.82
$Ag^+ + e^- \longrightarrow Ag(s)$	+0.80
$\frac{1}{2}Hg_2^{2+} + e^- \longrightarrow Hg(\ell)$	+0.79
$Hg^{2+} + 2e^- \longrightarrow Hg(\ell)$	+0.78
$NO_3^- + 2H^+ + e^- \longrightarrow NO_2(g) + H_2O$	+0.78
$Fe^{3+} + e^- \longrightarrow Fe^{2+}$	+0.77
$I_2(s) + 2e^- \longrightarrow 2I^-$	+0.53
$Cu^+ + e^- \longrightarrow Cu(s)$	+0.52
$Cu^{2+} + 2e^- \longrightarrow Cu(s)$	+0.34
$SO_4^{2-} + 4H^+ + 2e^- \longrightarrow SO_2(g) + 2H_2O$	+0.17
$Sn^{4+} + 2e^- \longrightarrow Sn^{2+}$	+0.15
$2H^+ + 2e^- \longrightarrow H_2(g)$	0.00
$Pb^{2+} + 2e^- \longrightarrow Pb(s)$	−0.13
$Sn^{2+} + 2e^- \longrightarrow Sn(s)$	−0.14
$Ni^{2+} + 2e^- \longrightarrow Ni(s)$	−0.25
$Co^{2+} + 2e^- \longrightarrow Co(s)$	−0.28
$2H^+(10^{-7}M) + 2e^- \longrightarrow H_2(g)$	−0.41
$Fe^{2+} + 2e^- \longrightarrow Fe(s)$	−0.44
$Cr^{3+} + 3e^- \longrightarrow Cr(s)$	−0.74
$Zn^{2+} + 2e^- \longrightarrow Zn(s)$	−0.76
$2H_2O + 2e^- \longrightarrow 2OH^- + H_2(g)$	−0.83
$Mn^{2+} + 2e^- \longrightarrow Mn(s)$	−1.18
$Al^{3+} + 3e^- \longrightarrow Al(s)$	−1.66
$Mg^{2+} + 2e^- \longrightarrow Mg(s)$	−2.37
$Na^+ + e^- \longrightarrow Na(s)$	−2.71
$Ca^{2+} + 2e^- \longrightarrow Ca(s)$	−2.87
$Sr^{2+} + 2e^- \longrightarrow Sr(s)$	−2.89
$Ba^{2+} + 2e^- \longrightarrow Ba(s)$	−2.90
$Cs^+ + e^- \longrightarrow Cs(s)$	−2.92
$K^+ + e^- \longrightarrow K(s)$	−2.92
$Rb^+ + e^- \longrightarrow Rb(s)$	−2.93
$Li^+ + e^- \longrightarrow Li(s)$	−3.00

12. Given the reaction: _Fe^{3+} + _Sn^{2+} → _Fe^{2+} + _Sn^{4+}.
    When the reaction is completely balanced using SMALLEST whole numbers, the coefficient of Fe^+ will be
    A. 1   B. 2   C. 3   D. 4

13. In the reaction $Zn + Cu^{2+} → Zn^{2+} + Cu$, the Cu^{2+} ions
    A. gain electrons   B. lose electrons
    C. gain protons   D. lose protons

14. In the reaction $2K + Cl_2 → 2KCl$, the species oxidized is
    A. Cl_2 B. Cl^- C. K   D. K^+

15. Indicate which of the following compounds will undergo a substitution reaction with chlorine.
    A. CH_4 B. C_2H_4 C. C_3H_6 D. C_4H_8

16. Which formula represents a hydrocarbon with a double covalent bond?
    A. CH_3Cl B. C_2H_3Cl C. C_2H_2 D. C_2H_4

17. Which compound is an isomer of 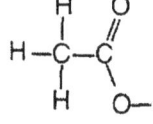 ?

    A. [structure]   B. [structure]
    C. [structure]   D. [structure]

18. The TOTAL number of covalent bonds in a molecule of methane is
    A. one   B. two   C. three   D. four

19. As an S^{2-} ion is oxidized to an S^0 atom, the number of protons in its nucleus
    A. decreases
    B. increases
    C. remains the same
    D. one cannot tell from the information given

20. As 1 gram of H₂O(g) changes to 1 gram of H₂O(ℓ), the entropy of the system

    A. decreases
    B. increases
    C. remains the same
    D. one cannot tell from the information given

20.____

21. The volume of a sample of hydrogen gas at STP is 1.00 liter. As the temperature decreases, pressure remaining constant, the volume of the sample

    A. decreases
    B. increases
    C. remains the same
    D. *one cannot tell* from the information given

21.____

Questions 22-23.

DIRECTIONS: Questions 22 and 23 are to be answered on the basis of the graph below. The graph shows the relationship between temperature and time as heat is added to one mole of a substance at a rate of 100 calories per minute. The substance is in the solid phase at Time = 0 minutes.

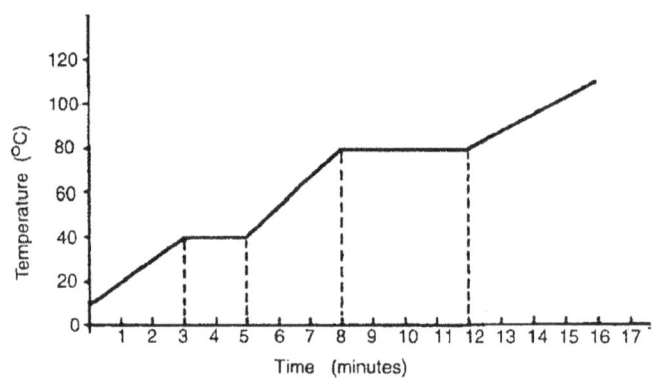

22. The temperature at which the substance begins to boil is _____ °C.

    A. 10   B. 40   C. 80   D. 110

22.____

23. From the time that the solid begins to melt, the MINIMUM number of calories required to completely melt the one mole sample is

    A. 100   B. 200   C. 400   D. 600

23.____

24. The pressure on 200. milliliters of a gas at constant temperature is changed from 380. torr to 760. torr. The NEW volume of the gas is _____ ml.

    A. 100.   B. 200.   C. 400.   D. 800.

24.____

25. The temperature of a substance changes from -173° C to 0° C. This change represents _____ Kelvin degrees.

    A. 100.   B. 173   C. 273   D. 446

25.____

26. How many kilocalories of heat are needed to raise the temperature of 500. grams of water from 10.0° C to 30.0° C? _____ kcal.

    A. 10.0 B. 25.0 C. 50.0 D. 40.0

27. Isotopes of the same element must have the same

    A. atomic number B. mass number
    C. number of nucleons D. number of neutrons

28. Which pair has identical electron configurations?

    A. S^{2-} and Cl^- B. S^0 and Ar^0
    C. K^0 and Na^+ D. Cl^- and K^0

29. The energy level with a principal quantum number (n) of 2 contains a total of _____ sub-levels.

    A. eight B. two C. three D. four

30. What is the TOTAL mass of a 10. gram sample of ^{42}K that will remain unchanged after 12.4 hours? _____ grams.

    A. 2.5 B. 5.0 C. 7.5 D. 10.

31. Which particle has a mass that is APPROXIMATELY 1/1,836 of the mass of a proton? A(n)

    A. gamma ray B. neutron
    C. alpha particle D. electron

32. The P-Cl bond in a molecule of PCl_3 is

    A. nonpolar covalent B. polar covalent
    C. coordinate covalent D. electrovalent

33. The formula H_2 represents one

    A. gram B. liter C. atom D. molecule

34. The predominate type of attraction between molecules of HF in the liquid state is _____ bonding.

    A. hydrogen B. electrovalent
    C. ionic D. covalent

35. Which substance contains positive ions immersed in a sea of mobile electrons?

    A. $O_2(s)$ B. $SiO_2(s)$ C. $Cu(s)$ D. $CuO(s)$

36. The radioactive isotope I-131 is used in

    A. geologic dating
    B. medical diagnosis
    C. controlling fission reactions
    D. controlling speeds of neutrons

37. Which measurement contains a total of three significant figures? 37.____
    _____ grams.
    A. 0.01 B. 0.010 C. 0.0100 D. 0.01000

38. The diagram at the right represents a portion of a triple beam balance. If the beams are in balance, with the riders in the position shown, what is the TOTAL mass in grams of the object being massed? 38.____
    A. 460.62
    B. 466.20
    C. 466.62
    D. 460.20

39. According to an accepted chemistry reference, the heat of vaporization of water is 540. calories per gram. A student determined in the laboratory that the heat of vaporization of water was 620. calories per gram. 39.____
    The student's results had a percent error of
    A. 12.9 B. 14.8 C. 80.0 D. 87.1

40. The data below were obtained by a student in order to determine the percent of water in a hydrate: 40.____
    Mass of the Hydrate   5.0 g
    Mass of the Anhydrous Compound   3.2 g
    The hydrate contains _____ percent water.
    A. 64 B. 56 C. 36 D. 22

KEY (CORRECT ANSWERS)

1. D	11. C	21. A	31. D
2. C	12. B	22. C	32. B
3. D	13. A	23. B	33. D
4. D	14. C	24. A	34. A
5. C	15. A	25. B	35. C
6. A	16. D	26. A	36. B
7. C	17. C	27. A	37. C
8. B	18. D	28. A	38. B
9. B	19. C	29. B	39. B
10. D	20. A	30. B	40. C

TEST 3

DIRECTIONS: Each question or incomplete statement is followed by several suggested answers or completions. Select the one that BEST answers the question or completes the statement. *PRINT THE LETTER OF THE CORRECT ANSWER IN THE SPACE AT THE RIGHT.*

1. Element A and element B chemically combine to form substance C. Substance C MUST be a(n) 1.____

    A. solution   B. compound   C. element   D. mixture

2. Which gas has properties that are MOST similar to those of an ideal gas? 2.____

    A. O_2 B. H_2 C. NH_3 D. HCl

3. When the vapor pressure of a liquid equals the pressure on its surface, the liquid will 3.____

    A. sublime   B. solidify   C. boil   D. melt

4. The energy required to change a unit mass of a solid to a liquid at constant temperature is called its heat of 4.____

    A. formation   B. vaporization
    C. combustion   D. fusion

5. A 1 liter flask of $CO_2(g)$ and a 1 liter flask of $H_2(g)$ are both at STP. The ratio of the number of molecules of $CO_2(g)$ to the number of molecules of $H_2(g)$ in the flasks is 5.____

    A. 1:1   B. 2:3   C. 3:2   D. 1:3

6. The number of protons in the nucleus of $^{32}_{15}P$ is 6.____

    A. 15   B. 17   C. 32   D. 47

7. Atomic mass is measured in atomic mass units (amu) that are based on an atom of_____ equal to_____ amu. 7.____

    A. ^{16}O; 16.000   B. ^{32}S; 32.000
    C. ^{12}C; 12.000   D. ^{14}N; 14.000

8. According to the chart at the right, which change requires the LEAST amount of energy?
   A. Li⁰(g) → Li⁺(g) + e⁻
   B. Rb⁰(g) → Rb⁺(g) + e⁻
   C. K⁰(g) → K⁺(g) + e⁻
   D. Na⁰(g) → Na⁺(g) + e⁻

9. An atom has the electron configuration $1s^2 2s^2 2p^6 3s^2 3p^5$. The electron dot symbol for this element is

   A. X: B. Ẋ: C. ·Ẋ: D. :Ẍ:

10. Which sublevel has a total of five orbitals?
    A. s   B. f   C. p   D. d

11. The MAXIMUM number of electrons that may be found in the third principal energy level is
    A. 8   B. 2   C. 18   D. 32

12. According to the chart at the right, a product of the radioactive decay of $^{226}_{88}$ is
    A. $^4_2$He
    B. $^{226}_{89}$U
    C. $^{\ \ 0}_{-1}$e
    D. $^{230}_{90}$U

13. In the balanced equation $2Na + 2H_2O \rightarrow H_2 + 2X$, the compound represented by X is
    A. Na_2O B. Na_2O_2 C. $NaOH$ D. NaH

14. Indicate which of the following elements has the LOWEST normal boiling point
    A. Ne   B. He   C. Ar   D. Kr

15. The CORRECT formula for sodium oxide is
    A. SO_2 B. S_2O C. NaO_2 D. Na_2O

16. The attraction which exists between carbon dioxide molecules in solid carbon dioxide is due to

    A. van der Waals forces
    B. molecule-ion forces
    C. ionic bonds
    D. hydrogen bonds

17. Given the reaction:
    The bond formed between the NH_3 and the H^+ is

    A. electrovalent
    B. ionic
    C. metallic
    D. coordinate covalent

    $$H \cdot \overset{x \; \cdot \cdot \; x}{\underset{\underset{H}{x \cdot}}{N}} \cdot H + H^+ \rightarrow \left[H \cdot \overset{x \; \cdot \cdot \; x}{\underset{\underset{H}{x \cdot}}{N}} \cdot H \right]^+$$

18. Which of the following compounds has the LEAST ionic character?

    A. KI   B. NO   C. HCl   D. MgS

19. What type of bond is present in diamonds?

    A. Covalent
    B. Ionic
    C. Electrovalent
    D. Metallic

20. All the elements in Period 3 have the same number of

    A. occupied sublevels
    B. principal energy levels
    C. electrons
    D. protons

21. More than two-thirds of the elements are classified as

    A. nonmetals
    B. metals
    C. metalloids
    D. noble gases

22. Which element in Group VA has the GREATEST metallic character?

    A. N   B. P   C. Sb   D. Bi

23. The element in Period 3 that has the LOWEST first ionization energy is a(n)

    A. alkali metal
    B. alkaline earth metal
    C. halogen
    D. noble gas

24. When fluorine reacts with a Group IA metal, it becomes an ion with a charge of

    A. 1^- B. 2^- C. 1^+ D. 2^+

25. The alkaline earth metals are in Group

    A. IA   B. IB   C. IIA   D. IIB

26. Which of the following metals has the LOWEST melting point?

    A. Copper   B. Mercury   C. Silver   D. Iron

27. A compound contains 0.5 mole of sodium, 0.5 mole of nitrogen, and 1.0 mole of hydrogen.
    The empirical formula of the compound is

    A. NaNH   B. Na_2NH C. $NaNH_2$ D. $Na(NH)_2$

28. The percent by mass of oxygen in CO is APPROXIMATELY _____ percent.   28._____

    A. 73   B. 57   C. 43   D. 17

29. The mass in grams of 1.00 mole of $CaSO_4 \cdot 2H_2O$ is _____ grams.   29._____

    A. 172   B. 154   C. 136   D. 118

30. The total number of sodium atoms in 46.0 grams of sodium is _____ $\times 10^{23}$.   30._____

    A. 3.01   B. 6.02   C. 12.0   D. 24.0

31. Given the reaction: 31._____
    $4NH_3(g) + 5O_2(g) \rightarrow 4NO(g) + 6H_2O(g)$.
    At STP, what is the TOTAL volume of $O_2(g)$ required to produce 80.0 liters of NO(g)?
    _____ ℓ.

    A. 5.00   B. 20.0   C. 80.0   D. 100.

32. What is the TOTAL number of grams of solute in 500. milliliters of 1 M CH_3COOH (formula mass = 60.)?   32._____
    _____ grams.

    A. 30.   B. 60.   C. 90.   D. 120

33. At 10° C, 23 grams of a substance saturates 100 grams of water.   33._____
    The substance could be

    A. $NaNO_3$ B. KNO_3 C. NH_4Cl D. KCl

34. The addition of a catalyst to a reaction will cause a change in the   34._____

    A. potential energy of the reactants
    B. potential energy of the products
    C. heat of reaction
    D. activation energy

35. Given the reaction at equilibrium: 35._____
    $A(g) + B(g) \rightleftharpoons C(g) + D(g)$.
    At constant temperature and pressure, an increase in the concentration of A(g) will cause a(n) _____ in the concentration of _____ .

    A. increase; B(g)   B. decrease; B(g)
    C. decrease; C(g)   D. decrease; D(g)

KEY (CORRECT ANSWERS)

1.	B	16.	A
2.	B	17.	D
3.	C	18.	B
4.	D	19.	A
5.	A	20.	B
6.	A	21.	A
7.	C	22.	D
8.	B	23.	A
9.	D	24.	A
10.	D	25.	C
11.	C	26.	B
12.	A	27.	C
13.	C	28.	B
14.	B	29.	A
15.	D	30.	C

31. D
32. A
33. C
34. D
35. B

CHEMICAL NOTES AND RESOURCES

TABLE OF CONTENTS

	Page
GLOSSARY OF CHEMICAL TERMS	
Absolute temperature ... Alkali	1
Alkylation ... Aniline	2
Anion ... Base	3
Base-formers ... Carat	4
Carbogen ... Chemical Equilibrium	5
Chemical Symbol ... Concentrated	6
Condensation ... DDT	7
Decomposition Reactions ... Drier	8
Dross ... Emulsifier	9
Emulsion ... Exposure	10
Exothermic ... Formula Weight	11
Fourdrinier Machine ... Heat of Formation	12
Heat of Neutralization ... Inert Substance	13
Inhibitor ... Kindling Temperature	14
Kinetic Energy ... Mass Action (Law Of)	15
Matte ... Monoclinic	16
Monomer ... Nitrogen Cycle	17
Nitrogen Fixation ... Oxidation	18
Oxygen-Carbon Dioxide Cycle ... Pickling	19
Pigment ... Proteins	20
Proton ... Resin	21
Rhombic ... Solder	22
Solubility Product Constant ... Supersaturated	23
Surface-Active Agent ... Thermoplastic Type of Plastics	24
Thermosetting Type of Plastics ... Vapor Tension	25
Vat Dyes ... Wetting Agents	26
X-Rays ... Zirconium	27
CHEMICAL LAWS	
Avogadro's Hypothesis ... Law of Conservation of Energy	27
Law of Conservation of Matter (Mass) ... Periodic Law (Moseley's)	28
GLOSSARY OF COMMON SUBSTANCES	
Alum ... Carbonic Acid Gas	29
Caustic potash ... Hypo	30
Kaolin ... Quicksilver	31
Rochelle Salt ... Zinc White	32
CHEMICAL ELEMENTS AND SYMBOLS	
Actinium ... Lanthanum	33
Lead ... Tungsten	34
Uranium ... Zirconium	35
PERIODIC TABLE OF THE ELEMENTS	36

CHEMICAL NOTES AND RESOURCES
GLOSSARY OF CHEMICAL TERMS
A

ABSOLUTE TEMPERATURE

Temperature on the Absolute scale whose zero is -273Centigrade.

ABSORPTION

A soaking up throughout the mass.

ACCELERATOR

Chemical additive which hastens or increases the speed of a chemical reaction. Used, for example, to improve the vulcanization of natural and synthetic rubber and latex compounds.

ACID

A water soluble chemical compound containing hydrogen replaceable by metals or basic radicals. An acid reacts with an alkali to form a salt and water. Example of acid: sulfuric acid, commonly used in storage batteries and many other applications.

ACID ANHYDRIDE

An oxide of a nonmetal capable of uniting with water to form an acid.

ACID-FORMERS

A property usually characteristic of those elements called nonmetals.

ACID SALT

A salt containing replaceable hydrogen.

ACID SULFITE

A salt formed by the union of a metal with the HSO ion.

ACRILAN

One of the synthetic fibers.

ADSORPTION

A condensation on the surface of a material.

ADSORPTION, ACTIVATED

That form of adsorption in which sufficient heat energy must be supplied before the film forms. This process is probably chemical in nature.

AERATED

Given an opportunity to dissolve or combine with air or some other gas.

AEROSOLS

Fog-like sprays.

AIR-SLAKED LIME

A mixture of calcium hydroxide and calcium carbonate formed by exploding calcium hydroxide to the air.

ALCOHOL

A compound containing an organic radical and one or more OH groups.

ALDEHYDE

An organic compound containing the CHO group.

ALIPHATIC

(Derived from Greek word for fat.) Pertaining to an open chain carbon compound. Usually applied to petroleum products derived from a paraffin base and having a straight or branched chain, saturated or unsaturated, molecular structure as distinguished from aromatic hydrocarbons which are built up from one or more benzene rings. Gasoline is a typical aliphatic hydrocarbon.

ALKALI

A compound that has the power to neutralize an acid and form a salt. Example: sodium hydroxide, referred to as caustic soda or lye. Used in soap manufacture and many other applications.

ALKYLATION
A process for rearranging straight chain hydrocarbons.

ALLOTROPISM
The ability of some elements to exist in more than one form.

ALLOY
A material composed of two or more metals.

ALPHA PARTICLES
Positively charged helium nuclei.

ALUM
The double sulfate of a monovalent and trivalent metal, containing a definite amount of water of hydration ($KAl(SO_4)_2 \cdot 12 H_2O$).

ALUMINOTHERMY
A thermite or similar reaction.

AMALGAM
An alloy of mercury with one or more other metals.

AMALGAMATION PROCESS
A process of extracting gold from ore by amalgamating the gold with mercury.

AMINO ACIDS
The "building blocks" from which the giant protein molecules are constructed.

AMMONIA (NH_3)
Nitrogen and hydrogen compound, a colorless gas liquefied by compression. Dissolves in water to form aqueous ammonia. Synthetic ammonia is main source of nitrogen for fertilizer and chemical production.

AMMONIUM ION. NH_4^+
This is a cation produced by the ionization of an ammonium salt.

AMMONIUM RADICAL, NH_4
An ammonium radical is a group of atoms which plays the role of a metal in certain salts (e.g., NH_4Cl).

AMORPHOUS
This is a substance without crystalline structure. The atoms or molecules are not arranged in a definite pattern.

AMPERE
An Ampere is one coulomb of electricity per second. That current which deposits .00lll8g. silver per second.

AMPHOTERIC
Referring to a compound which may ionize as a base in the presence of a strong acid, and as an acid in the presence of a strong base.

ANGSTROM UNIT (A)
= 10^{-8} cm.

ANHYDRIDE
A compound, usually an oxide of a metal or a nonmetal, capable of uniting with water to form a base or an acid.

ANHYDROUS
Material from which the water has been removed.

ANILINE ($C_6H_5NH_2$)
One of the most important of organics derived from coal. Building block for many dyes and drugs.

ANION
An anion is a negatively charged ion. It is attracted to the anode (+electrode) during electrolysis.

ANODE
The positive terminal of an electric cell.

ANTIBIOTIC
A substance either synethesized chemically or produced by a microorganism, usually a mold or fungus, which kills other organisms, or retards, or completely represses their growth, normally without harm to higher orders of life. Antibiotics retain highly germicidial properties even in dilute concentrations.

ANTICHLOR
A chemical which acts against chlorine, such as a solution of sodium thiosulfate.

ANTIOXIDANT
A compound added to rubber and other substances to prevent deterioration by oxidation.

AQUA AMMONIA
A solution of ammonia gas in water.

AQUA REGIA
A mixture of concentrated nitric and hydrochloric acids capable of dissolving gold.

ARC-TYPE FURNACE
One that has an electric arc jumping the gap between carbon electrodes.

AROMATIC
Applied to group of hydrocarbons derived from or characterized by presence of the benzene nucleus (molecular ring structure). Sometimes called "cyclic solvents" or "cyclic hydrocarbons."

ASSOCIATION
A joining together of small molecules to form larger molecules.

ATOM
A chemical unit, the smallest part of an element which remains unchanged during any chemical reaction yet may undergo physical changes to other atoms as in atomic fission. Believed to be made up of a complex system whose electrically charged components are in rapid orbital motion.

ATOMIC NUMBER
A number identifying an element, equal to the number of protons in its atoms.

ATOMIC WEIGHT
The average relative weight of the atoms of an element compared with those of oxygen taken as a standard and given a value of 16.

B

BACITRACIN
One of the newer antibiotics.

BAKING SODA
The compound sodium hydrogen carbonate used in baking powders and for other purposes

BAROMETER
An apparatus for measuring atmospheric pressure.

BASE
A compound containing the hydroxyl group which, when dissolved in water, forms no negative ions but hydroxyl ions.

BASE-FORMERS
A property usually characteristic of metals.
BASIC ANHYDRIDE
An oxide of a metal capable of reacting with water to form a base. **BASIC SALT**
A salt containing replaceable oxygen or hydroxyl groups.
BENZENE (C_6H_6)
Major organic intermediate derived from coal or petroleum. Ring-shaped (cyclic) molecular structure makes it broadly useful as chemical building block.
BESSEMER CONVERTER
An egg-shaped converter which changes pig iron into steel by burning out impurities with an air blast.
BETA PARTICLES
Negatively charged particles, actually electrons, emitted by some radioactive materials.
BETATRON
One of the types of "atom-smashing" machines for bombarding atomic nuclei.
BINARY
Binary compounds are made up of only two elements.
BISQUE
A porous porcelain product that has been fired only once.
BLOCK TIN
Solid tin, as distinguished from tin-plate.
BOILING POINT
The temperature at which the vapor pressure of a liquid reaches atmospheric pressure.
BOTTLED GAS
Propane, butane, or a mixture of both, stored under pressure in steel cylinders and used as a fuel.
BREEDER REACTOR
A reactor which uses some fissionable material to produce energy and a greater quantity of fissionable material.
BRITISH THERMAL UNIT (B.T.U.)
The quantity of heat necessary to raise the temperature of one pound of water one degree Fahrenheit.
BROWNIAN MOVEMENT
The zigzag movement of colloidal particles through the medium in which they are suspended.
BUFFER
A suitable mixture of salt and acid (or salt and base) that regulates or stabilizes the pH of a solution.

<u>C</u>

CALCINE
A partially refined copper ore.
CALORIE
A unit for measuring heat, equal to the amount of heat necessary to raise one gram of water one degree Centigrade.
CALORIMETER
A vessel used in measuring the heat evolved in chemical or physical changes.
CARAT
A unit of weight used for gems, equal to 200 milligrams.

CARBOGEN

A mixture of oxygen with 5% to 10% of carbon dioxide.

CARBOHYDRATES

Compounds containing carbon, hydrogen, and oxygen, usually with the hydrogen and oxygen present in the ratio of two to one.

CARBONATED BEVERAGES

Beverages which contain dissolved carbon dioxide.

CARBOXYL

The COOH group in organic compounds as found in organic acids.

CARBURETOR

The second or middle chamber of a water gas apparatus in which the gas is often enriched by spraying in oil or by adding propane.

CATALYST

A substance which through acceleration or retardation changes the spread of a chemical reaction and effects a definite change in composition and/or properties of the end product. In paint manufacture, catalysts generally become part of the final product. In most uses, however, they do not.

CATHODE

The negative electrode or terminal.

CATION

(1) A positively charged ion. (2) The ion attracted to the cathode in electrolysis.

CAUSTIC

A substance that attacks skin, hair, or such materials by chemical action.

CELLULOSE ($C_5H_{10}O_{5n}$)

A carbohydrate which makes up the structural material of vegetable tissues and fibers. Purest forms: chemical cotton and chemical pulp. Basis of rayon, acetate and cellophane.

CEMENT

A mixture made from limestone and clay which, after mixing with water, sets to a hard mass.

CEMENTATION

A process formerly used for making steel by heating wrought iron in red-hot charcoal for a long period of time.

CENTIGRADE TEMPERATURE

Temperature on the Centigrade scale which has $0°$ for the freezing point of water and $100°$ for the boiling point at a pressure of 760 mm.

CHAIN REACTION

A reaction in which the material or energy which starts the reaction is also a product.

CHAMBER PROCESS

A process for making sulfuric acid in large lead chambers, using oxides of nitrogen to promote the necessary reaction.

CHECKERWORK

Loosely-stacked firebricks in a chamber providing a circuitous passage for fuel gas or air.

CHEMICAL CHANGE

A change which produces a new substance with new properties.

CHEMICAL EQUATION

A qualitative and quantitative expression of a chemical change.

CHEMICAL EQUILIBRIUM

A reaction in which the products unite to form the original reactants at the same speed at which the reactants are forming the product.

CHEMICAL SYMBOL
Either one or two letters used as an abbreviation for an element.
CHEMOTHERAPY
Use of chemicals of particular molecular structure in the treatment of specific disorders on the assumption that known structures exhibit an affinity for certain parts of cells of affected tissues and thereby eliminate the causative factors.
CHEMURGY
That branch of applied chemistry devoted to industrial utilization of organic raw materials, especially farm products, as in the use of pine tree cellulose for rayon and paper, and soy bean oil for paints and varnishes.
CHLORINATION
Adding chlorine to a material.
CHLOROMYCETIN
One of the antibiotics.
CHLOROPHYLL
Green coloring matter in leaves which acts as a catalyst for photosynthesis.
CHLORTETRACYCLINE
One of the antibiotics, formerly called aureomycin.
CHROMOPHORS
Certain groups whose presence results in compounds having a color.
COAL GAS
A fuel gas obtained by the destructive distillation of soft coal.
COKE OVEN CHEMICALS
Those organic compounds derived from bituminous coal in the production of metallurgical coke. This major chemical raw materials source provides a base for thousands of chemicals.
COLLOID
A particle in an extremely fine state of subdivision.
COMBINATION REACTIONS
Those in which one element reacts with another to form a compound.
COMBINING WEIGHT
The number of grams of an element that will combine with or replace 8 grams of oxygen or its equivalent.
COMBUSTION
Oxidation accompanied by noticeable light and heat.
COMMON-ION EFFECT
The addition of a substance containing an ion common to that already present, causing the reaction to be driven in a definite direction.
COMPONENT
One of a minimum number of substances necessary to give the composition of a system.
COMPOST
A product of the decay of plant material.
COMPOUND
A substance composed of two or more elements joined according to the laws of chemical combination. Each compound has its own characteristic properties different from those of its elements.
CONCENTRATED
Containing much of a material, the opposite of dilute.

CONDENSATION
(1) Changing a material such as vapor to a liquid;
(2) Increasing the size of very small particles up to colloidal size;
(3) A reaction between raw materials in the making of a plastic that results in the formation of water as one of the products.

CONTACT PROCESS
A process for making sulfuric acid in which the sulfur dioxide and oxygen come in contact with a catalyst.

COORDINATE VALENCE
A kind of chemical bonding somewhat similar to co-valence, but in which there is only one donor atom.

CORTISONE
A compound of animal origin, used particularly for athritis.

COSMIC RAYS
These are rays which come to the earth from somewhere in space, perhaps beyond the solar system.

COTTRELL PRECIPITATOR
A device for precipitating colloidal dust with electricity of high voltage.

COUNTERCURRENTS
Two currents proceeding in opposite directions through an apparatus.

COVALENCE
A kind of chemical bonding in which two atoms share an electron with each other. C.P.
Abbreviation for "chemically pure."

CRACKING
Breaking large or complex molecules into simpler, smaller molecules.

CRITICAL PRESSURE
The pressure of a system at its critical temperature.

CRITICAL SIZE
The smallest amount of fissionable material which can sustain a chain reaction.

CRITICAL TEMPERATURE
The highest temperature at which a liquid and its vapor can co-exist as separate phases.

CRYSTALLOID
A term applied to materials that crystallize easily and pass through a semi-permeable membrane without difficulty.

CRYSTALS
Solids separated from solutions having a definite shape or structure.

GULLET
Broken glass that is re-melted with raw materials in a new batch of glass.

CUPELLATION
A process of separating gold and silver from a base metal such as lead. An oxidizing flame converts the lead to the oxide(PbO), which is removed by a stream of air or is absorbed in the porous bottom of the reverberatory furnace. The silver-gold residue remains unchanged.

CYCLOTRON
One of the atom-smashing machines used to bombard the nuclei of atoms.

D

DACRON
One of the synthetic fibers.

DDT
Letters stand for dichloro-diphenyl-trichloroethane, an insecticide.

DECOMPOSITION REACTIONS
Those in which a compound is decomposed by heat, light, or electricity into simpler compounds.

DECREPITATION
The expulsion of water with a crackling sound when some crystals are heated.

DEHYDRATION
The removal of water from a substance.

DELIQUESCENCE
The process of picking up enough water to become wet.

DENSITY
Mass per unit volume, e.g., grams per cubic centimeter.

DESTRUCTIVE DISTILLATION
The process of heating wood, coal, bones, etc., in a closed vessel, resulting in a breaking down to simpler materials.

DETERGENT
An agent that removes dirt.

DEUTERIUM
An isotope of hydrogen of mass 2.

DEUTERON
The nucleus of the deuterium atom.

DEVELOPING
A process in photography in which the reduction of the silver compound, started by light, is promoted by the action of an alkaline, organic, reducing agent.

DIALYSIS
A process in which a semi-permeable membrane is used to separate colloidal particles from substances in true solution.

DIBASIC
A term applied to acids that have two replaceable hydrogen atoms.

DIESELENE
A petroleum fuel for Diesel engines.

DIFFUSION
The intermingling of liquids and gases.

DILUENT
A diluting agent, such as water in a solution, or turpentine in paint.

DIPOLES
Molecules with unbalanced charges so that one end may be positive and the other end negative.

DISINFECTANTS
Agents that kill, not merely arrest, the growth of bacteria.

DISSOCIATION
The separation of the ions of an electrovalent compound by the action of a solvent.

DISTILLATION
The process of evaporation followed by condensation of the vapors in a separate vessel.

DOUBLE REPLACEMENT REACTIONS
Those in which two compounds exchange ions to produce two new compounds.

DOUBLE SALT
A salt in which two metal atoms are combined with one acid radical or one metal is combined with two acid radicals, e.g., $KAl(SO_4)_2 \cdot 12 H_2O$.

DRIER
Catalysts, such as oxides of lead and manganese, added to paint to promote the drying of the paint.

DROSS

A powdery scum that floats on top of melted metal.

DUCTILITY

That property of a substance which permits its being drawn into wire.

DUTCH PROCESS

A process for making white lead using lead buckles, acetic acid, and decomposing tanbark or manure.

DYNAMITE

An explosive made by absorbing nitroglycerin in wood flour mixed with sodium nitrate.

DYNE

A unit of force. The force necessary to give a mass of one gram an acceleration of one centimeter per second per second.

DYNEL

One of the synthetic fibers.

EFFERVESCENCE

The process of giving off bubbles of gas from a liquid.

EFFLORESCENCE

The property of giving off water vapor to the air.

ELASTOMER

Actually, it is any flexible or elastic material but, in a more limited sense, a synthetic rubber or soft or rubbery plastic with some degree of elasticity at room temperature.

ELECTRIC POTENTIAL

Electrical pressure or voltage between terminals.

ELECTRODE

A terminal of an electric circuit where the current either enters or leaves.

ELECTROLYTE

A compound whose water solution conducts an electric current.

ELECTRON

A unit particle of negative electricity. Its mass is 1/1845 of the hydrogen atom.

ELECTRON VOLT

That quantity of energy which is equal to the kinetic energy of an electron accelerated by a potential difference of 1 volt.

ELECTRONEGATIVE ELEMENT

An element which has a tendency to take up electrons.

ELECTROPLATING

Deposition of metals on a surface by means of an electric current.

ELECTROTYPES

Copper plates from which the pages of a book are printed.

ELECTROVALENCE

Type of chemical bonding where one or more electrons are transferred from one atom to another.

ELEMENT

Solid, liquid or gaseous matter consisting of atoms of one type which cannot be further decomposed by chemical means. The atoms of an element may differ physically but do not differ chemically. Example: chlorine. Known elements: 101.

EMULSIFIER, EMULSIFYING AGENT

A chemical that mixes and disperses dissimilar materials to produce an emulsion and keep it stable. Casein, for example is a natural emulsi-fier in milk, keeping butter fat droplets emulsified.

EMULSION
Suspension of insoluble fine particles or globules of a liquid in another liquid.

ENDOTHERMIC
Pertaining to a reaction which absorbs heat.

ENERGY
The capacity for doing work.

ENZYME
An organic secretion that acts as a catalyst.

EQUATION
An expression which shows, by the use of symbols and formulas, the changes in arrangement of the atoms which occur during a chemical reaction.

EQUILIBRIUM
A reaction in which the products unite to form the original reactants at the same speed at which the reactants are forming the products.

EQUILIBRIUM (CHEMICAL)
A state in which a chemical reaction and the reverse reaction are taking place at the same rate. The concentrations (at equilibrium) of all substances remain constant.

EQUILIBRIUM CONSTANT
An equilibrium constant (K) is the ratio (number) obtained by dividing the product of the active concentrations of the substances produced in a reaction by the product of the active concentrations of the reactants, after equilibrium has been reached.

ERG
The work done by a force of one dyne per centimeter.

ESTER
A compound formed by the reaction between an acid and an alcohol.

ESTERIFICATION
The process of preparing esters by adding acid to an alcohol

ETHANE (C_2H_6)
A saturated hydrocarbon (maximum number of hydrogen atoms attached to each carbon) derived from petroleum or natural gas, important for organic synthesis. Ethylene derived from it.

ETHANOL (ETHYL ALCOHOL) (C_2H_5OH)
Organic compound derived through either a fermentation process or via synthesis from petroleum or natural gas. Wide use as solvent and for chemical synthesis.

ETHYLENE (C_2H_4)
Gaseous organic compound prepared in cracking of petroleum or by passing natural gas through heated tube. Removal of two hydrogen atoms from ethane component of petroleum or natural gas makes this unsaturated hydrocarbon of wide use as petrochemical base for numerous chemical reactions, notably plastic material manufacture.

ETHYLENE GLYCOL
Colorless liquid which is a useful humectant since it absorbs approximately twice its weight of water at room temperature and 100% humidity. A major use: anti-freeze. Among many other uses -chemical synthesis, as in producing alkyd resins.

EUTECTIC
A mixture of two or more substances with the lowest melting point.

EXPLOSIVE RANGE
A pair of percentages below or above which the gas will not form an explosive mixture with air.

EXPOSURE
In photography, the act of admitting light to the film or plate.

EXOTHERMIC
Pertaining to a reaction which liberates heat.
EXTRUDED
Forced through a die by pressure.

F

FAHRENHEIT TEMPERATURE
Temperature on the Fahrenheit scale with 32° as the freezing point of water and 212° as the boiling point at a pressure of 760 mm.
FAMILY OF ELEMENTS
A group of elements with more or less similar properties.
FATS
Glyceryl esters of certain organic acids.
FELDSPARS
Complex silicates, usually aluminum silicate with either sodium or potassium silicate.
FERMENTATION
A chemical reaction caused by living organisms or enzymes.
FERTILIZER
Plant food, or material, that contains compounds of the elements needed by plants for growth.
FILTRATION
The process of removing suspended material from a liquid by allowing the liquid to pass through a material such as filter paper or a layer of sand.
FISSION
The disintegration of an atom into two nyclei with nearly equal mass.
FIXATION OF NITROGEN
A process in which atmospheric nitrogen is converted into useful compounds.
FIXING
In photography the operation of removing unchanged silver salts after the picture has been developed, thereby fixing the image on the film or plate.
FLOTATION (ORE)
A process in which crushed ore is agitated in water containing a fro-ther (pine oil) and a collector (potassium ethyl xanthate). The valuable mineral particles are attached to the froth and rise to the surface from which they are removed.
FLOTATION REAGENT
Chemical used in flotation separation of minerals. Added to pulverized mixture of solids, water and oil, causes preferential oil-wetting of certain solid particles, making possible the flotation and separation of un-wet particles.
FLUIDITY
The reciprocal of viscosity.
FLUORESCENT
Giving off light after exposure to sunlight.
FLOWERS OF SULFUR
Finely-divided sulfur formed by the condensation of sulfur vapors on a cool surface.
FLUX
A material added to unite with impurities to form an easily melted product.
FORMULA
A collection of chemical symbols indicating what elements and how many atoms of each are present in a compound.
FORMULA WEIGHT
The sum of the weights of the atoms in a formula.

FOURDRINIER MACHINE
A machine that converts a suspension of taper fibers into sheets.

FRACTIONAL CRYSTALLIZATION
Separation of two dissolved solids by evaporating until the less soluble solid separates while the more soluble solid remains in solution.

FRACTIONATION
The process of separating a mixture by careful evaporation, depending upon the materials having different boiling points.

FROTH-FLOTATION
A process for concentrating powdered ore by causing the good ore to cling to bubbles which float above liquid, while the worthless rocky material sinks to the bottom of the container.

FUNGICIDE
Any one of a group of chemicals used to prevent or inhibit the growth of fungi or bacteria. Among these are: plant fungicides, wood preservatives, mildew or mold preventives and disinfectants.

<u>G</u>

GALVANIZE
To coat iron or steel with zinc.

GAMMA RAYS
High energy X-rays emitted from a radioactive material.

GANGUE
Worthless material, rock or earth, present in an ore.

GEIGER COUNTER
A device used to detect the presence of radiation from radioactive material.

GEL
A jelly-like solid.

GENERATOR
In chemistry, the vessel in which a reaction occurs between chemicals.

GERMAN SILVER
An alloy containing copper, nickel, and zinc.

GRAM
Basic unit of weight in the metric system, equal to 1/1000 of the standard kilogram.

GRAM-EQUIVALENT WEIGHT
The weight of an element that will combine with or replace one gram of hydrogen.

GRAM-FORMULA WEIGHT
The number of grams of a substance that equal its formula weight.

GRAM-MOLECULAR VOLUME
The volume, 22.4 liters, occupied by one gram-molecular weight at any gast at S.T.P.

GRAM-MOLECULAR WEIGHT
That number of grams of any substance that equal its molecular weight, also called a MOLE of that substance

<u>H</u>

HALF-LIFE
The time required for one-half the atoms of a mass of radioactive material to decompose.

HALOGEN
The name given to the family of elements having seven valence electrons.

HEAT OF FORMATION
The heat which is given out or absorbed when a compound is formed from elements.

HEAT OF NEUTRALIZATION
The number of calories liberated in the formation of 18g. of water from hydrogen and hydroxyl ions.

HEAVY WATER
Water containing deuterium atoms in place of ordinary hydrogen atoms.

HEMOGLOBIN
The red coloring matter in blood.

HERBICIDE
A weed-killing agent. Most of these are specific in their action and therefore not intended for indiscriminate use. Label indicates particular purposes and gives directions for most effective application.

HOMOLOGOUS SERIES
A series of compounds each of which can be represented by a type of formula, such as C_nH_{2n+2}.

HUMIDITY, RELATIVE
The ratio of the actual amount of water vapor in atmosphere to the amount necessary for saturation at the same temperature.

HYDRATE
Crystals that contain water of hydration.

HYDRATED LIME
Calcium hydroxide, the product formed when water unites with calcium oxide.

HYDROCARBONS
Organic compounds composed solely of caron and hydrogen. Myriad variety of molecular combinations of C and H. Basic building block of all organic chemicals. Main chemical industry course of hydrocarbons: petroleum, natural gas and coal.

HYDROFORMING
The process of improving gasoline by heating it with hydrogen in the presence of a catalyst.

HYDROGENATION
The addition of hydrogen to a material.

HYDROLYSIS
The reaction of water with a salt to form the acid and the base of which the salt was a product; it opposes neutralization reactions.

HYDROPONICS
The science of gardening without the use of oil.

HYGROSCOPIC
Having a tendency to pick up water vapor.

I

INACTIVE SUBSTANCE
One which reacts, but not very readily, with other substances.

INDICATOR
A substance used to show, by means of a color change, whether an acid or a base is present.

INERT ELEMENT
An element of the zero group of the periodic table. Elements in this group have no chemical properties.

INERT SUBSTANCE
One which does not react at all with other substances under the usual conditions of chemical reactions.

INHIBITOR
(1) A material used to prevent or retard rust or corrosion.
(2) An agent which arrests or slows chemical action.

INORGANIC
Term used to designate chemicals that generally do not contain carbon. Source: matter, other than vegetable or animal. Example: chlorine is an inorganic chemical derived from salt.

INSECTICIDE
Any one of a group of chemicals used to kill or control insects.

INTERMEDIATE
An organic chemical formed as a "middle-step" between the initial material and the one or frequently several ultimate end products.

INVERSION
The combination of cane sugar with water to form two molecules of simple sugars.

ION
An atom or group of atoms which carries an electric charge.

ION-EXCHANGE RESINS
Granules of resins that absorb either positive or negative ions.

IONIC EQUILIBRIUM
The balance attained when the rate of dissociation equals the rate of association.

IOOTZATION
The formation of ions from polar compounds by action of a solvent.

IONIZATION CONSTANT
The product of the concentration of the ions divided by the concentration of the unionized molecules of solute (electrolyte).

IONIZATION POTENTIAL
The energy necessary to remove an electron from a gaseous atom to form an ion. This energy is expressed in electron volts.

IRRADIATION
Subjected to light, especially ultraviolet light.

ISOBARES
Atoms of the same atomic weight but having different atomic numbers are isobares.

ISOMERS
Compounds having the same composition but different structure.

ISOTOPE
One of two or more atomic species of an element differing in weight but having the same nuclear charge (atomic number). For example, in the element, chlorine, the atomic weight is the mean of the two isotopes making up the element.

K

KAOLIN
A fine, white clay composed of hydrated aluminum silicate.

KERNEL
All of the atom except the valence electrons.

KILN
A type of furnace used for producing quicklime, making glass, baking pottery, etc.

KILOCALORIES
Units equal to one thousand calories.

KILOGRAM
The standard of weight in the metric system equal to 1000 grams.

KINDLING TEMPERATURE
The lowest temperature at which a substance takes fire. This temperature varies with the physical state of the substance.

KINETIC ENERGY
Energy of motion.
KINETIC THEORY
The theory of matter which assumes that all molecules of matter are always in motion.
KNOCKING
A pounding sound produced in automobile engines by too rapid combustion of the mixture of gasoline vapor and air.

L

LAC OF SULPHUR
Precipitated sulfur.
LATENT HEAT
The heat absorbed or liberated in changing a mole of substance from one state to another at a fixed temperature, e.g., converting 18g. water to water vapor at $100°$ C.
LATEX
Original meaning: Milky extract from rubber tree. Now also applied to water emulsions of synthetic rubbers or resins. In emulsion paints, the film-forming resin is in the form of latex.
LAW, LeCHATELIER'S
A system in equilibrium, if disturbed by external factors such as temperature and pressure, will adjust itself in such a way that the effect of the disturbing factors will be reduced to a minimum.
LEHR
A cooling oven for annealing glass.
LIGNIN
Major non-carbohydrate constituent of wood and woody plants; functions as binder for the cellulose fibers. Removed from wood in pulp manufacture. Extracted from waste sulfite liquor. Research underway on chemical applications. Current use as adhesive base, for boiler water treatment and for road binders.
LIGNITE
A partially mineralized peat.
LIME
A term loosely used for all calcium compounds but properly belonging to calcium oxide, although often used for calcium hydroxide and calcium carbonate.
L.P.G., or LIQUEFIED PETROLEUM GAS
A compressed or liquefied gas comprised of pure propane, or a butane, or a combination of propane and butane; obtained as a by-product in petroleum refining or gasoline manufacture. Used in chemical synthesis.
LITER
The basic unit of volume in the metric system.
LITHOPANE
A paint base composed of barium sulfate and zinc sulfide.
LITMUS
A dye extracted from lichens which is used as an indicator.
LYE
A term used for either sodium hydroxide or potassium hydroxide.

M

MASS
The property of a substance (body) that determines the acceleration it will acquire when acted upon by a given force.
MASS ACTION, LAW OF
The speed of a chemical change is proportional to the concentration of the reacting substances.

MATTE
A mixture of sulfides produced in a partially refined ore.

MATTER
Anything which occupies space and has weight.

METALLURGY
The science of extracting and refining metals.

METALS
Elements with a luster that are good conductors of heat and electricity and are electropositive.

MERCERIZING
Treating stretched cotton with sodium hydroxide solution.

METAMORPHIC
Applied to rocks that have undergone a change in form due to heat or pressure.

METER
The basic unit of the metric system, equal to 39.37 inches.

METHANE (CH_4)
The simplest saturated hydrocarbon, chief component of most natural gas. Chemical raw material.

METHYL ALCOHOL (METHANOL, WOOD ALCOHOL) (CH_3OH)
Organic compound important for chemical synthesis; also used in denaturing alcohol; solvent and many other uses.

MILLILITER
One-thousandth of a liter.

MILK OF SULFUR
Precipitated sulfur.

MIXTURE
Two or more substances which, when combined, do not lose their identity and may be separated by mechanical means.

MODERATOR
A substance which slows down fast neutrons.

MOLAL SOLUTION
One mole of a substance dissolved in 1000g. of solvent.

MOLAR SOLUTION
One gram-molecular weight of a substance dissolved in enough solvent to make one liter of solution.

MOLE
That number of grams of a substance which is exactly equal to its molecular weight.

MOLECULAR VOLUME
The volume occupied by a mole of any gas at $0°$ C. and 760 mm pressure, e.g., 22.4 liters.

MOLECULAR WEIGHT
The sum of the weights of the atoms in a molecule.

MOLECULE
The chemical combination of two or more like or unlike atoms.

MONATOMIC
Molecules made up of one atom.

MONOBASIC ACID
An acid having one replaceable hydrogen atom per molecule.

MONOCLINIC
Referring to those crystals having one oblique axis.

MONOMER
A compound of relatively low molecular weight which, under certain conditions, either alone or with another monomer, forms various types and lengths of molecular chains called polymers or copolymers of high molecular weight. Example: styrene is a monomer which polymerizes readily to make the polymer, polystyrene.

MORTAR
A mixture of lime, sand, and water.

MOTHER LIQUOR
The liquid which is left after a crop of crystals has separated from a solution.

N

NAPHTHALENE ($C_{10}H_8$)
A white solid crystalline hydrocarbon found as a mineral and obtained from coal tar by distillation. Used as a moth repellent and a basic material in the manufacture of dyestuffs, synthetic resins, lubricants and other products.

NAPHTHENES
Hydrocarbons having a ring structure.

NASCENT
At the instant an element is liberated from a compound it is said to be in the nascent state. Nascent dryogen is probably atomic hydrogen.

NATIVE METAL
A metal found as an element, rather than as a compound, in the ground.

NATURAL GAS
A combustible gas composed largely of methane and other hydrocarbons with variable amounts of nitrogen and non-combustible gases; obtained from natural earth fissures or from driven wells. Among other things, used as a fuel, in the manufacture of carbon black and in chemical synthesis of many products.

NEON (Ne)
A rare gaseous element which forms no chemical compounds and is derived by fractional distillation of liquid air. Used mostly in luminescent electric tubes.

NEUTRALIZATION
The union of hydrogen ions of an acid with hydroxyl ions of a base to form water.

NEUTRON
A neutral particle found in the atom.

NIACIN ($C_6H_5O_2N$)
The anti-pellagra factor of the vitamin B complex; present in animal tissues, in fish, milk and green leafy vegetables.

NITER (KNO_3)
A white salt widely distributed in nature and formed in soils from nitrogenous organic bodies by the action of bacteria. Used in making gunpowder, medicinals and other products.

NITRIC ACID (HNO_3)
A colorless to yellowish fuming liquid with powerful corrosive properties. Manufactured by several methods, it is used in organic synthesis, in etching metals and ore flotation, in the manufacture of explosives, medicines, and other products.

NITROCELLULOSE
A powerful explosive made by treating cellulose with nitric and sul-furic acids.

NITROGATION
Adding of nitrogen compounds to the soil.

NITROGEN CYCLE
The cycle of changes through which nitrogen passes, starting with nitrates in the soil which become, in turn, plant proteins, animal proteins, dead matter, ammonia, nitrites, and then nitrates again.

NITROGEN FIXATION
Process of combining nitrogen of the atmosphere into any of the various stable chemical compounds valuable to the manufacture of fertilizers, and ammonia, among others.
NITROGLYCERIN
Glyceryl trinitrate, a powerful and sensitive explosive.
NITROUS OXIDE (NO_2)
A colorless gas of sweetish odor and taste; used as an anesthetic. Also called laughing gas.
NONELECTROLYTE
A compound whose water solution does not conduct electric current. NONMETALS
Elements that are usually poor conductors of heat and electricity and are electro-negative.
NORMAL SALT
A salt containing neither replaceable hydrogen nor hydroxyl.
NORMAL SOLUTION
A solution that contains one gram-equivalent of a substance dissolved in enough solvent to make one liter of solution.
NUCLEONS
The fundamental constituents of atomic nuclei(protons and neutrons).

O

OCCLUSION
The adsorption of gases by solids.
OCTANE RATING
A number indicating how a gasoline behaves with regard to knocking when compared with a test fuel given an arbitrary rating of 100.
OCTET
The term applied to a group of eight electrons in the highest energy levels of atoms.
ONE ATMOSPHERE
The average pressure of the atmosphere at sea level,equal to 760 mm. of mercury.
OPEN-HEARTH PROCESS
A process for making steel in a large, shallow pool.
ORBIT
The path of an electron about the nucleus of an atom.
ORGANIC
Term used to designate that group of chemicals that contain carbon. Approximately 300,000 such compounds have been identified,many occurring in nature,others produced by chemical synthesis. Sources: petroleum and coal tar by fractional distillation; soft coal and wood by destructive distillation; wood by chemical treatment; grains and fruits by fermentation; grains, vegetables and fruit by mechanical and chemical separation of starch and sugar; cotton by mechanical and chemical treatment; animals, seeds and nuts, by mechanical extraction of fats and oils.
ORLON
One of the synthetic fibers.
OSMOSIS
The passage of liquids and gases through porous membranes.
OXIDATION
Process of combining oxygen with some other substance.

OXYGEN-CARBON DIOXIDE CYCLE

The cycle of events whereby plants take in carbon dioxide and give off oxygen in photosynthesis, whereas animals take in oxygen and give off carbon dioxide in respiration.

OZONE

An allotropic form of oxygen containing three atoms per molecule.

P

PAINT BASE

The particles suspended in the oil of a paint.

PAINT VEHICLE

A quick drying oil that forms a flexible horn-like film. The paint base is suspended in this oil.

PARAFFINS, PARAFFIN SERIES (From parun affinis-small affinity)

Those hydrocarbon components of crude oil and natural gas whose molecules are saturated (i.e., carbon atoms attached to each other by single bonds) and therefore very stable. Examples: methane, ethane.

PARKERIZED

Dipped into a hot alkaline solution of sodium phosphate.

PARKES PROCESS

A method of separating silver from molten, crude lead by adding zinc.

PEPTIZATION

A breaking up of coarse particles into a finer state of subdivision.

PERIODIC TABLE

An arrangement of the elements in the order of their atomic numbers.

PH

A numerical scale that indicates the concentration of hydrogen ions in a solution; 7 is neutral, less than 7 is acid, and greater than 7 is basic.

PHENOL (C_6H_5OH)

Popularly known as carbolic acid. Important chemical intermediate intermediate derived primarily from coal tar and produced by chemical synthesis. Base for plastics, Pharmaceuticals, explosives, anti-septics, and many other end products.

PHENOLPHTHALEIN

An indicator which turns red in the presence of an excess of hydroxyl ions.

PHOSPHORS

Compounds that fluoresce under ultraviolet light.

PHOSPHORESCENCE

A faint glow similar in appearance to that emitted by phosphorus when it is exposed to the air in a dark room.

PHOTON

A unit of light (a particle of light).

PHOTOSYNTHESIS

The process by which plants build carbohydrate foods with the aid of sunlight, using carbon dioxide and water as the raw materials and chlorophyll as the catalyst.

PHYSICAL CHANGE

A change in color, size of particle, temperature, or other physical property that does not produce a new substance.

PHYSICAL EQUILIBRIUM

A condition of balance when the rate of a physical change in one direction is equal to an opposite physical change.

PICKLING

Treating a metal with acid to remove surface coatings of oxide.

PIGMENT
A substance that adds color to a mixture.

PLASTICIZERS
Organic chemicals used in modifying plastics, synthetic rubber and similar materials to give such special properties as elongation, flexibility and toughness as may be essential to their end uses.

PLASTICS
Officially defined as any one of a large and varied group of materials which consists of, or contains as an essential ingredient, an organic substance of large molecular weight; and which, while solid in the finished state, at some stage in its manufacture has been or can be formed (cast calendered, extruded, molded, etc.) into various shapes by flow - usually through application of heat and pressure singly or together. Each plastic has individual physical, chemical and electrical properties. Two basic types: thermosetting and thermoplastic. Prior to processing, plastic materials often are referred to as resins. Final form may be as film, sheet, solid, or foam; flexible or rigid.

POLAR MOLECULE
A molecule with an unsymmetrical electron distribution.

POLING
The use of green wood in the refining of copper ore to reduce the traces of copper oxide present.

POLYMER
A high molecular weight material containing a large number of repeating units. These may be hundreds or even thousands of the original molecules (monomers) which have linked together end to end. Rubber and cellulose are naturally occurring polymers. Most resins are chemically produced polymers. Polymers may be formed by polymerization or condensation. For instance, the polymer, polyethylene, is polymerized from the monomer, ethylene. An example of condensation is the production of phenol formaldehyde resins with the incidental formation of water or some simple substance.

POLYMERIZATION
A physical reaction by which polymers are formed from the linkage of monomers.

POLYMORPHISM
The ability to exist in two or more crystalline forms.

PORCELAIN
A product made from pure, white clay mixed with powdered feldspar and usually fired twice in a kiln.

POSITRON
A unit charge of positive electricity of approximately the same mass as the electron.

POTASH
Source of potassium, essential plant nutrient (other two basic nutrients: nitrogen, phosphorus). Potash value in a fertilizer is expressed in terms of equivalent amount of potassium oxide K_2O.

PRECIPITATE
An insoluble solid formed by adding one solution to another.

PRODUCER GAS
A cheap fuel gas for industrial purposes made by blowing a blast of steam and air through red-hot coke.

PROPERTIES
The characteristics by which we identify materials.

PROTEINS
Complex organic compounds necessary for the growth of living things or the repair of worn-out tissue.

PROTON
A positively charged particle found in the atom.

Q

QUICKLIME
Calcium oxide, often called unslaked lime.

R

RADICAL
A group of atoms which acts like a single atom in forming compounds.

RADIOACTIVITY
Emission of energy in waves or moving particles from the nucleus of an atom. Always involves change of one kind of atom into a different kind. A few elements such as radium are naturally radioactive. Other radiactive forms are induced (see RADIOISOTOPE).

RADIOCHEMICALS
Any compound or mixture containing a sufficient portion of radioactive elements to be detected by Geiger counter.

RADIOISOTOPE
An isotopic form of an element that exhibits radioactivity,whether naturally found or produced by fission and other induced nuclear changes. The latter are used in biological tracer work and industrial control operations. More than 500 radioactive substances have been produced.

RADON
A gaseous element produced by the disintegration of radium atoms.

REACTANTS
The elements or compounds entering into a chemical reaction.

REAGENT
Any substance used in a chemical reaction to produce another substance or to detect its composition.

REDOX REACTION
A reaction in which oxidation and reduction take place.

REDUCING AGENT
An agent that removes oxygen from a material.

REDUCTION
(1) Removal of oxygen. (2) The gain in electrons by an element.

REFRACTORY
Pertaining to a substance that is not easily melted.

REGENERATIVE HEATING
A system whereby the heat of outgoing flue gases is used to preheat incoming fuel gas and air.

RELATIVE HUMIDITY
The amount of moisture present in the air as a vapor compared with the total amount of moisture the air could hold at that temperature.

REPLACEMENT SERIES
The arrangement of the metals in the order of their decreasing chemical activity.

RESIN
A solid or semisolid amorphous organic compound or mixture of such compounds with no definite melting point and no tendency to crystallize. Resins may be of vegetable,animal or synthetic origin. Natural resins may be distinguished from gums in that they are insoluble in water.However, certain synthetic water soluble materials are referred to as resins or resin

stages. There are many types, each with distinctive physical and chemical properties. Some types of resin materials may be molded, cast, or extruded. Others are used for adhesives, for the treatment of textiles and paper, and for protective coatings. Still others are rolled or extruded into continuous sheets and films of various thicknesses. All, broadly speaking, have plastic use.

RHOMBIC
Referring to crystals having equilateral edges and oblique angles.

RIFFLES
Grooves in a sluice for catching gold in hydraulic mining operations.

S

SACRIFICIAL METAL
The more active of a pair of metals which is oxidized by an electric cell action.

SALTS
Crystalline compounds made up of metals and non-metals. Example: table salt is sodium and chlorine.

SAPONIFICATION
The process of making soap by adding lye to a glyceryl ester.

SARAN
One of the synthetic fibers.

SATURATED SOLUTION
A solution in which the solute in solution is in equilibrium with undissolved solute.

SEDIMENTARY
A term applied to rocks formed from sediment that has been deposited in layers.

SHELL-FILLER
An explosive that requires a severe shock to set it off.

SHERARDIZING
Coating with zinc by allowing zinc vapor to condense on the object.

SILICONES
Unique new group of polymers made by molecular combination of the inorganic chemical, silicone dioxide, with organic chemicals. Produced in variety of forms including silicone fluids, resins and rubber. Silicones have special properties, such as water-repellensy, wide temperature resistance, durability and dielectric property

SILT
A soil which is coarser than clay but finer than sand.

SINGLE REPLACEMENT REACTION
One in which an element replaces another in a compound.

SINTERING
Heating until fusion just begins.

SLAG
A by-product of smelting. It is formed by the action of low melting material (flux) on impurities in the ore. Slags contain calcium and aluminum silicates.

SLAKED LIME
Calcium hydroxide, or calcium oxide, that has united with water.

SMOKELESS POWDER
A nitrocellulose explosive.

SOAP
The sodium or potassium salts of a fatty acid, e.g., $NaC_{18}H_{35}O_2$.

SOLDER
An easily melted alloy, especially one of tin and lead.

SOLUBILITY PRODUCT CONSTANT

The product of the concentrations of the ions of slightly soluble salt at saturation.

SOLUTION

Mixture in which the identities of components are lost as such.

SOLVENT

A substance, usually an organic compound, which dissolves another substance.

SPECIFIC GRAVITY (GASES)

The ratio of the weight of one liter of air to the weight of one liter of the gas.

SPECIFIC GRAVITY (SOLID OR LIQUID)

The ratio of the weight of a unit volume of a substance to the weight of the same volume of water.

SPECIFIC HEAT

The heat required to raise the temperature of one gram of a substance one degree centigrade.

SPECIFIC VOLUME

The volume of one gram of a substance.

SPINNERETS

Thimble-like plates with tiny holes for extruding synthetic fibers.

STALACTITES

Icicle-like masses of calcium carbonate hanging from the roof of limestone caves.

STALAGMITES

Masses of calcium carbonate rising from the floor of limestone caves, formed by dripping of calcium bicarbonate solution from the cave roof.

STANDARD CONDITIONS

$0°$ C. and 1 atmosphere pressure (760 mm.).

STANDARD PRESSURE

A pressure equal to that furnished by a column of mercury 760 mm. high.

STANDARD TEMPERATURE

Zero degrees Centigrade.

STERLING

Containing 92.5% silver, or 925 fine.

S.T.P.

Abbreviation for "standard temperature and pressure."

STRONG ACID

One which is completely ionized in water solutions.

STRONG ELECTROLYTE

One which is ionized almost completely.

STRUCTURE FORMULAS

Formulas that tell how the atoms are joined in the molecules.

SUBLIMATION

A process in which a solid is vaporized and condensed to a solid without passing through the liquid state.

SUPERHEATED WATER

Water heated under pressure to a temperature above the normal boiling point.

SUPERPHOSPHATE

Phosphorus-bearing material made by action or sulfuric acid on phosphate rock to make phosphorus available as a plant nutrient. Phosphorus in soluble form is one of the three essential plant nutrients. (Other two: nitrogen, potassium.)

SUPERSATURATED

Pertaining to a solution saturated at a high temperature which retains the solute in solution as it cools.

SURFACE-ACTIVE AGENT
Any of a group of compounds added to a liquid to modify surface or interface tension. In the case of synthetic detergents, best known surface-active agent, reduction of tension provides cleansing action. Term also includes dispersing, emulsifying, foaming, penetrating and wetting agents. Usually synthetic organic in origin.

SURFACE COATINGS
Term used to cover paint, lacquer, varnish and other chemical compositions used for protecting and/or decorating surfaces.

SURFACTANT
A coined word which means "surface-active agent."

SYNCHROTRON
One of the "atom-smashing" machines for bombarding atomic nuclei.

SYNERGIST
A material which, in combination with another, improves the effectiveness of the combination to a degree in excess of the sum of the effects of the two materials taken independently.

SYNTHESIS
The reaction, or series of reactions, by which a complex compound is obtained from simpler compounds or elements.

SYNTHETIC DETERGENTS
Chemically-tailored cleaning agents soluble in water. Originally developed as soap substitute. Because they do not form insoluble precipitates, they are especially valuable in hard water. See SURFACE-ACTIVE AGENT.

SYNTHETIC RUBBER
Nab-made polymeric chemical with rubber-like attributes. Various types with varying composition and properties. Major types designated as S-type, butyl, neoprene (chloroprene polymers), and N-type.

T

TALL OIL
(Name derived from Swedish TALLOLJA; material first investigated in Sweden-not synonymous with our pine oil.)

Natural mixture of rosin acids, fatty acids, sterols, high molecular weight alcohols and other materials, derived primarily from waste liquors of wood pulp manufacture. Dark brown, viscous, oily liquid often called liquid rosin. Recent encyclopedia lists 38 major industry uses.

TANKAGE
A fertilizer made from slaughter house scraps.

TAR CRUDE
Basic organic raw material derived from distillation of coal tar and used for chemical manufacture.

TEMPERING
Regulation of the iron carbide, and thus the hardness of a piece of steel, by heating and sudden cooling.

TERNARY
Composed of three elements.

TERNE PLATE
Sheet iron coated with an alloy of tin and lead.

THERMITE REACTION
The replacement reaction between a metal, such as aluminum, and an oxide, such as ferric oxide, which liberates much heat.

THERMOPLASTIC TYPE OF PLASTICS
Those that can repeatedly melt or soften with heat and harden on cooling. Examples: vinyls, acrylics, polyethylene.

THERMOSETTING TYPE OF PLASTICS
Those that are heat-set in their final processing to a permanently hard state. Examples: phenolics, ureas and melamines.

THINNER
A liquid, such as turpentine, used in paint to make it spread more easily and penetrate better

TINCTURE
A solution the solvent of which is alcohol, e.g., tincture of iodine.

TITRATION
Determination of the concentration of a solution by comparing it with a standard solution, usually employing burettes for the operation.

TOLUENE ($CH_3C_6H_5$)
Hydrocarbon derived mainly from petroleum but also from coal. Base for TNT, lacquers, saccharin and many other chemicals.

TRIADS
Group of three elements in the same vertical column of the periodic table.

TRIBASIC ACID
An acid containing three replaceable hydrogen atoms per molecule.

TRIPLE SUPERPHOSPHATE
Phosphorus fertilizer of higher phosphorus content than in superphosphate; produced by addition of phosphoric acid to phosphate rock.

TUYERES
The nozzles of the blowpipes of a blast furnace.

TYNDALL EFFECT
The dispersion of a beam of light as it passes through a colloidal solution.

U

ULTRAVIOLET RAYS
Invisible radiations having a shorter wave length than violet light.

UNSLAKED LIME
Calcium oxide, or line to which water has not been added.

U.S.P.
Abbreviation for <u>United States Pharmacopoeia,</u> an official book that specifies strengths and degrees of purity of official remedies.

V

VALENCE
The number of electrons gained, lost, or shared in forming a chemical bond.

VALENCE ELECTRONS
Electrons in the outermost orbit which may be gained or lost in chemical reactions.

VAPOR
A gas that can be converted into a liquid at that temperature by pressure alone.

VAPOR DENSITY
The ratio of the weight of a gas to the weight of an equal volume of hydrogen measured under the same conditions.

VAPOR PRESSURE
The (partial) pressure exerted by a vapor.

VAPOR TENSION
The pressure which a vapor exerts on a liquid when the liquid and vapor are in equilibrium at a given temperature (the maximum vapor pressure for the given temperature).

VAT DYES
Water-insoluble,complex coal tar dyes that can be chemically reduced in a heated solution to a soluble form that will impregnate fibers. Subsequent oxidation then produces insoluble colored dye-stuff remarkably fast to washing, light and chemicals.

VEHICLE
The liquid portion of paint,such as linseed oil,used to hold the paint base in suspension.

VERMICULITE
Mica that has bean expanded with steam to make a light,porous material.

VISCOSITY
(1) The resistance to flow of a liquid.
(2) The internal friction of a liquid.

VITRIFIED
Heated to the point where melting just begins,thus closing pores.

VITRIOL
An acid substance.

VOLUME-VOLUME PROBLEMS
Those in which a known volume of one material is given and the volume of another material involved in the reaction is sought.

VOLT
The electrical pressure required to make a current of one ampere through a resistance of one ohm.

VULCANIZATION
Process of combining rubber (natural, synthetic, or latex) with sulfur and various other additives usually under heat and pressure, in order to eliminate tackiness when warm and brittleness when cool, and to change permanently the material from a thermoplastic to a thermosetting composition. Finally to otherwise improve strength, elasticity, and abrasive resistance.

W

WARFARIN
A new kind of rat poison.

WATER GAS
A fuel gas made by blowing a bast of steam through a bed of red-hot coke.

WATER GLASS
A syrupy solution of sodium silicate.

WATER OF HYDRATION
Water that has united with some chemicals as they form crystals called hydrates.

WEAK ACID
An acid which is but slightly ionized in water solutions.

WEAK ELECTROLYTE
One that is but slightly ionized.

WEIGHTED SILK
Silk that has been dipped in solutions of certain tin salts.

WEIGHT-WEIGHT PROBLEMS
Those in which a known quantity of one material is given and the amount of another material involved in the reaction is sought.

WEIGHT-VOLUME PROBLEMS
Those in which the weight or volume of one material is given and either the weight or volume of another material involved in the reaction is sought

WETTING AGENTS
Materials that reduce the surface tension of a liquid, causing it to spread out better.

X

X-RAYS
Light radiations of high frequency and very short wave length.

Z

ZEOLITES
Naturally occurring minerals, such as an aluminate of either sodium or potassium.

ZIRCONIUM
A metallic element with an exceedingly high melting point.

CHEMICAL LAWS

1. AVOGADRO'S HYPOTHESIS

Equal volumes of gases, under the same conditions of temperature and pressure, contain the same number of molecules.

A liter of oxygen contains the same number of molecules as a liter of hydrogen measured under the same conditions of temperature and pressure.

2. BOYLE'S LAW

If the temperature remains constant, the volume of a given mass of gas is inversely proportional to the pressure.

$$\frac{V_1}{V_2} = \frac{P_2}{P_1}$$

Example: If the pressure on a gas is doubled and the temperature is constant, the new volume is one-half the original volume.

3. CHARLES' LAW

If the pressure remains constant, the volume of a gas caries directly with the Absolute temperature.

$$\frac{V_1}{V_2} \quad \frac{T_1}{T_2}$$

Example: If the Absolute temperature of a gas is doubled, the volume is also doubled.

4. GAY-LUSSAC'S LAW OF COMBINING VOLUMES OF GASES

The relative combining volumes of gases and their products, if gaseous, may be expressed by small whole numbers.

Example: One volume of chlorine combines with one volume of hydrogen forming two volumes of hydrogen chloride.

5. HENRY'S LAW OF GAS SOLUBILITY

If the temperature is held constant, the weight of a gas which dissolves in a given volume is proportional to the pressure.

Example: The greater the pressure, the larger the volume of gas which can be dissolved. Suppose that one liter of water can dissolve 2 grams of carbon dioxide at 1 atmosphere of pressure. If the temperature remains the same, 4 grams can be dissolved if the pressure is increased to 2 atmospheres.

6. LAW OF CONSERVATION OF ENERGY

Energy can neither be created nor destroyed; it may, however, be changed from one form to another.

Example: When coal is burned, stored chemical energy is converted and released as heat energy.

7. LAW OF CONSERVATION OF MATTER (MASS)
Matter can neither be created nor destroyed. If the matter is changed from one form to another, the new products produced have the same mass as the original substances.

8. LAW OF MASS ENERGY
This law expresses the equivalence of mass and energy. It states that energy (E) is equal to mass (m) times the square of the velocity of light (c) in centimeters per second.

$$E = mc^2$$

9. LAW OF DEFINITE PROPORTIONS
Every chemical compound has a definite composition of weight.

Example: If pure water is analyzed its composition will never vary.

There will always be eight times as much oxygen by weight as hydrogen.

10. LAW OF MASS ACTION
The speed of a chemical reaction is proportional to the product of the molecular concentration of the reacting substances.

Example: Mass action refers to the changing of the equilibrium of a reaction by varying the concentration of one or more of the reactants. Thus, the law states that in a reversible reaction the speed at which it occurs depends on the concentration of the reactants.

11. LAW OF MULTIPLE PROPORTIONS
When two elements unite to form more than one compound, the weights of one element which combine with a fixed weight of the other are in the ratio of small whole numbers.

Example: In the compound carbon monoxide (CO), there are 12 grams of carbon and 16 grams of oxygen. In the compound carbon dioxide (CO_2), there are 12 grams of carbon and 16 grams of oxygen. Therefore,

$$\frac{\text{weight of oxygen in CO}}{\text{weight of oxygen in CO}_2} = \frac{1}{2}$$

12. LE CHATELIER'S PRINCIPLE
If a system which is in equilibrium is affected by a change in temperature or pressure, it will adjust itself so that the effect of the change will be reduced to a minimum.

Example: If the pressure on a system in equilibrium is increased, the system will adjust itself so that it will occupy less volume.

13. PERIODIC LAW (MOSELEY'S)
The chemical properties of the elements are a periodic function of their atomic numbers.

GLOSSARY OF COMMON SUBSTANCE

A

COMMON NAME	CHEMICAL NAME	FORMULA
Alum	Potassium aluminum sulfate	$K_2SO_4 \cdot Al_2(SO_4)_3 \cdot 24H_2O$
Alumina	Aluminum oxide	Al_2O_3
Alundum	Fused aluminum oxide	Al_2O_3
Ammonia water	Ammonium hydroxide	NH_4OH
Aniline	Phenyl amine	$C_6H_5NH_2$
Aqua ammonia	A solution of NH_3 in H_2O	NH_4OH
Aqua fortis	Nitric acid	HNO_3
Aqua regia	Hydrochloric and nitric acids	$3 HCl + HNO_3$
Asbestos (principal form)	Hydrated magnesium silicate	$3 MgO \cdot 2 SiO_2 \cdot 2H_2O$
Aspirin	Acetylsalicylic acid	$C_6H_4(COOH)OCOCH_3$

B

COMMON NAME	CHEMICAL NAME	FORMULA
Babbitt	Alloy of Sn, Sb, and Cu	
Bakelite	Resin from phenol and formaldehyde	
Baking powder	A mixture of $NaHCO_3$, an acid ingredient, and starch	
Baking soda	Sodium bicarbonate	$NaHCO$
Bauxite	Hydrated aluminum oxide	$Al_2O_3 \cdot 3H_2O$ and $Al_2O_3 \cdot H_2O$
Bleaching powder	Calcium oxychloride	$CaOCl_2$
Blue vitriol	Cupric sulfate	$CuSO_4$
Bluestone	Cupric sulfate	$CuSO_4$
Bone ash	Calcium phosphate (impure)	$Ca_3(PO_4)_2$
Bone black	Animal charcoal	C
Boracic acid	Boric acid	H_3BO_3
Borax	Sodium tetraborate	$Na_2B_4O_7 \cdot 10 H_2O$
Brass	Alloy of Cu and Zn	
Brimstone	Volcanic sulfur	Impure S
Brine	Sodium chloride solution	NaCl and H_2O
Bronze	Alloy of Cu, Sn, and Zn	

C

COMMON NAME	CHEMICAL NAME	FORMULA
Cadium yellow	Cadmium sulfide	CdS
Calcite	Calcium carbonate	$CaCO_3$
Calich	Sodium nitrate (impure)	$NaNO_3$
Calomel	Mercurous chloride	HgCl
Camphor, artificial	Pinene chloride	$C_{10}H_{17}Cl$
Cane sugar	Sucrose	$C_{12}H_{22}O_{11}$
Carbolic acid	Phenol	C_6H_5OH
Carbonic acid gas	Carbon dioxide	CO_2

GLOSSARY OF COMMON SUBSTANCES (CONT'D)

COMMON NAME	CHEMICAL NAME	FORMULA
Caustic potash	Potassium hydroxide	KOH
Caustic soda	Sodium hydroxide	$NaOH$
Ceruse	Basic lead carbonate	$2\,PbCo_3 \cdot Pb(OH)_2$
Chalk	Calcium carbonate (impure)	$CaCO_3$
Chile saltpeter	Sodium nitrate (impure)	$NaNO_3$
China clay	Aluminum silicate	$Al_2O_3 \cdot 2SiO_2 \cdot 2H_2O$
Chloride of lime	Calcium oxychloride	$CaOCl_2$
Chrome alum	Potassium chromium sulfate	$K_2SO_4 \cdot Cr_2(SO_4)_3 \cdot 24\,H_2O$
Cinnabar	Mercuric sulfide	HgS
Coke	Carbon (impure)	C
Common salt	Sodium chloride	$NaCl$
Copperas	Ferrous sulfate	$FeSO_4 \cdot 7H_2O$
Corrosive sublimate	Mercuric chloride	$HgCl_2$
Corundum	Aluminum oxide	$Al2O_3$
Cream of tartar	Potassium hydrogen tartrate	$KHC_4H_4O_6$

D

Dextrose	Glucose	$C_6H_{12}O_6$
Diamond	Carbon	C
Dry ice	Solid carbon dioxide	CO_2

E

Epsom salts	Magnesium sulfate	$MgSO_4$

F

Feldspar (one form)	Potassium aluminum silicate	$KalSi_3O_8$
Firedamp	Methane	CH_4
Flowers of sulfur	Sulfur	S
Fluorspar	Calcium fluoride	CaF_2
Fool1 s gold	Iron pyrite	FeS_2

G

Galena	Lead sulfide	PbS
Glass	A solid solution containing a mixture of silicates	
Glauber's salt	Sodium sulfate	$Na_2SO_4 \cdot 10H_2O$
Glucose	Dextrose	$C_6H_{12}O_6$
Glycerin	Glycerol	$C_3H_5(OH)_3$
Grain alcohol	Ethyl alcohol	C_2H_5OH
Graphite	Carbon	C
Green vitriol	Ferrous sulfate	$FeSO_4$
Gypsum	Calcium sulfate	$CaSO_4 \cdot 2H_2O$

H

Horn silver	Silver chloride	$AgCl$
Household ammonia	Ammonium hydroxide	NH_4OH
Hypo	Sodium thiosulfate	$Na_2S_2O_3 \cdot 5H_2O$

GLOSSARY OF COMMON SUBSTANCES (CONT'D)

COMMON NAME	CHEMICAL NAME	FORMULA

K

Kaolin	Hydrogen aluminum silicate	$H_2Al_2(SiO_4)_2 \cdot H_2O$

L

Lampblack	Carbon (impure)	C
Lanolin	Cholesterol	$C_{27}H_{46}O$
Laughing gas	Nitrous oxide	N_2O
Levulose	Fructose	$C_6H_{12}O_6$
Lime, hydrated	Calcium hydroxide	$Ca(OH)_2$
Lime, quick	Calcium oxide	CaO
Lime, slaked	Calcium hydroxide	$Ca(OH)_2$
Limestone	Calcium carbonate	$CaCO_3$
Limewater	Calcium hydroxide solution	$Ca(OH)_2$
Litharge	Lead oxide	PbO
Lithopone	Zinc sulfide and barium sulfate	ZnS and $BaSO_4$
Lunar caustic	Silver nitrate	$AgNO_3$
Lye	Sodium hydroxide	NaOH
Magnesia	Magnesium oxide	MgO
Magnesite	Magnesium carbonate	$MgCO_3$
Malachite	Basic copper carbonate	$CuCo_3 \cdot Cu(OH)_2$
Marble	Calcium carbonate (impure)	$CaCO_3$
Marsh gas	Methane	CH_4
Methanol	Methyl alcohol	CH_3OH
Minium	Lead tetroxide	Pb_3O_4
Moth balls	Naphthalene	$C_{10}H_8$
Muriate of potash	Potassium chloride	KCl
Muriatic acid	Hydrochloric acid	HCl

N

Niter	Potassium nitrate	KNO_3

O

Oil of bitter almonds	Benzaldehyde	C_6H_5CHO
Oil of vitriol	Sulfuric acid	H_3SO_4
Oil of wintergreen	Methyl salicylate	$CH_3COOC_6H_4OH$
Oileum	Fuming sulfuric acid	$H_2SO_4 \cdot SO_3$

P

Pearl	Calcium carbonate	$CaCO_3$
Phosgene	Carbonyl chloride	$COCl_2$
Plaster of Paris	Calcium sulfate	$2CaSO_4 \cdot H_2O$
Potash	Potassium carbonate or potassium hydroxide	K_2CO_3 or KOH
Pyrolusite	Manganese dioxide	MnO_2

Q

Quicklime	Calcium oxide	CaO
Quicksilver	Mercury	Hg

GLOSSARY OF COMMON SUBSTANCES (CONT'D)

COMMON NAME	CHEMICAL NAME	FORMULA
R		
Rochelle salt	Potassium sodium tartrate	$KNaC_4H_4O_6$
Route	Ferric oxide	Fe_2O_3
S		
Sal ammoniac	Ammonium chloride	NH_4Cl
Sal soda	Sodium carbonate	Na_2CO_3
Salt of sorrell	Potassium acid oxalate	$KHC_2O_4 \cdot H_2O$
Saltpeter	Sodium nitrate	$NaNO_3$
Sand	Silicon dioxide	SiO_2
Silica	Silicon dioxide	SiO_2
Slaked lime	Calcium hydroxide	$Ca(OH)_2$
Soda lime	Calcium oxide & sodium hydroxide	CaO and NaOH
Soap (one kind)	Sodium stearate	$C_{17}H_{35}COONa$
Spirit of hartshorn	Ammonium hydroxide	NH_4OH
Spirit of wine	Ethyl alcohol	C_2H_5OH
Sugar	Sucrose	$C_{12}H_{22}O_{11}$
Sugar of lead	Lead acetate	$Pb(C_2H_3O_2)$
Superphosphate	Calcium sulfate & calcium acid phosphate	$CaSO_4$ and $Ca(H_2PO_4)_2$
T		
TABLE SALT	Sodium chloride	NaCl
TALC	Hydrated magnesium silicate	$3\,MgO \cdot 4SiO_2 \cdot H_2O$
TARTAR EMETIC	Potassium antimonyl tartrate	$2\,K(SbO)C_4H_4O_6 \cdot H_2O$
V		
Vinegar	Acetic acid, dilute	$HC_2H_3O_2$
W		
Water glass	Sodium silicate	Na_2SiO_3
White lead	Basic lead carbonate	$2PbCO_3 \cdot Pb(OH)_2$
White vitriol	Zinc sulfate	$ZnSO_4$
Whiting	Calcium carbonate	$CaCO_3$
Wood alcohol	Methyl alcohol	CH_3OH
Z		
Zinc blende	Zinc sulfide	ZnS
Zinc white	Zinc oxide	ZnO

CHEMICAL ELEMENTS AND SYMBOLS

NAME OF ELEMENT	SYMBOL	ATOMIC NUMBER	ATOMIC WEIGHT
A			
Actinium	Ac	89	227.0
Aluminum	Al	13	26.98
Americium	Am	95	[243]
Antimony	Sb	51	121.76
Argon	A	18	39.944
Arsenic	As	33	74.91
Astatine	At	85	[210]
B			
Barium	Ba	56	137.36
Berkelium	Bk	97	[245]
Beryllium	Be	4	9.013
Bismuth	Bi	83	209.00
Boron	B	5	10.82
Bromine	Br	35	79.916
C			
Cadmium	Cd	48	112.41
Calcium	Ca	20	40.08
Californium	Cf	98	[246]
Carbon	C	6	12.011
Cerium	Cc	58	140.13
Cesium	Cs	55	132.91
Chlorine	Cl	17	35.457
Chromium	Cr	24	52.01
Cobalt	Co	27	58.94
Copper	Cu	29	63.54
Curium	Cm	96	[243]
D			
Dysprosium	Dy	66	162.46
E			
Erbium	Er	68	167.2
Europium	Eu	63	152.0
F			
Fluorine	F	9	19.00
Francium	Fr	87	[223]
G			
Gadolinium	Gd	64	156.9
Gallium	Ga	31	69.72
Germanium	Ge	32	72.60
Gold	Au	79	197.0
H			
Hafnium	Hf	72	178.6
Helium	He	2	4.003
Holmium	Ho	67	164.94
Hydrogen	H	1	1.0080
I			
Indium	In	49	114.76
Iodine	I	53	126.91
Iridium	Ir	77	192.2
Iron	Fe	26	55.85
K			
Krypton	Kr	36	83.80
L			
Lanthanum	La	57	138.92

CHEMICAL ELEMENTS AND SYMBOLS (CONT'D)

NAME OF ELEMENT	SYMBOL	ATOMIC NUMBER	ATOMIC WEIGHT
Lead	Pb	82	207.21
Lithium	Li	3	6.940
Lutetium	Lu	71	174.99
M			
Magnesium	Mg	12	24.32
Manganese	Mn	25	54.94
Mercury	Hg	80	200.61
Molybdenum	Mo	42	95.95
N			
Neodymium	Nd	60	144.27
Neon	Ne	10	20.183
Neptunium	Np	93	[2373]
Nickel	Ni	28	58.69
Niobium	Nb	41	92.91
Nitrogen	N	7	14.008
O			
Osmium	Os	76	190.2
Oxygen	O	8	16.0000
P			
Palladium	Pd	46	106.7
Phosphorus	P	15	30.975
Platinum	Pt	78	195.23
Plutonium	Pu	94	[242]
Polonium	Po	84	210.0
Potassium	K	19	39.100
Praseodymium	Pr	59	140.92
Promethium	Pm	61	[145]
Protactinium	Pa	91	231.
R			
Radium	Ra	88	226.05
Radon	Rn	86	222.
Rhenium	Re	75	186.31
Rhodium	Rh	45	102.91
Rubidium	Rb	37	85.48
Ruthenium	Ru	44	101.1
S			
Samarium	Sm	62	150.43
Scandium	Sc	21	44.96
Selenium	Se	34	78.96
Silicon	Si	14	28.09
Silver	Ag	47	107.880
Sodium	Na	11	22.991
Strontium	Sr	38	87.63
Sulfur	S	16	32.066
T			
Tantalum	Ta	73	180.95
Technetium	Tc	43	[99]
Tellurium	Te	52	127.61
Terbium	Tb	65	158.93
Thallium	Tl	81	204.39
Thorium	Th	90	232.05
Thulium	Tm	69	168.94
Tin	Sn	50	118.70
Titanium	Ti	22	47.90
Tungsten	W	74	183.92

U
Uranium	U	92	238.07

V
Vanadium	V	23	50.95

X
Xenon	Xe	54	131.3

Y
Ytterbium	Yb	70	173.04
Yttrium	Y	39	88.92

Z
Zinc	Zn	30	65.38
Zirconium	Zr	40	91.22

(NOTE: Brackets indicate the isotope of longest known half-life.)

PERIODIC TABLE OF THE ELEMENTS

IA	IIA	IIIB	IVB	VB	VIB	VIIB	VIIIB			IB	IIB	IIIA	IVA	VA	VIA	VIIA	Noble gases
1 H 1.008																	2 He 4.003
3 Li 6.941	4 Be 9.012											5 B 10.81	6 C 12.011	7 N 14.007	8 O 15.999	9 F 18.998	10 Ne 20.179
11 Na 22.990	12 Mg 24.305											13 Al 26.982	14 Si 28.086	15 P 30.974	16 S 32.06	17 Cl 35.453	18 Ar 39.948
19 K 39.102	20 Ca 40.08	21 Sc 44.956	22 Ti 47.90	23 V 50.941	24 Cr 51.996	25 Mn 54.938	26 Fe 55.847	27 Co 58.933	28 Ni 58.71	29 Cu 63.546	30 Zn 65.37	31 Ga 69.72	32 Ge 72.59	33 As 74.922	34 Se 78.96	35 Br 79.904	36 Kr 83.80
37 Rb 85.468	38 Sr 87.62	39 Y 88.906	40 Zr 91.22	41 Nb 92.906	42 Mo 95.94	43 Tc 98.602	44 Ru 101.07	45 Rh 102.905	46 Pd 106.4	47 Ag 107.868	48 Cd 112.40	49 In 114.82	50 Sn 118.69	51 Sb 121.75	52 Te 127.60	53 I 126.905	54 Xe 131.30
55 Cs 132.905	56 Ba 137.34	57 La 138.905	72 Hf 178.49	73 Ta 180.948	74 W 183.85	75 Re 186.2	76 Os 190.2	77 Ir 192.22	78 Pt 195.09	79 Au 196.966	80 Hg 200.59	81 Tl 204.37	82 Pb 207.19	83 Bi 208.2	84 Po (~210)	85 At ~210	86 Rn (~222)
87 Fr (223)	88 Ra 226.02	89 Ac (227)	104	105													

58 Ce 140.12	59 Pr 140.907	60 Nd 144.24	61 Pm (145)	62 Sm 150.4	63 Eu 151.96	64 Gd 157.25	65 Tb 158.925	66 Dy 162.50	67 Ho 164.930	68 Er 167.26	69 Tm 168.934	70 Yb 173.04	71 Lu 174.97
90 Th 232.038	91 Pa 231.036	92 U 238.029	93 Np 237.048	94 Pu (244)	95 Am (243)	96 Cm (247)	97 Bk (247)	98 Cf (251)	99 Es (254)	100 Fm (257)	101 Md (256)	102 No (254)	103 Lr (257)

www.ingramcontent.com/pod-product-compliance
Lightning Source LLC
Chambersburg PA
CBHW082038300426
44117CB00015B/2522